Thomas D. Butler

Poetry and Prose of Marie Radcliffe Butler

Thomas D. Butler

Poetry and Prose of Marie Radcliffe Butler

ISBN/EAN: 9783337369996

Printed in Europe, USA, Canada, Australia, Japan

Cover: Foto ©Thomas Meinert / pixelio.de

More available books at **www.hansebooks.com**

POETRY AND PROSE

OF

MARIE RADCLIFFE BUTLER

EDITED BY

THOMAS D. BUTLER

CINCINNATI

STANDARD PUBLISHING COMPANY

1884

TO .

Mrs. Fannie H. Christopher,

THE DEVOTED FRIEND AND LIFELONG COMPANION

OF THE AUTHOR,

THIS WORK

IS DUTIFULLY AND AFFECTIONATELY INSCRIBED.

TABLE OF CONTENTS.

PART I.—POETRY.

The Christian Standard on the	An Acre of Graves . . . 61
Field of Armageddon . . 1	Desolation 63
The Falling Leaf 4	Charles Dickens 64
A Baby's Face 5	O Bright and Silent Sun ˙ . . 65
Spirit Musings 6	The Bridge 67
Spirit Changes 8	Lost 68
Earth-Anchors 10	Lines on the Death of a Theologi-
A Mother's Anniversary . . 11	cal Student 70
Broken Dreams 12	Love's Crosses 71
" Broken Wings " 14	My Prayer 74
Muscle and Brain . . . 16	The Little Sower's Prize Poem . 76
The Royal Road of Duty . . 18	Little Quarrels 78
The Poet of the Hearth . . 20	Our Children 80
My Half-way House to Heaven . 23	Grandfather 81
Snow 26	Grandmother 83
Snow 28	Our Baby 85
The Ships of Doom . . . 30	Robed in White 87
Camp Nelson. 31	Song of the Christmas Eve . . 88
Lines on the Death of a Friend . 32	The Evening Story . . . 89
Thorns 33	A Letter to the Children . . 91
Life's Timepiece 34	Where Jesus is 93
An Hour of Sabbath . . . 36	My Letter from the King . . 94
Midnight 37	Our Nation's Destiny . . . 96
Midnight Angels 39	The Angels 98
Out of Tune 40	Lines, with a Bible Presented . 100
Murdered Days 41	My Life and I . : . . 100
The Ocean Cable . . . 42	My Theory 102
" War on the Continent " . . 44	My Creed 103
The Death Mystery . . . 46	Nearer God 105
The Minister's Problem . . . 48	After a While 106
Immanuel 52	Dr. L. L. Pinkerton . . . 108
Iconoclasm 54	My Vesper Song 109
The Ships of Life 55	Women—Mission Workers . . 111
Three Pictures of Faith . . 57	My Sunset Window . . . 113
" In Memoriam " . . . 59	A Prayer 114
At the Aid Society 59	Across the Sea 116
Partnership 60	Reticence 118

John the Baptist 119	What of the Day ? 149
The Greatest Prophet . . . 120	Life's Service 149
The Second Miracle . . . 121	Rivers of Song 152
God 121	My Ideal 153
A Response 124	A Voice in the Storm . . . 155
The Cross of Christ . . . 127	Lines to my Husband on the At-
Pentecostal Voices . . . 129	lantic—Outward Bound . . 156
As our Day shall our Strength be 130	Lines to M. C. Ramsey, with a
Christmas Poems . . . 131	Bible, presented by his Choir 158
The Angels' Song . . . 132	Change 158
The Wise Men's Song of Worship 132	Is it Best ? 159
Fragments 133	A Reply 161
A Face in a Crowd . . . 134	Ye have not Lived in Vain . . 162
The Only Daughter . . . 136	Lines to my Mother . . . 163
Going on a Journey . . . 137	Lines to a Stranger, whose Writ-
When shall I see Thee, Mother	ings I had Read . . . 164
Mine ? 138	A Wish, for a Friend, who re-
Satisfaction 140	quested it 166
A Reverie 140	Lines to my Sister . . . 167
Madaline 141	Lines written in a Friend's Album 167
One Day with God . . . 142	Loneliness 168
Something More 143	A Dream of the Past . . . 169
Guessing at the Unknown . . 144	My Secret 170
The Iron Horse 146	A Prayer 171
At Rest 146	The Half-way House . . . 172
From Sun to Sun 147	Thy Will be Done 173
My Friend and Christ's . . 148	Waves of Galilee 174

PART II.—PROSE.

The Fight of Patience . . . 175	Deacons as Evangelists . . . 253
The Bible Stage of Christianity . 179	Ordination 270
These Temples 183	Little by Little 280
A Sermon from the Pew . . 185	"Put out the Light" . . . 283
The Lever of Archimedes . . 191	Christmas 286
Pilate's Wash-basin . . . 197	What our Souls tell us . . . 292
The Leaven of the Pharisees . 201	"The Realm of Change" . . 308
The Wonderful Will . . . 204	Keeping Time 313
Latest from Paris 208	The Broken Evergreen . . . 318
A Social Rampage 213	Rays from an Old Memory . . 326
Pens and Patience 217	Under the Dome 334
Life-Work ; or, Raised from the	A Page of History and a Line of
Depths 223	Revelation 343

INTRODUCTION.

Had the wishes of friends, near and far, expressed by every style of communication, from time to time, been acceded to, most of these productions, which have appeared in leading religious and secular journals, would have appeared in book form many years ago.

The insuperable hindrance to earlier publication was interposed by the author herself; and this she did persistently, as she would declare that she had not yet produced anything worthy of such honor, and moreover, she always expected to write a longer poem to lead all the others. That longer poem was never written.

Only a few hours before she winged her way to the heights of glory, of which even the poets only dream, she committed these pieces into my hands for preparation and publication. She calmly realized that the volume of her book was at last finished, and sanctioned its going forth to work on for the pleasure and profit of the people. I therefore send it forth as her message still speaking in our ears, the things which took the forms of beauty, and sang in musical strains first in her own soul, hoping that the full measure and perfectly rounded sum of the many-sided good she desired to accomplish may be successfully wrought thereby, and that these eloquent pages may speak her thoughts in her own words,

"Though her lips are now frozen and dumb."

This gifted, saintly, and now glorified woman, who for nearly twenty-three years was the inestimable helpmate of Thomas D. Butler, was born at Jordan, Onondaga Co., N. Y., Feb. 15, 1839. About two years after this event, her parents removed to Cuyahoga

Falls, Summit Co., O., where, in her thirteenth year, she wrote the
earliest of her preserved poems, entitled "The Falling Leaf," published in its original form many years afterwards, in the *Christian
Standard.* In 1853, her parents removed to Wheeling, Va., where
her father, not long after, died during an epidemic of cholera. Her
mother now opened a school for instruction in music, drawing and
embroidery, having select classes in other towns, in which Marie
became an efficient assistant. While living in Wheeling, she gained
the first prize awarded at the county fair for a series of pencil
sketches, which her family still hold as treasures. In 1857, Mrs.
Radcliffe accepted the position of governess in a private boarding-
school at Brownsboro, Oldham Co., Ky., with Marie as assistant.
Here the mother was married to Deacon John S. Christopher, of
Louisville, Ky., and soon afterwards Marie entered the Female
High School of that city to finish her education. Although always
hampered and enfeebled by a violent and exhausting cough, and
faithful beyond limit in her department of domestic duty, she performed the exceptional and unparalleled task of crowding the four
years' course into two years, and graduated with an unusually brilliant class. George D. Prentice, the famous editor of the Louisville
Journal, who had written most eulogistically of her poetical contri-
butions to his paper, wrote the following concerning her graduating
essay : "It would be invidious to speak separately of the essays of
the members of the graduating class, but we can not refrain from
mentioning that upon 'Disunion,' read by Miss Rachel Gibbous,
and the remarkable dissertation upon 'Woman and Dreams,' by
Miss Marie Radcliffe. The former displayed great wit and strong
intellect ; the latter, a maturity of thought very rare in young girls.
The strong-mindedness was, indeed, an objectionable feature, eman-

ating from so lovely a girl, whose business in life is to brighten a fireside, and not to discuss woman's rights." (This was twenty-four years ago.)

In August 22, 1861, she became the consort of Thomas D. Butler, then and for fourteen years afterwards a resident of Louisville. During her residence in this city, her six children were born, and nearly all her literary work was done. During all her subsequent journeyings, Louisville was home, sweet home; and she rests there in God's acre.

None but her family knew the vast labor, the ever-present suffering, and the all-sustaining and all-conquering heroism that made up her daily life. As she said once, and only once, "I have never drawn a well breath in all my life."

Although measurably keeping up her habit of reading only the best books, and devoutly exercising her gifts as a writer, she was a most diligent, careful and painstaking mother, as the fruits of her loving heart and busy, skillful fingers will testify long after her latest boy is a man, or with her in glory.

At the request of the editor of the *Christian Standard*, she occupied the first column of the first page of the first number with a long poem, thus introducing the first copy to its friends. For several years afterwards she wrote almost exclusively for the pages of the *Standard*, and many of her pieces in prose and poetry were copied into leading religious and secular journals of this and other countries. A number of her poems were published in the New York *Independent*.

That paper, in announcing her death, said: "The Louisville *Commercial* announces the death of Mrs. Marie Radcliffe Butler, wife of Rev. T. D. Butler. Mrs. Butler will be recalled by the

older readers and subscribers of the *Independent* as a former contributor to our columns. She wrote verses which were greatly admired
at the time of their appearance."

Other papers sought her services as a contributor. She wrote
some prize poems about this time, iu all of which, I think, she was
distinctly successful. For some months about the year 1871, she
performed editorial service on the *Standard* during the absence of
its editor at various places filling engagements. In this work, which
she very much enjoyed, she wrote many editorial articles of great
beauty of diction, and of striking originality of thought. While
in Cincinnati, she produced a singularly beautiful and powerful
article, entitled "A Page of History and a Line of Revelation,"
for the pages of the *Christian Quarterly*. This was the only
article, I believe, ever contributed by a woman to that scholarly
review.

In 1872, Bosworth, Chase & Hall, of Cincinnati, published her
two books—"Riverside" and "Grandma's Patience"—two serials
which had appeared in the *Standard*. She also edited two small
books written by her mother, Mrs. Fannie H. Christopher, entitled
"Duke Christopher" and "Bartholet Milon."

Intensely and unceasingly devoted to gospel truth, she was in no
sense or degree a sectarian. She loved her church, and labored for
its prosperity and honor with untiring zeal and fidelity.

The project of organizing the C. W. B. M. had peculiar interest
for her. She longed and prayed for it years before its formation.
When finally it came to be a fact in the history of our missionary
undertakings, she was grievously disappointed that she was too sick
to attend the first annual meeting, in connection with the General
Convention held at Cincinnati, October 20, 1874. She was then

lying, as we feared, near the gate of death. But in this, as in everything else, she did what she could. Full of weakness and pain, while her poor body was pillowed in her bed, her great, loving soul sent its own message in its own way, in a poem of twenty-two stanzas, to be read as her offering to the Convention of Christian Women. This poem was read by Miss Ida Hood, of Cincinnati.

From this time a great change came over her life and work. Nursed and tended with the utmost care and skill, she was preserved through the ensuing winter and spring, when, in charge of her devoted mother and a nurse, she went with her children to the home of bishop B. U. Watkins, Maine Prairie, Minn., on the quiet shore of whose "Silver Lake" her only brother had been resting for many months. From her far northern retreat she sent her eloquent and immortal lines to the memory of Dr. L. L. Pinkerton, which, in lieu of a worthy poet to sing to her memory, we will apply to her as equally appropriate and fitting.

Her disease being arrested, she felt that as God had given her another, although a frail, lease of life, she would devote herself particularly to pursuits of the highest and deepest practical importance. She was fortunate in having for her mother a woman of unusual culture, piety and practical philanthropy. She led her daughter into all such fields, often, as I know, requiring the highest moral courage and the deepest self-sacrifice, and was more than content afterwards to follow the larger leadership of her more gifted child. As during the dark and bitter years of the war from 1861 to 1865, both mother and daughter were conspicuous for their loyalty to the Government, for their laborious work in behalf of the sick soldiers —converting their home into a hospital for many months—and unabated service in hospital and camp until peace came, so the temperance cause took hold of them, and the soul of our departed one was filled with zeal and her lips with burning words.

Making her home in Detroit in 1876, she at once associated herself with the W. C. T. U., and notwithstanding her physical energy had lost much of its vitality, she was an indefatigable, fearless and efficient worker in the departments specially assigned her—with direct reference to her preëminent intellectual capabilities. Her name and fame in Michigan, Ohio, Pennsylvania, and other States, rest almost all together upon her public work as a lecturer in the temperance field and a preacher of the gospel of Jesus Christ. Many persons who heard her in these gospel temperance meetings have said that they did not know there was so much temperance in the Bible until they heard her speak. It was a joy to her to *unite* the various denominations in practical, as they were separated in *theoretical*, Christianity, as she often did in union gospel temperance meetings.

The beginnings of her twofold public work were, in our judgment, strikingly providential. She had lived to be thirty-seven years of age, in a quiet and modest, but withal a useful Christian life, with the daily satisfaction of doing the duty of the hour. And for this she always had the courage of a true purpose. While she never cherished a prejudice or a resentment, her eye was always single and clear and steadfast. To her the supreme question was, Is it right ? This settled, while she would as a child sit at the feet of others, if need be, to learn methods, she never held her convictions and her duty subject for a moment to any one. It was hers to do her duty, and as she used to say, she "had not the *time* or *strength* or *disposition* to discuss the question with objectors and critics." Her path lay above them. Her public work in temperance was utterly unsought by her. The Sunday afternoon meeting of the W. C. T. U. in Detroit was an immense popular assembly all the year round. The preachers of the city discoursed there, as I did on several occasions. In 1877, Francis Murphy was announced to address the meeting, but the President of the Union, Mrs. B. B. Hudson, who was also President of the State organization, fearing that for some reason he might disappoint them, applied to Mrs. Butler, and urged her to prepare herself to speak on that uncertain occasion. The time came, and she had to fill the vacancy under such trying conditions. This was the first time in her life that she stood before an audience for such a work. Her earnestness and the gravity of her message more than compensated, as inspiration, for the unfamiliarity of her task and the shrinking sense of her inability for the work. But with her soul on fire, she spoke with quiet but intense fluency, and with consummate effectiveness, for the space of an hour and more. A city paper thus noticed the address:

"The gospel temperance meeting on Sunday afternoon was addressed by Mrs. T. D. Butler, of this city. Her effort is commended as one of the most eloquent, sympathetic and practical that the Union has had the pleasure of listening to."

Some time afterwards she accompanied me to an annual meeting in the county north of Grand Rapids, where brethren and sisters spoke to me with regard to asking her to preach at the meetings. As I had to go, after the first day of meeting, to fill an engagement at Charlotte, I told them that they had my consent for her to preach, provided she did not speak in the open air meetings. When we met again at home the next week, I learned that she had preached four successive evenings in the public hall. At first she refused, for the work was strange and solemn, and she knew she would be subjected to misunderstandings and unkind criticisms, and finally consented to preach only from night to night, as her work might be vindicated by the good she was able to do. During these evenings, Bro. Grice, the pastor, received, I think, fifteen confessions of persons directly influenced by her words. Thus into the temperance and gospel work she was constrained by irresistible moral forces, simply for the good she might do for God and man. She knew she was right, and did it, as many will testify to her honor in time and eternity. They will tell the good she has done.

About this time (1877–8) she edited for one year a weekly temperance paper in Detroit, called " Truth for the People."

Her fame as a lecturer and preacher traveled fast and far. At Bailey, north of Grand Rapids, there never was a church of any kind. There was preaching by two or three preachers in the school-house, and the foundation was in course of preparation for a United Brethren house of worship. As missionary and evangelist of the third district of Michigan, she labored in that school-house for three weeks, and took the hearts of the people so much that the town was profoundly interested. Scores were converted, and among them leading people. A church was at once organized, and a good house was erected, and Bro. Grice employed as preacher.

For a year she was preacher of the church at Byron, south of Grand Rapids. In both of these places, as elsewhere, she is enshrined in the hearts of hundreds.

In July, 1881 a temperance mass meeting was held on the fair grounds in Akron, O., continuing through Saturday and Sunday. At this meeting the leading temperance men of the State were present—Samuel F. Cary, of Cincinnati; I. A. Justice, of Youngstown; S. G. McKee, of Alliance, and Col. I. W. Tucker, of Columbus. On Lord's day morning, religious services were held, when Mrs. Butler delivered a temperance sermon. Meeting General Cary in the afternoon, he remarked, "If you can preach as well as your wife, you are a good preacher."

At the General Convention, at Louisville, in 1880, she spoke for the C. W. B. M., and at various State and district conventions she was heard on the many important questions included in gospel temperance and missionary work during every year since that time.

As late as the last winter she labored in the northeastern part of the State of Pennsylvania, delivering twenty-eight discourses, usually an hour in length, in twenty-five days, besides shorter talks and addresses in addition. In her labors among the churches she sought to arouse Christian women to organize auxiliary societies of the C. W. B. M. The other arm of her work was to organize Christian women into auxiliaries of the W. C. T. U. In both of these works, which lay so near to her heart, she was very successful. Early in this year she was appointed a State organizer of the N. W. C. T. U., and was preparing to prosecute this mission when her little remaining strength finally failed her. Her persistent labors had been performed in great feebleness and suffering. From the first she did not waste her strength, but scrupulously husbanded it for her work. She spoke calmly, deliberately, and with the least possible physical exertion. Her clear and precise articulation enabled her to be heard by a very large audience in her usually easy tone of voice, without ever straining her powers. Her speaking seemed to strengthen her chest and lungs, and on the whole her health appeared to be benefited by her work.

After the flood which happened in Louisville more than a year ago, she was instrumental in promoting the religious awakening in our churches in that city—more particularly among the sisters. Bro. A. I. Hobbs, describing the workers in the *Old-Path Guide*, said : "Justice to Sister Marie R. Butler requires me to say that much of this good work is due, under God, to her clear brain, warm heart, and eloquent tongue."

During my labors at Troy, Pa., in the first part of February, she preached for me, as her custom was. Those sermons on February 3d and 10th were her last. The final one, entitled "The Scarlet Thread," was listened to by a large audience, many of whom were the leading people of the community. Reports tell me that she spoke like one inspired. Such a theme—the blood of Christ running through the Christian system like a scarlet thread, was her poetical conception of Christ's all-pervasiveness. Spurgeon says that Paul was such a preacher that he was ready, after preaching, to walk down from his pulpit and lie down in his coffin. It was so with her. The next time she entered the church she was in her shroud.

She went to church and to her engagements as president of the W. C. T. U., in Johnstown, as long as she could drag one foot after another. Her errands were all in these directions. She labored as long as she could move, and, like Neander, who worked to the last, saying good-bye, and composed himself to sleep in Jesus, and also like Calvin, who asked to be supported while he wrote with his dying fingers, saying, "I want the Master, when he comes, to find me working," so she, who used to say, "If I wait until I am well, or even better than sick, I shall never do anything," only when she had done all she could, and when she could do no more, complacently lay down upon her bed, and without a doubt or anxiety, as without ecstasy or depression, she confidently waited for the coming of the Lord. We read to her precious words from her Book—especially her favorite, the 23d Psalm. And we sang precious words from the Hymn and Tune-Book, "Abide with me," and "Yes, for me," etc., which seemed to refresh her. The ladies of her own and other churches, and the W. C. T. U., who nursed her, have many precious thoughts which she expressed. "What can poor sinners do when they come to die without a dear Saviour to lean upon?" George Whitfield used to say that the Lord would not require him to give any testimony when he came to his dying hour, for he had borne so much testimony for him during his active life. So was it with Mrs. Butler. She asked her physicians to tell her the whole truth concerning her case, adding, "It will make no difference to me, as I have been for many years preparing for this time." She prayed for her release; she asked the Saviour to take her, for life was pain, and it never had been otherwise. The physicians and many Christian women had done their utmost. Hundreds had prayed for her. And as her feet touched the cold waters, she raised her large eyes to the faces of mother, husband and children, and with the plea of a departing soul, like the cry of the dying Christ, she said with infinite yearning, "Pray for me," and fell asleep.

Just afternoon of the day,
Just afternoon of her life.

Hearts are stricken sorely at home, and measurably everywhere. The story of her life and work and departure will be told for many a day in all the religious circles of this community, and others where she has lived. She belonged denominationally to one, but practically, as the Presbyterian preacher said at her funeral, to all the churches and all the people of the town, and as another preacher added, to the State, the nation, and the world at large.

Funeral services were held in the Christian Church in Johns-town, in which some of the leading preachers most feelingly partic-ipated, and a large concourse of workers for humanity from all the churches were present, After the services, a sorrowful procession followed her remains to the P. R. R. Depot, *en route* to Louisville, Ky. On this final day, appropriate services were held in her own church, at Fourth and Walnut, by Elders A. I. Hobbs and Geo. E. Walk, the former of whom delivered a most discriminating address. And then we laid her to rest by the side of her children in the beau-tiful cemetery of her old home, from which disease banished her while living, but most gracefully and hospitably received her again to a peaceful sepulcher.

And so her memory rests embalmed in the hearts of the Christian and philanthropic people of the town where she spent her last months ; and no less tenderly embalmed is it in the hearts of the same classes of Christian workers in the city of Louisville, as in many another place.   THOMAS D. BUTLER.

PART I.

—

POETRY.

—

THE CHRISTIAN STANDARD ON THE FIELD OF ARMAGEDDON.

Once, faint, and weary of the world around me —
    The mists before me, and the clouds behind —
My spirit drooping with the flesh that bound me,
    And growing fainter as my faith declined;

Strange doubting heresies grew o'er my spirit —
    The noisome fungi of a stagnant soul;
The Good and Evil that our lives inherit
    Lost their proportions in a darkened whole.

While doubt loomed darkly on the side of Error,
    Faith glimmered feebly on the brink of night —
I deemed the struggle far too full of horror,
    And too unequal to be just and right.

Could Love Eternal give us nothing better? —
    But here my weary questioning soul grew still —
Dropped all unconscious every earthly fetter,
    And wandered gladly at its own wild will;

But paused at length upon the gleaming sky-way
  O'er which the angels on their missions come,
To lead us over God's celestial highway,
  When we are weary and are going home.

Beneath my feet the struggling world was lying,
  And to my spirit's sight was then revealed;
Eternal Wisdom, to my soul replying,
  Solved the deep mystery that Life concealed.

This was our birthright: as each being entered,
  He sought his place amid the deadly strife;
Found some bright standard where his high hopes
      centered,   `
  And fought his battle on the field of Life.

Here Mammon's banner on the wind was flying,
  Catching the sunlight with its bars of gold;
And there Ambition flaunted o'er the dying
  The mocking purple of each gorgeous fold.

There was no rest, and death the only ending —
  The winds were laden with the flags unfurled,
And streamed forever o'er the wild contending,
  The sin-born splendors of a groaning world.

In the wild centre of the vast upheaving,
  Rose the white standard of the Christian Faith,
Just where the strife grew deadliest, and the living
  Seemed most unequal in the grasp of Death.

Like a white sail upon the breast of ocean,
  Riding triumphant while the storm-winds blow,
That radiant banner through the fierce commotion,
  Floated in calmness o'er the strife below.

While legions struggled for the mocking splendors
    Of gaudy banners on the dim air flung;
That standard rallied but a few defenders,
    Though Earth and Heaven were in the balance hung.

Oh dark eclipse! would human sin and blindness
    Defy alike the wrath and love of God?
And would the banner of His loving-kindness
    Float unregarded where the Saviour trod?—

Were there no echoes in the wild winds sleeping,
    Of Him who suffered that we might be blessed?
Had earth no relics in her holy keeping—
    No blood-stained mem'ries on her scar-worn breast?

Infinite Knowledge, with its deep divining,
    Had surely fathomed what His wisdom planned?
A sweet contentment hushed my wild repining—
    The good and evil struggled in His hand,

Nor vainly struggled; for beyond the river,
    Across the bridge from faith to promise spanned,
God's angels led his war-worn heroes over,
    To bear His standard in the Peaceful Land.

These patient heroes who had won promotion,
    To wear their honors on a bleeding breast,
Rose from the chaos and the wild commotion,
    To the calm presence of Eternal Rest.

Passing o'er fields rich with eternal flowers,
    That drink the sunshine that is always there;
They waved their standard from the shining towers,
    In the white radiance of the heavenly air.

The sin-stained earth with other blood must redden :
They had gone upward to their great reward ;
While we upon the field of Armageddon,
Were fighting still the battles of the Lord.

We were co-workers with the great All-Father,
In the deep mystery of His wondrous plan ; —
The good and evil of the ages gather
For final struggle in the fate of man.

We *know* the issue of the fearful trial :
He holds the evil as his smiting-rod ;
We read the shadows on His wondrous dial,
And we are wiser than the "Sons of God."

What are the banners of the earth before us ?
For he who "brought upon the earth a sword "
Gave with the standard that is streaming o'er us,
Strength from His arm, and wisdom from the Lord.

Holding our standard with a firmer grasping,
We stand transfigured in its radiant light ;
For all the promises of God are clasping
Their rainbow glories o'er its stainless white.

THE FALLING LEAF.

(WRITTEN IN HER THIRTEENTH YEAR.)

The falling leaf! it sinks to earth
So gently, and it seems to say :
My little work is finished now,
My race is run, I go my way —
Swept by the winds, to earth I bow.

'T was but a day — see thou and learn —
And I was beautiful and gay,
  The glory of the summer tree —
But ah! my beauty fades to-day;
  Learn from the withered thing you see.

So with thy life, all glory fades;
So strength and power, like me, decay;
  So sweetness, grace and worth must die —
Fall like the summer leaves away —
  All things of earth with me must lie.

Thy youth is blooming green and fair;
But age will come to thee at last;
  Thy form will bend, thine eye grow dull,
Thou 'lt fall like me before the blast; —
  And thus the course of ages roll.

A BABY'S FACE.

'T is the beautiful work of the hand Divine,
Where a soul-ray sleeps in an earthly shrine;
'T is pure as an angel's heaven-lit brow,
Or thoughts that well up in its bosom now;
And oh! how I wish for some mystic art
To unveil the thoughts in a baby's heart.

And when sleep has kissed the fluttering breast,
And the dewy lips, and the soul to rest;
When the eyelids close o'er their wells of blue
As the petals hide the rose's dew —
Lest glances of love, like the sun's bright ray,
Should steal the dew from their depths away;

I 've longed to know if the spirit lies,
Like the half-veiled light in the sleeper's eyes,
Unconsciously holding a hidden power,
That will wake to life in a future hour,
With all the sweet, unspoken things
That sleep like angels with folded wings.

But most of all, I have tried to dream
What clouds will o'ershadow thy pure life-stream,
And how many blushes, and smiles, and tears
Are waiting for thee in the future years;
What hopes will blossom, what love decay,
What lights will pass from thy soul away.

O fair young child, with thy spotless brow,
So fresh from the hand of thy Maker now —
Though the fingers of Time with the iron of care
Shall engrave deep lines of sorrow there —
May no dark sin, with its earthly stain
Rest there, till thou goest to God again.

But life has many a snare, sweet child,
And many a path that 's dark and wild.
There shadows fall in eternal night,
Which only the smile of God can light;
And only those who trust in Him
Shall safely pass through the shadows dim.

SPIRIT MUSINGS.

Only a picture upon the wall;
A beautiful picture — that is all.

A little form for my heart to hold;
A little face that will ne'er grow old.

But a mother's heart is a holy cell,
Where the faces and forms of her children dwell.

My heart, like a ship on the sea of life,
If it weathers the gale and storm and strife,

By soft winds favored or rough winds driven,
Will carry that little face to Heaven.

But 't is a dream and nothing more;
It will not stand on the blessed shore,

To welcome me when my toil is done,
· And my battle of life is fought and won:

But the angels will finish what I began,
And develop the child to a perfect man;

And my soul's sweet bud in Heaven will grow
To a fairer thing than the earth could know.

Whose being expands in the airs of Heaven,
Must grow to the stature Christ has given;

And I shall look up to my radiant child,
And down on the little face that smiled.

Will vague regret for my earthly toy
Dim the glory that crowns my boy?

Or will the picture I loved of yore,
Be a beautiful picture — nothing more?

SPIRIT–CHANGES.

Like Ocean in its hoarse unrest —
Wild surges of the sea —
My moaning thoughts break on the shores
Of brooding Memory.

My idle hands have lost their work,
My life its sweet employ,
For precious plans lie folded up,
And buried with my boy.

And all the earth is changed to me:
If I am sad or gay,
No shining sun can ever bring
The light of yesterday.   ·

We sometimes pass from childhood on,
Through youth and riper years,
Nor note the changes as they come
Through varying hopes and fears;

But sometimes in our journeying,
A landmark on the way
Remains, to tell us whence we bore
An older heart away.

A little milestone it may be,
But when Life's sun is low,
It casts a shadow far across
The lengthened way we go.

So all the earth is changed to me :
If I am sad or gay,

No rising sun can ever bring
   The light of yesterday.

I know I stand on higher ground,
   To view Life's earnest plan —
I see with more prophetic eyes
   The hope and toil of man.

Older and wiser, better too
   My struggling soul has grown, —
Beyond Life's dark horizon line,
   It wandered forth alone;

And Heaven was opened to my view,
   I saw a vision blest —
A child that on my bosom grew
   Slept on the Father's breast;

And, echoed from the jasper walls,
   A whisper came to me —
"She thought to lead *him*, but *his hands*
   Shall lead *her* up to Thee."

And then the gates of pearl swung back,
   And shut the glory in,
And I was standing here alone
   With sorrow, earth and sin.

So all the earth is changed to me,
   My life and labor too.
Father, ordain me for Thy work,
   And teach me *what* to do.

Though darkness o'er my soul has come,
   I may not question why —

This is the wind and storm and fire
That now is passing by.

But when the "still small Voice" shall float
In calmness out to me,
My soul shall know its higher life,
And read its destiny.

EARTH-ANCHORS.

Above my head the pitying stars are shining,
    As if their holy eyes were dim with tears,
While I, life's mystery but half divining,
    Look up and onward to the coming years.

Softly the shadows fall away that cover
    The future from the present, where I stand;
And I, like ancient Israel, looking over,
    Catch the far hill-tops of the Promised Land.

But I am mortal, and my eye grows weary
    With its far flight into the heavenly air;
And lesser lights, along life's pathway dreary,
    Eclipse the splendor of the glory there.

I love the earth with all its teeming beauty—
    The vineyard and the garden of our Lord;
I see fair flowers grow on the hills of duty,
    And toil may pluck them as its sweet reward.

And dear hands draw us with a touch so tender,
    Our hearts forgive the earthward impetus;

And dear eyes hold us with their loving splendor,
Till Earth alone seems Heaven enough for us.

'T is not idolatry that holds my spirit:
My soul turns ever to the farther shore;
But from the Earth, our mother, we inherit
Ties that will bind us here for evermore,

Till on her bosom, in a quiet slumber,
The spirit's warfare with the flesh is o'er,
And God shall add us to the holy number
Who rise all stainless from the chains they wore.

And even then, where trod the dear Redeemer,
Earthward our souls may wander to and fro;
And some tired heart, like Israel's ancient dreamer,
May watch the angels as they come and go.

A MOTHER'S ANNIVERSARY.

A year ago, my darling boy —
A year of sadness, tears and joy,
Of Heavenly trust, with Earth's alloy —

My grief and faith stood side by side,
I could not think that thou hadst died,
But only left me purified;

No more a child for earth and me,
Through life and death, passed on to be
An heir of immortality.

The wound that bleeds with long regret
May heal at last, but never yet
A mother's heart could quite forget.

Though I have toiled and prayed and striven,
A calm like thine has not been given;
For thou hast been a year in Heaven.

I am a child to-day, and thou —
Ah! yes, thou art God's hand, I know,
Stretched out to guide me here below.

In changed relation to my child, ·
I grope a pathway dark and wild,
To where thy love-framed image smiled.

But thy white feet, unsoiled by sin,
Above the clouds that hem me in,
Still walk in paths where God has been.

Infinite tides of glory drop
Into thy soul's expanded cup,
To fill thy empty being up.

Across the boundary I lean
To catch what thy dear eyes have seen,—
But still the veil must intervene.

BROKEN DREAMS.

The broken ways of change
Are rugged steps whereon our souls may rise,

Ere yet the miracle that we call death,
Embalms them for the skies.

And when at last we stand
Upon that far-off summit we must climb,
To take our first look of the world beyond—
The last of earth and time;

Upon each radiant spot,
Where we have tarried in our onward way,
We shall but see a grave where some lost hope,
Or sunny dream-child lay.

But love may gather up
Our broken dreams, just as the scattered rain
Is all collected by the potent sun,
To fill the streams again.

So when the silver cord
Is snapped asunder, and the heart is stilled,
Perhaps each soul may find in heaven
Its dreams are all fulfilled.

Perhaps the severed links
They mourned so sadly, while on earth they trod,
Bound them more firmly than unbroken chains,
About the feet of God.

Perhaps our earthly dreams
Are but the glimmerings of eternal light,
That pierce the veil that still must hide
God's glory from our sight,

Till like the veil of old,
That hid the Presence in the holiest place,

It shall be rended, and the light
Stream from His shining face.

When from the spirit falls—
Falls the last fold of the enwrapping clay—
Fades the last shadow of the soul's eclipse,
In Heaven's eternal day,

Perhaps the golden threads,
Broken and tangled in earth's weary strife,
Will all be woven in the shining web
Of everlasting life.

And all the endless years,
Like golden orbits for our souls shall seem;
While we remember life's sad pilgrimage
But as a broken dream.

"BROKEN WINGS."

It sometimes seems the saddest lot
To walk through Fate's uneven ways,
And find, when hardest tasks are done,
Unequal shares of blame and praise.

To know our souls are true and firm,
Determined, if at last we fall,
To scale heroic heights, and die
Like sentries on the outer wall;

Yet tread amid a careless throng
That see not where the triumph lies,

Nor stop to mark with altar-stone
The spot whereon a hero dies.

Ah! this is sad, but those who toil
For crowns immortal, do not mourn,
When drooping laurels they have won
On other brows are proudly worn.

It may be sad, but still at last
Our highest praise is found with Him
Before whose smile the lesser lights
Of mortal fame grow vague and dim.

But there is something sadder still—
The non-fulfillment of a dream
Whose purpose lies across our lives
Like broken bridges o'er a stream,

That seem to touch the farther side,
Inviting effort o'er and o'er,
Yet rise and fall with every tide,
And leave us waiting on the shore,

Waiting, until the sun is set,
And all the way is yet untrod,
And nothing, but our shapeless dreams,
Is left to offer up to God.

Ah! sense of powers that hidden lie
Beneath some mountain weight of care,
And wings that never upward fly,
To circle in the vital air!

Ah! sense of something yet to be,
And yet which might have been before,

Something we long and strive to find,
Yet may not clasp for evermore!

Poor souls, that climb a weary height,
To find at last the topmost tower
That crowned a life's exalted dream,
One step beyond their blighted power!

Those bear the saddest lots, who could
Have made of life a grander thing,
But for the purpose unfulfilled,
Or reached upon a broken wing.

MUSCLE AND BRAIN.

Walk in the light of thy beautiful dreaming—
Dreams are the wings that may raise thee to God,
Light-pinioned angels our weakness redeeming—
Soul leading Sense up the wearisome road.
Make human and real
Thy grandest ideal,
Embody thy dream with thy muscle and brain.

Stand by the rock of thy purpose and mould it,
With chisel and hammer strike blow upon blow—
Thy angel lies hid, but thy work shall reveal it,
Thou art hewing for God in His quarry below.
Hoping, believing,
Not blindly achieving,
Toil for the Lord with thy muscle and brain.

Stand at the loom of thy destiny weaving,
A miracle warp is before thee outspread—

Who weaves for the world for himself is achieving,
For God is beside him to double the thread.
Waiting the issues
Of wonderful tissues,
Toil for the world with thy muscle and brain.

Stand at the helm while thy life-ship is riding
Over the turbulent billows of Fate;
We break from the arms of Omnipotent guiding
Unless we endeavor, and labor, and wait.
An angel beside us
Shall strengthen and guide us,
Who toil at the helm with our muscle and brain.

Earth's glory goes on like the change of the seasons;
God turns a new leaf for each oncoming age;
And each with its failures, successes and reasons,
Contributes an ill or a well written page.
A thought that is grand
Will live on and expand
Slowly rounded to form by our muscle and brain.

Stand on the hill, twixt the now and the morrow,
Catch the first glimpse of the incoming dawn;
Behind press the feet that are heaving with sorrow,
Before are the feet of the children unborn.
O Father, renew us,
Shine in us and through us,
To will and to do with our muscle and brain.

Look with the eyes of a great inspiration
Up where the pathway lies farthest and dim.
In the thought of to-day lies the fate of a nation;
Be sure He ordains us to lead it to Him.

Are we ready, if straightway
Shall open the gateway
To grander achievements of muscle and brain?

Strike with God's hammer and trust Him forever,—
Strike on the resonant anvil of Time;
Soft opportunities wrought by endeavor
Harden to deeds that are grand and sublime.
Providence waits for us,
Forging our fates for us,
Striking *her* blows with *our* muscle and brain.

The clouds have rolled back, and our glorified vision
Sees God in the conflict, and Jesus is there,
And the Book of all books, with its holy commission,
Borne on by our lips and embalmed by our prayers.
God's light hath unbound us,
The workmen crowd round us:
Ordain for thy service our muscle and brain.

THE ROYAL ROAD OF DUTY.

Why stand ye gazing up to God?
There are no footprints in the air;
Feet were ordained to walk the sod,
And angels meet us everywhere.

When on our homeward march sublime
We bear the victor's gathered spoil,
'T will be but things of sense and time—
The daily worship of our toil.

For duty hath no soiling hand,
  And labor never leaves a stain,
But purposes divine and grand
  Are wrought by human toil and pain.

Sublime ideals meet our eyes
  Bent o'er ascending stairs of hope,
But by successive steps we rise
  To beings of immortal scope,

Not when we idly fold our hands—
  For muscle only grows with pain;
And evermore the soul expands
  With pulses of an aching brain.

How dare we look to Heaven in prayer
  Unless we toil along the way,
And through our daily pain and care
  Grow nearer God from day to day?

We only ask to be like Him;
  We only hope when life is gone
To bridge the river dark and dim
  With these strong words: Thy will be done.

Yet not in words that will was done;
  But Christ, in toil and sweat and blood,
His great eternal kingdom won,
  And on the brink of glory stood.

His life began in emptiness,
  And struggled on through pain, to rise
O'er boundless heights of love, to bless
  The world at last with sacrifice.

His prayers were echoes of his deeds,
    Prophetic of their future yield—
God's blessing on the scattered seeds
    Of an eternal harvest field,

Whose boundaries stretch through earth and time,
    Beyond the sun-touched hills of prayer,
Far into a serener clime
    Where God's immortal reapers are.*

Ah! broken winged are prayers that rise
    Where idle feet the vineyard trod;
Poor stranger-birds in Paradise,
    And aliens in the home of God.

THE POET OF THE HEARTH.

O Poet of the hearth!
Though Earth may mar thy spirit's heavenly calm,
Yet grief, and love, and changeless trust, are still
    The rhythm of its psalm.

Some wondrous hands have swept
Across thy spirit's sweet Æolian strings,
And left their echo in the melody
    Thy spirit sits and sings.

O vessel of God's love!
He gives thee less than man, yet gives thee more—
Less power to carve thy thoughts in deeds
    That were but dreams before;

* "And the reapers are the angels."

More power of human love,
To make a palace for thy dreaming soul,—
To see o'er all life's tangled, broken things,
    The beauty of the whole;

More power to catch the sun
With the bright lenses of thy cheerful eyes,
Or, bended o'er the storm-drenched hills of life,
    God's rainbow in the skies;

More power to take His gifts,
And bind them fondly to a thankful breast,
And when his hand withdraws them, stronger faith
    To follow to His rest.

The saints of old were men—
The priests and prophets of Jehovah's reign;
But Christ, the Saviour, came and dignified
    Our womanhood again.

How with His holy plans
Thy destiny was woven, who shall tell?
But from thy patient heart, like rusted chains
    The curse of Eden fell.

And when the Logos came
To wear the garment of our flesh and blood,
The stream was thine, O woman; thine alone,
    The parentage of God.

Upon thy virgin breast
The holy Child was laid by hands divine;
The purest bosom for his earthly rest,
    O womanhood, was thine.

And through the lowly life,
Where not a stain but tears could e'er be found,
When weary feet bore weary heart and brain,
Upon their weary round,

His only glimpse of rest—
His glimpse of what a human home *might* be—
Was with the faithful hearts that loved him best,
In quiet Bethany.

A woman's ointment soothed
The holy breast that bore the scourging rod,—
No woman's lips denied, nor kiss betrayed
The wounded Son of God.

But then, His bleeding hands
Swept o'er thy spirit's sweet Æolian strings,
And left an echo in the melody
Thy spirit sits and sings.

The passing years, that keep
The faithful record for the Book above,
Repeat the sacred story that was told
Of woman's faithful love.

Still, as the world goes on,
Proud brains will question and proud hearts rebel;
Yet seldom on a woman's heart the blight
And *curse of doubting* fell.

Through ages yet to come
Thy holy birthright shall be handed down;
And thou in faith shalt bear the heaviest cross,
And win the brightest crown.

MY HALF-WAY HOUSE TO HEAVEN.

I sit and work till shadows fall
    Dim o'er the sun's bright golden way,
And lids of evening softly close
    The dazzled eyes of weary day;

Then fling my garb of toil aside,
    For the soft robe of rest and dream,
And if my hands have caught a stain
    I wash them in the silver stream

Of Truth, that o'er the plains of Life
    Still flows along, a crystal tide,
And bears no tinge of earth to stain
    Life's river on the other side.

The dust that gathers on my brow,
    The dust of labor and of care,
An angel wipes with golden wings
    That stir the depths of slumberous air.

The cross is lifted from my heart,
    A crown laid on my grief-worn brow,
And down the channels of my face
    No bitter rain is falling now.

Fate stands beside me all the while
    To watch my soul in beauty dressed,
But hides her frowning with a smile—
    For I shall be the angels' guest.

I hear a murmur in the air,
  The rushing sound of coming wings;
And I forget my toil and care,
  With all earth's sad and sordid things.

A something brighter still than light
  Is sifted over crystal walls;
And backward o'er the gloom of night,
  A glory like a curtain falls.

This is my half-way house to Heaven,
  The lighted palace of my dreams;
And here I meet the loved and lost,
  And all is real here that seems.

I hold no forms of beauteous mould
  That reason tells me are but clay;
I kiss no waxen eyelids down
  O'er eyes whose light has passed away.

And dear ones that the earth forgot—
  She hid them in her breast so long—
Are singing, but no sad refrain
  Comes like the haunting ghost of song.

For here no wailing undertone
  Rings through each sweet and happy sound;
And where the palm trees meet the sun,
  They cast no shadow on the ground.

And where the nodding roses bloom,
  They hide no withered leaves away;
For summer here is endless June—
  A thousand years are but a day.

Here in my half-way house to Heaven,
  Beyond the blight of pain or sin,
Within the palace of my dreams,
  A shining circle hems me in;

And in the radiant air they sit,
  Each in the golden light, a gem,
For when they left the world below
  They trailed the sunshine after them.

And day by day I follow them
  Up o'er this shining track of gold,
And these poor yearning arms embrace
  What earth can never more behold.

And then a little angel comes
  To nestle in the dear old place,
And all my being warms beneath
  The radiance of one little face.

But soon I kiss the shining brow,
  And lift the angel from my breast,
For in this half-way house to Heaven
  I am not dweller—only guest.

And Fate is standing at the door,
  And beckoning down the shining track;
But when the task she sets is done
  My yearning soul will wander back.

There youth eternal crowns them all,
  No face shall ever fade away;
For in the palace of my dreams
  A thousand years are but a day.

SNOW.

I looked from my window, one dark winter eve :
Earth seemed like a captive to murmur and grieve,
Her poor fettered bosom so wounded and bare
In the chains of the frost that were forged in the air;
She seemed like a soul in the bondage of sin,
As blasted without and as hopeless within;
    The shriek of the wind
    Seemed the howl of a fiend
O'er a soul that at last irredeemably sinned.

In the morning I looked from my window, and, lo!
The earth was redeemed from her bondage and woe;
She stood like a Magdalene garmented white,
Her pardon revealed in the gloom of the night,
When love with soft fingers had covered the sin
That blasted her bosom without and within,
    Like a soul that has passed
    Through a night overcast,
To stand in the infinite glory at last.

O beautiful vision, O lesson of heaven,
Old things are forgotten as well as forgiven;
The past is sealed up, and this drapery white
Is the peace which comes down from the "Father of
    Light"—
The wings of His love o'er a desert unfurled,
His "mantle of charity" over the world,—
    To cover her storm-
    Beaten bosom, till warm
She springs into gladness and verdure and form.

That morn, how the snow lay unbroken and deep,
And white o'er the world as it wakened from sleep ;
And 'the sunshine streamed down from the glory
 above,
Like a broad flowing river of infinite love,
Whose measureless waves from their fountain o'er-
 ran
To break on the desolate dwelling of man!
 Their surges lay white
 On the shores of the night,
And the snow was a crystallized ocean of light.

But alas for the spoiling that morning would bring!
That beauty would pass for a valueless thing;
And the half-blinded vision of worldly-wise men
Would pass by the picture again and again,
Till the snow would be blackened by toiling and
 strife,—
Those dark counter-currents of hurrying life,
 In whose waves men are hurled,
 And hurried and whirled
In a maelstrom, whose vortex is vast as the world.

Ah! let us like children rejoice as we go,
In the earth, and the air, and the light, and the
 snow;
These pictures are wrought by the wonderful Giver
To hang on the walls of our memory forever,
Expanding our dreams of the glory and bliss
Of the world that's to come, by the beauty of this,
 Making it clearer,
 And better and dearer,
Seen through a glass darkly, yet plainer and nearer.

But the picture has passed from the gazing of men,
For the snow was all blackened when night came again,
Like humanity clinging to earth and the sod,
Losing the glory and likeness of God;
Till it only can hope to dissolve like the snow
In the sunshine of love and lie sleeping below,
     Losing the stain
     Of earth's contact, and then
Rise like the vapor to heaven again.

SNOW.

I watch the white snow-flakes that flutter and fly,
With their millions of wings, from the snow-burdened
     sky;
As silent and soft as the answer to prayer,
They fall on the earth, or they brood in the air;
And cover earth's frozen and desolate things
With the marvelous down of their beautiful wings.
     The crystals are shed
     On the graves of our dead,
And where our lost living, forgetting us, tread.

The earth has ungirdled the garb of her toil,
And put off the stain of humanity's soil;
Like a queen, in her ermine, resplendent and white,
No foot-print of man on her vesture to-night;
She sits in the glimmer, and sparkle, and glow,
Her lap full of jewels,—the glittering snow;—
     But the sorrow and sin,
     That to-night are shut in,
Will walk where, unsullied, the snow-flakes have been.

Like a soft-folded curtain, bespangled with gleams,
The snow flutters down, and trails over my dreams—
My Childhood comes back with its clamor and din,
The sky is shut out, and the earth is shut in;
The snow-drifts are miracle mountains, that rise
From the snow on the earth to the snow in the
    skies,
        A Babel of snow
        And confusion and glow—
A chaos of crystal above and below.

Now the snow-flakes that hurry and gather o'er-
    head
Drift down on the vanishing face of the dead;—
I shriek and call after, but still they go on,
And here in the snow I am dreaming alone;
And yet not alone, though they slumber below,
Wrapped in their downy white blanket of snow;
        For their spirits are free
        Where their dwelling must be,—
And perhaps they are watching and waiting for
    me.

Has the snow touched the spring where the tear-
    fountain lies?
Or is it the flakes that fall into my eyes?
Ah! yes, I remember—I can not forget,
For the clouds of the morning hang over me yet;
But God has been with me, and these are not tears
That water the desert of sorrowing years;
        But the snow-drift, that lay
        On my spirit to-day,
In the light of His presence is melting away.

THE SHIPS OF DOOM.

"The wicked shall be banished from the presence of the Lord,
and the glory of His power."

Away from our Father, and Heaven, and Light,
    Far off in Eternity drifting,
In a ship that went out from the harbor of Life,
To be lost in the chaos, where infinite night
    Its infinite shadows is lifting—

Sailing out from the Earth through the ocean of sky,
    Where cloud-isles in glory are lying,
To catch a last glimpse of the headlands of Heaven,
But to bid them a longing, eternal good-bye,
    And drift out in the dark with the dying—

In a doom-guided ship without compass or helm,
    To be daring the darkness forever,
With a shroud for a sail, while the desolate mast
Is cleaving a path through the desolate realm
    That the living and dying must sever.

O terrible voyage where God will forsake!
    O voyage with never an ending,
And never a place to cast anchor again,
While the horror of darkness that covers our wake
    With the horror before us is blending,

Till the eye and the ear forget vision and sound,
    In the silence to darkness replying;
And e'en the dread power of dissolving in space
Would be bliss, to the soul in its loneliness bound,
    Where living is infinite dying.

CAMP NELSON.

'T is May; and on the hillside green
The apple blossoms fall,
And clovers set their roots between
The boulders in the wall.

Above the pond the tall trees bend,
To watch its quiet rest;
And, murmuring, chide the winds that send
A ripple o'er its breast.

The blue of heaven is mirrored there;
And stars, reflected bright,
Have gazed, until the waters fair
Have buried half their light.

But see, what fearful shadows creep
Where stars of heaven look down;
While round "Camp Nelson's" rocky steep
The fearful lines move on—

Move on to mar the green hillside,
And apple blossoms fair;
With ashen spaces black and wide—
The barren steps of war.

And where the shining grasses catch
The blossoms as they fall,
The midnight guard shall walk and watch,
In silence over all.

And when the morning sun shall kiss
  The tears of night away,
The wandering wind shall sigh,. to miss
  The bloom of yesterday.

And where the dainty clovers love
  The kisses of the sun,
The cannon's breath shall ruin strew
  Before the day is done.

So loving Nature, weaving bloom,
  Spends all her patient hours ;
Man marks his way with death and doom,
  And Nature hers with flowers.

LINES ON THE DEATH OF A FRIEND.

Farewell, dear friend, a long farewell,
  For earth has lost thee now ;
And silence gathers round thy heart,
  And grave-dust on thy brow.

But where perpetual sunbeams lie,
  And never mortal trod,
Without a stain of earthly touch,
  Thy spirit walks with God.

And all the truths sublime and deep,
  We strive and long to find,
Infinite Love unfoldeth now
  To an immortal mind.

The "tree of knowledge" only grows
  Within the walls of Heaven;
And only to immortal lips
  The blessed fruit is given.

And Love, sweet bud of Heaven, grew here
  Where Christ and angels trod,
Yet could not bloom; it pined to feel
  The living smile of God.

It never blossoms here on earth,
  Though watered by our tears;
In the Hereafter it will bloom,
  Through God's eternal years.

And on thy fair, transfigured brow,
  Its blossoms angels twine;
For Heaven has not a gift too fair,
  Too precious to be thine.

THORNS.

To toil for knowledge, and to toil in vain;
  To grant forgiveness, and receive but hate;
To long for friendship which we can not gain;
  To read a mystery a day too late;
To love the beautiful, and only tread
  A stony pathway where we find no flowers;
To hear a whisper of a sin long dead
  And long repented, when the sin was ours;
To read a brother and to read him wrong—
  To lay our friendship at the feet of truth,

And then to mourn in spirit, sore and long,
  The hasty judgment of a hasty youth;
To do our duty for the Saviour's sake,
  To those who curse us when our toil is done;
To make a sacrifice though heart should break,
  And none be wiser for the battle won;
To kiss the lips that we shall press no more—
  To lay our darling in the pure white snow;
To love a being whose contempt we bore,
  And hold the secret that *he may not know;*
To weep in agony beside the dead,
  And plead for pardon in a useless prayer;
To feel remorse upon a guilty head,
  And gather curses that our sins prepare;
To die in horror as we shriek *"too late,"*
  And seal misfortune by reproaching Fate:
These are the wounding thorns of earth, and we
  With blood and tears work all our destiny;
These are the blossomings of sin and woe,
The bitter harvest of the long-ago.
  Keep us, Father, in our blindness;
  Hold us in Thy loving kindness.

LIFE'S TIMEPIECE.

Alone to-day and yesterday,
And hills on hills stretch far and gray,
Till Time's last sands shall fall away.

And yet with mine these hills were trod
By feet that found a greener sod
Upon the sunset hills of God.

I linger, but they send no token;
I listen, but no word is spoken—
The endless silence is unbroken,

Save by my weary, plodding feet,
That like twin echoes still repeat
My heart's perpetual ebbing beat.

But though my pulses creep or bound
Through dull routine of sense or sound,
My brain keeps on its weary round,

As some weird time-piece, strange and old,
Above a hearthstone dark and cold,
Ticks on through ruin, dust and mold;

Ticks on through childhood, youth and prime,
And marks with still, unvarying chime
The lowest tidal ebb of Time.

O sentient being, manifold,
That keeps its strange tenacious hold
On life, and heeds not growing old.

It grows not old, the soul divine,
Nor heeds each gathering human sign
That marks the casket's slow decline.

Till soon a loving hand will stay
The strange, mysterious, patient play
That wears the wheels of life away;

And, with these wondrous wheels, grow still
All sense of coming good or ill,
With human power, and hope, and will.

But Love, far-seeing and sublime,
In some far-off, eternal clime,
Will set them to a sweeter chime—

A chime of long, perpetual day,
Wherein no light shall fade away,
Nor years bring ruin and decay;

Where all the wheels of life shall roll
In grooves of God's divine control,
And leave no friction on the soul;

Where, through the cycles as they run,
Unmarked by dawn or setting sun,
The perfect will of God is done:

The Time-piece shall be wound again,
And nevermore by human strain
The silver cord be snapped in twain.

AN HOUR OF SABBATH.

Night is falling, calm and holy
    On the Sabbath free from care,
Like the hand of God descending
    On His children bowed in prayer.
Silence is His benediction,
    When His Spirit draweth nigh,
And His children in the darkness
    Touch His mantle, trailing by—

Touch His mantle, and grow stronger—
  Stronger for the march of Time,
For the cross that Faith endureth,
  For the heights that Love must climb;
For the light of heavenly beacons,
  Seen through tear-drops' bitter rain,
Broken into rainbow splendors
  By these drops of human pain.

What, though we should wake to-morrow
  With the cares we lose to-night
Looming up like mountain ranges,
  Shutting heaven from our sight;
Surely we are better, stronger,
  Higher lifted from the sod,
With a faith more surely anchored
  To the steadfast throne of God.

For where, on our heavenly journey,
  Prayers and praise alternate rise,
Build we of our earthly altars
  Golden stairways to the skies —
Highways, where our prayers, ascending
  To the palace of our King,
Keep ajar the golden doorways,
  While we linger faltering.

MIDNIGHT.

Night above the slumbering city,
  Night in many a weary heart,
Where some dear beloved blossom,
  Some sweet hope-bud fell apart;

Night above the murmuring forest,
　　Night upon mid-ocean waves,
·Night around a thousand couches,
　　Night above a thousand graves.

Holy Midnight, tender watcher,
　　Sitting on God's footstool down,
O'er the couch of weary nature,
　　Watching till her sleep has flown,

See : thy dusky mantle traileth
　　Darkly over half the globe—
Round my shadow-haunted spirit,
　　Let me fold thy dusky robe.

I would haste beneath thy pinions
　　To a far-off Eastern shore,
Where a fair young dreamer sleepeth,
　　Who is mine for evermore.

Softly wrap thy mantling shadows
　　Round the sleeper's heart and brain ;
Let him dream of me—'t will banish
　　Every dream-remembered pain.

In his heart my face is pictured
　　On a glory-tinted ground ;
Wrapped in olden dreams of beauty,
　　Love immortal frames it round.

So I leave him in thy keeping,
　　Guardian angel of the night.
Watch his pillow while he dreameth
　　Of the swiftly coming light.

For I know that God will call us
From these paths diverse and dim,
And my thoughts, like many rivers,
Rise in gratitude to Him.

MIDNIGHT ANGELS.

Soft shadows fall upon the stilly earth,
And silence, peace and holy rest are brought
On angel pinions from the spirit land.
What is this holy presence? What the power
That guides us through the boundless fields of
    thought;
And with a mystic key unlocks the fount
Of hopes and joys, undreamt of and untasted?
Do happy spirits from the unseen land,
Leaving a world of glory and of light,
Come softly mingling with the shadows gray,
To bear our spirits from the darkening earth,
Away from all its sorrow, toil and pain,
To revel gladly for one happy hour
In the atmosphere of heaven?
Or do God's ministers, the angels, bring
Upon their balmy wings a zephyr from
The breeze divine that floats in paradise?
Whate'er it be, we feel the wondrous spell,
Akin to what the soul at rest must feel.
Father, we thank thee for a glimpse of Heaven.

OUT OF TUNE.

Her heart was over-brimming,
   And the fancies in her brain
With thought were interweaving
   All their variegated skein.

She saw the sun uprising
   Through the golden days of June,
Till the glory rippled over
   All the summer afternoon.

At eve she saw him pillowed
   On the dusky shores of day,
On the clouds up-piled in darkness—
   And the glory ebbed away.

In spring she saw the mountains
   Put their blooming garlands on,
To woo the soft caresses
   Of the ardent summer sun,

Then she knew the earth grew warmer
   On a thousand happy farms,
And from spring it blushed to summer
   In the sun's impassioned arms,

Till the autumn's chilly fingers
   Froze the blushes on her brow,
And she lay at last deserted,
   In her bridal robe of snow.

So all her visions ended
   In a shadow or a tomb,

And round her brightest fancies
  Lay a border-line of gloom.

'T was not her care' or toiling,
  But the weary, vague unrest
Of a soul whom doubt divideth
  From the Father's loving breast.

The earth was full of music,
  But her heart was out of tune
With the sweet poetic rhythm
  Of the golden afternoon.

For Nature never falters
  In her consecrated song,
To whose music all the planets
  In their orbits move along.

But in vain we long and listen,
  And the spirit toils and strives,
Until we put in harmony
  The key-note of our lives.

MURDERED DAYS.

WRITTEN ON NEW YEAR'S EVE.

The Night has put her mourning on,
  And Nature sheds her tears of dew,
While round the solemn, vaulted sky
  The stars are shining, far and few.

And now the Moon, repentant, comes
  When all the funeral pomp is done,
To hold above the grave of Day
  The wasted torches of the Sun.
The day is dead, and cold, and still,
The victim of our wanton will.

The *year* is dead, and on its brow
  Are scored the furrows of our pain,
And on its tender bosom still
  The scars of all our sins remain;
For every sin must leave a scar,
  Though long has healed the bleeding wound;
In all the years that glide away,
  Can any unscarred days be found?—
Of this our only hope is born,
They wait no resurrection morn.

Yet, ghosts upon the wings of air,
  Our souls shall feel their pinions sweep,
To trouble, through the dreams of night,
  The quiet waters of our sleep.
And, ah! those murdered days may come
  Across our way that leads to God,
And hanging on our garment's hem
  Detain us long upon the road,
Till He who trod the way before,
And waiteth long, has shut the door.

THE OCEAN CABLE.

A swift-winged message came across the sea:
  In silent depths the mystic race was run,

Ere yet the winds, that wander far and free,
   Unfurled the damp wings of the morning sun —
Who rose at last to find his crown was won,
   His ancient crown that never rival wore,
     Won by the lightning with his harness on, —
Across a track no rival ventures o'er, —
Beneath the bosom of the deep from shore to shore.

This is the wedding of the East and West,
   This close communion of divided lands ;
And children shall " rise up and call them blessed "
   Who o'er this ocean cable join their hands.
" These lines go out through all the earth," these
    bands
Unite the world's divided hopes and fears ;
   These are prophetic hours, and Times low sands
Are dropping out the days, when, sown in tears,
The world's broad harvest ripens for millennial years.

This is the miracle of later days, —
   The mind's last triumph o'er material things ;
We draw the lightning from his cloud-lined ways,
   And bind our thoughts upon his fiery wings.
   Thus all the universe its tribute brings
To man, who waiteth for his crown and throne ;
   And we, descended from a line of kings,
Find in all kingdoms subjects for our own ; —
Our own, which is not yet, till these in wreck are
    strewn.

Men plan and struggle, but the years fulfill
   Prophetic marches on the destined road ;
Believing grandly in a finite will,.
   We doubt the wisdom and the power of God ;

E'en o'er the footprints where the Saviour trod
We plow a furrow through the sea's expanse,
And lay in faith our deep divining-rod,
And words go out to Earth's far ends, yet thence
Bring back to us no echo of omnipotence.

Ah! better is the blindest faith, that sees
Clay is not master of its fellow clay,
Than doubt, which makes us transient things like
these,
Things that live, die, and dying pass away; —
Faith tells sublimer things, that we shall sway
When Death prepares our kingdom : until then,
We are but kings uncrowned, and watch and pray,
And gather subjects for the endless reign
That waits our spirit's short minority of pain.

"WAR ON THE CONTINENT."

"War on the Continent!" rumors abroad
Of a battle to-day, and there flies on
The thick sultry air the presage of a storm
That has broke on the eastern horizon.

"War on the Continent!" wherefore and why?
Is a race or a nation defending
A right that 's entailed for the ages to come?
Or is Lust with Ambition contending?

I listen; but, catching the echoes that come,
My blood is not stirred with the story;
In fancy I hear the loud thunders of war,
But not a sweet anthem of glory.

There's a string that is silent, a chord that's un-
touched,
That bindeth the nations together—
The justice that lies with the weakness of one
At the pitiless feet of the other.

This chord runs unbroken through distance and time;
In humanity's ear its vibrations
Make ours, through the centuries covered with dust,
The sorrows and triumphs of nations.

"War on the Continent!" Kings in unrest,
Solving the problem of sages,
That never was solved and that never shall be,
Till we halt in the march of the ages

And bury the dead that encumber the train
With things that are broken and hoary,
Yet rule with their sceptres of iron, that bar
The wide-open gateway of glory.

The problem shall vex, while the world shall grow old,
And power be unbalanced forever;
While Ambition upholds it, and Justice shall hang
On the opposite arm of the lever.

"War on the Continent!" Kingdoms and kings,
Forsaking the gold for the gilding,
With their perishing arms, in the shadow of Death,
Their thrones of dominion upholding.

They will borrow to-day of the ages to come
A strength, and be poorer to-morrow
For the loan in the blood of their children consumed,
And the terrible usury, sorrow.

Ah! when will the half-blinded vision of men
Grow tired of these blood-written pages,
And read in the light of the sunset of time,
There are thrones in the heart of the ages.

There are thrones that are vacant, and kingdoms to
come ;
And the ranks of Humanity standing
On the hills of To-day, as they form into line,
The plains of the world are commanding.

With an infinite faith in the kingdom to be,
They are watching the fast-closing suture
In the brow of the promise that 's born in our time,
To inherit the crown of the Future.

When Authority sits in the lawgiver's seat,
And Truth shall be Lord of Opinion,
The Right, which is older than kingdoms and kings,
Shall trample the thrones of Dominion.

THE DEATH MYSTERY.

Dying, all haloed round with faith,
Calm, beautiful she lay,
With sleepless eyes, whose vision caught
Gleams of eternal day.
She saw the lights of heaven grow bright
O'er ways her feet must climb,
And calmly waited for the end
Of earth, and change, and time.

And so the heedless sunshod days,
　All smiling, hastened down
To where the eves in splendor wore
　Their purple-golden crown ;
But day by day those tireless eyes,
　Beyond the paths we trod,
Transfigured by a light divine,
　Seemed growing nearer God.

Some souls above their crumbling clay
　Can in the shadow stand,
And clasp across Life's breaking threads
　The Father's outstretched hand.
These feel before they reach the shore
　The tide of Life set in,
And ere the finite ebbs away
　The infinite begin.

So once this pair of dying eyes—
　By God's own angel sealed
For Life Eternal — even here
　This mystery revealed :
That death is not a slumber, where
　Our being falls apart,
Wrapt in the vague, dim mists, that lie
　Like dreams around the heart.

She left — and Heaven seemed far and dim,
　And mists on mists arise ;
But naught can cloud the memory of
　Those glory-lighted eyes.
Set in the midnight sky of death,
　Like beacon stars they shone,
And in my dreams of Heaven to-night
　They still are shining on.

Ah ! if such quenchless rays of light
  Flash out from dying eyes,
How can the spirit slumber while
  The clay robe folded lies —
Sleep on till the Redeemer comes
  To claim Earth's solemn trust,
And with His breath to re-create
  Our bodies from the dust ?

When not a star that sets at dawn
  In slumber veils its light,
And never sun at sunset hour
  Sleeps on the couch of night;
How can the soul, a breath of God,
  Fold up its restless wings,
And slumber at the door of Heaven,
  With grave-bound mortal things?

For soul to slumber, is to die :
  No passive life is known —
God's orbit is the universe,
  Its centre is His throne :
Our souls, which are a spark of God,
  Can ne'er be slumber-bound ;
In lesser orbits they but turn
  The everlasting round.

THE MINISTER'S PROBLEM.

The Minister sat in his easy chair,
The sunshine played in his faded hair, —

Where the snows of life were falling fast,
O'er the track of the golden summers past.

The sun, descending behind the hill,
Cast a gleam aslant o'er the window-sill.

It quivered and fell on the open book,
Like a finger beck'ning to rise and look; —

And the page grew bright that was dull before,
But he moved, and, abashed, it sought the floor.

Still he followed the author's "proofs of God,"
With his weary brain's theological plod; —

He read till the arguments deeper grew,
And the lines on his forehead deepened too;

But the lines that crossed and furrowed his face
Were not half so tangled and hard to trace.

A half-grown form in the parsonage door
Cast a full grown shadow across the floor.

The father's form and the shadow grim
In picture blended, vague and dim;

A likeness at once and a prophecy, —
For the father was as the boy would be

When a growth in all but his faith and joy
Had inwrought its marvels to change the boy.

Now the child stood up where the sunset bright
Flung o'er him a mantle of golden light;

And a beautiful faith, unstained and wild,
Flowed over the lips of the beautiful child:

"O Father, I know that the clouds must lie
Nearer to heaven than you and I; —

"For, oh! see — they catch in each purple fold,
The light that comes down from the streets of gold.

"It is not the light of the setting sun,
Or his backward smile o'er his journey done;

"For his light comes down o'er the garden wall
On you, and the roses, and in the hall;

"But no light from heaven is shining through,
O'er the garden wall, and the flowers, and you.

"And if we look down, we can not see, even
The light that flows over the threshold of Heaven.

"Yet if we were up in the changing sky,
We might look into heaven — you and I.

"For looking upward we see the shine
The angels hang out for a golden sign.

"I 've been watching the clouds in the purple air,
For I know that the home of God is there.

"How strange it is that man ever can doubt
When the evening glory its sign hangs out!"

The father looked up, and a vision bright
Fell over the sunbeam's line of light;

The radiant sky and the clouds were riven
By a golden bridge from the earth to heaven.

He was here alone, and in heaven was God,
And just half-way over his darling stood,

On the golden bridge, o'er the vast abyss
That divides the eternal world from this.

A terrible pain like a swift eclipse
Passed over the minister's brow and lips.

The boy stood up in the parsonage door,
But he cast no shadow across the floor.

The sunbeam that fell like a golden rod
To the earth from the palace-home of God,

No longer quivered beside his chair,
But it left the light of its presence there.

He severed at once the tangled skein
Whose threads had wearied his aching brain.

When next the Lord's day evening came,
And flooded the chapel aisles with flame —

When "the heavens declared the glory of God,"
He followed the shining sunbeam's rod

Up the slanting bridge to the dying sun,
Whose Lord's-day journey was almost done,

And cried, " *O Father, we never can doubt*
When the evening glory its sign hangs out."

Then a ship of prayer through the summer even
Sailed over the shoals of doubt to Heaven,

And anchored there with a great Amen,
That rolled up o'er the golden bridge again.

IMMANUEL.

His is the power sublime
That filled eternity and boundless space;
    Before creation at the birth of Time.
Beheld His radiant face.

His is the power supreme
That o'er the chaos of eternal night
    All smiling looked, and like a sun-lit dream
Creation woke to light.

His is the wondrous power
That breathed the soul-light into forms of clay;
    To shine forever from that glorious hour,—
Lamps of immortal ray.

His loving, watchful eye,
Looked down in pity while the angels wept;
    When man — God's image — taught by sin to die,
In earth's dark bosom slept.

But when the earth grew dim,
Dark with the shadow of its many graves;
    And souls went hopeless through the shadows grim,
O'er Death's unsounded waves—

His was the soul of love
That stooped in pity from His shining throne;
　Left the bright angels and the bliss above,
To suffer here alone;

　To suffer and to die,
Meekly descending to the shrouded tomb;
　Where generations of the years gone by
Slept in mysterious gloom.

　His was the mighty hand.
That swept the shadows from the grave away,
　And lit the portals of the spirit-land
With Hope's undying ray.

　And many a tear-dimmed eye.
Grows bright and brighter with each graveward view;
　Till at the door they lay their burdens by,
And pass with angels through.

　Far in the future lies
An hour, when golden suns shall cease to burn;
　And when the tear-stained earth and smiling skies
To chaos shall return.

　But when that hour shall be,
When time and all earth's monuments in wreck
　Float darkly out upon eternity,
A dimly fading speck;

　When suns and stars are fled,
And all the Universe waits dark and lone;
　When in his shroud e'en Death at last lies dead
Beside his crumbled throne;

The souls with Christ who trod
Through weary suffering to perfection on,
    Shall gem with holy light the realms of God,
Like stars set round the sun.

ICONOCLASM.

I have heard of storied columns,
    Standing in some eastern clime,
Telling, in a language solemn,
    Of a far-off olden time,
When fair temples rose in splendor,
    Mocking with their columned stone
Time, that lightly touched and left them
    In their grandeur, proud and lone,

Deeming only God could shake them,
    In His solemn anger, down;
Time, his footprints left and passed them
    With a murmur and a frown;
And the name of God was echoed
    In a mocking tone, and spurned,
While the incense of devotion
    On an idol's altar burned.

So God left them in their blindness,
    And the face of heaven grew dim,
While the smoke of burning incense
    Rose in mockery to Him.
How they crowned insensate idols,
    All but legend has forgot;
What their faith and worship promised,
    Even legend answers not.

Not your temples God has shattered,
　Not your altars in His wrath,
But your holiest things, your idols,
　He has crumbled in His path;
But your temples, weak profaners,
　Reared defiant o'er their head,
Stand like broken mausoleums,
　O'er a worship lying dead.

Dead the idols and their worship,
　Dead the toilers and their trust;
And no worshipers come after,
　For their gods were only dust.
Like the "Wandering Jew," their temples
　Through the lonely centuries stand,
Strange and hoary — unforgiven,
　Like a shadow on the land.

But that God whom we have worshiped
　Shall be worthy of our trust
When the temples we have builded
　Shall have moldered into dust;
When the walls forget the echoes
　Of our prayers, like incense given,
And the altars are remembered
　But as stepping-stones to Heaven.

THE SHIPS OF LIFE.

When, standing on the shores of time,
　We seaward bend our eyes,
How many fair, love-freighted ships
　On our rapt vision rise!

How much of joy they bear away;
How much of love they hold;
How much of sunlight from the earth,
Those shining sails enfold!

While we upon the busy shore
Are standing day by day,
Those heaven-bound ships, with gleaming sails,
Our treasures bear away.
With eager eyes we follow them;
And some go down in sight:
These are the hopes which could not bloom
· In Heaven's unclouded light.

Some vain ambition, selfish love
Is lost, or worldly pride;
And so, although we mourn them dead,
'T is well when they have died.
Some barks glide on, as if from God
A charméd life were given:
These bear the treasures that we know
Shall all be ours in Heaven.

For all the ships of life go out,
And all are heavenward bound,
Save here and there a white-winged bark,
With glory circled round.
And these bear little heaven-born souls,
The Father evermore
Sends floating down the waves of life,
To anchor on the shore.

Some ships go out as stars go down,
And shroud our souls in night:

These bear our precious ones away,
  Our love-lamps from our sight.
Yet though their light is hid from us,
  As stars grow dim awhile,
We know the boundless fields of heaven
  Are lighted by their smile.

How dear, how beautiful they look,
  When fair belovéd hands
Wave the last signal to depart
  For the eternal lands!
"Fear not, fear not that we are lost,"
  Their smiling seems to say;
"For, from the shores of time, we bear
  No earth-born things away.

"With eager hands, in holy trust,
  Our farewell signal 's given;
We leave the shores of Time, to seek
  The golden port of Heaven.
Our sails unfurled, the breezes blow,
  We may not look behind;
For faith is standing at the bow,
  And God is in the wind."

THREE PICTURES OF FAITH.

I saw a pure child, in whose beautiful eyes
Were blended the gleam and the blue of the skies,
When Sin, the dark angel of sorrow and blight,
Wearing the crown of an angel of light,
Tempted the child by the paradise gleams
Of bright blooming gardens and murmuring streams—

Gardens with bloom of the deadliest breath,
And streams whose dark waters flowed downward to
    death.
But light from our Father was shed on the way,
Ere the dear little pilgrim had wandered astray;
His lips to his heart spoke an answer to prayer:
''I see not Thy face, but I know Thou art there.''

I saw a lone pilgrim, who gazed with distrust
On all things: his idols had crumbled to dust;
And the slow wheels of Time had relentlessly rolled
O'er his heart's broken altars, where passion grew
    cold;
And o'er the smooth brow the deep wheel-ruts were
    worn,
That tell of a spirit dark passions have torn.
So the soul sat in darkness, and ashes, and gloom,
As the high-priest of Ruin might dwell in a tomb;
Till leaving the wrecks that God's mercy had strewn,
The lone-drifting dreamer looked up to the Throne;
Then down through the dark came an answer to
    prayer,
And the soul cried aloud—''Thou art there, Thou
    art there.''

I saw a lone pilgrim, slow wending his way
Through the deepening twilight of evening gray;
For long the tired feet had been turned to the west,
And the world-weary spirit was seeking for rest.
Where far in the distance Life's sun goeth down,
An angel was bearing a robe and a crown.
He flings off his garment of sackcloth and dust,
From his eyes fall the scales, from his spirit the rust;
For a moment, transfigured, he stood in my sight,

Then passed through the wide open doorway of
  Light:
And a whisper came down through the glorified air,
"My God and my Saviour, I know Thou art there."

"IN MEMORIAM."

(MY SISTER DIED NOVEMBER 1ST, 1860.)

Another Sunbeam gone from earth;
  Another Star declined;
Another Love-bud called to be
  In Christ's own garland twined;

Another Eye has softly shut
  Its blue-veined curtain down;
Another Soul has left its cross,
  To wear in heaven a crown;

Another Flower, its love-cup filled,
  Folds all its sweetness in;
Another Soul is born in heaven,
  Without a spot of sin;
Once more the crystal gates of light
  Have shut an Angel in.

AT THE AID SOCIETY.

Fold them up, they are warm and soft
  As the delicate knitter's heart and hand —

A pair of soft, blue woolen socks,
And love knit in with every strand.

More than this — there are dreams and prayers
Wove in like a mystic, golden thread —
Dreams that may stir a soldier's heart,
And prayers to bless a dying head.

It is not vain, it is not vain,
For love is blest, and prayer is strong,
To move the Arm that surely guides
The breasts that stem the tide of wrong.

And those who praying still believe,
Shall know the strength of human will;
They dream prophetic histories,
And through their *faith* their hopes fulfill.

PARTNERSHIP.

"We are but two, a little band;
    Be faithful till we die;
Shoulder to shoulder let us stand,
    Till side by side we lie."—WORDSWORTH.

But now, O miracles of love!
    Two added, we are four —
In earth or heaven, ours or God's
    May these be evermore.

In partnership with Him we bend
    These new-born souls above,
And tremblingly the contract sign
    Whose only bonds are love.

Then creature and Creator fold
    Alike this tender clay —
One, to sustain us all; and two,
    To guard them day by day.

O human love, on which is hung
    God's vast, eternal plan!
O love creative, shadowed in
    The finite love of man!

Both forge the glowing links of Life
    And weld a chain sublime,
The only finite, endless thing —
    Eternal, born in Time.

O wisdom of the heart of God,
    That for a signal still
Keeps through all wrecks, this golden string
    Unbroken as his will—

The chain of love, that holds alike
    The living and the dead,
And runs through all the universe,
    The only vital thread.

AN ACRE OF GRAVES.

Kentucky river, winding by
    A forest-guarded bank,
And stalwart trees that mutely stand,
    Like grenadiers in rank;

While flinging solemn shadows o'er
  The river's tranquil flow,
They keep, through ages, patient guard
  Upon the cliffs below—

Those towering cliffs, where eagles build,
  And man has never trod—
Where only soaring wings can touch
  The finger-prints of God;
Where Nature stretches in repose,
  Or sits in holy calm,
Teaching the sighing winds to chant
  Their sweet thanksgiving psalm.

And when the morning sun is low,
  Deep shadows, long and wide,
Stretch from the forest-guarded cliffs,
  Like bridges on the tide,
O'er which the first bright sunbeams come
  Like couriers sent before,
To tell the rushes on the bank
  The sun will soon be o'er.

A rising hill, a grassy plain,
  Below the river's sweep,
And silent trees that guard the place
  Where willows bend and weep;
And fields of golden-tasselled corn
  Fill up the perfect plan,
To show how kindly Nature works
  In partnership with Man.

Yet still the willows bend and weep,
  As if a grave were there;

Though not a sound or shadow stirs
  The pulses of the air,
Some dark and thrilling tragedy
  Is borne upon the flood,
And e'en these placid waters tell
  Of human strife and blood.

And here beneath these cliffs, that bare
  Their foreheads to the west,
Long billowy lines of sods are laid,
  Each on a soldier's breast:
So fair Kentucky's war-worn face
  Is dotted o'er with stains;
Not all the dews of heaven can cleanse
  The blue-grass of her plains.

DESOLATION.

Soul, wrap around thee thy garments of gloom,
Lay my dead heart in its desolate tomb;
Still'd are its throbbings, quiet at last,
Lethe, flow over my dreams of the past.

Strange now how passionless Memory seems,
While thought travels over the graves of her dreams;
But, O Desolation, my hope and my trust
Lie buried, with pain, in thy ashes and dust.

Alas, how the soul stills its pulses of fire,
Where the flames at the fountain grow cold and ex-
    pire!
Alas, that the heart with its music should die;
Its echo forever be only a sigh!

But, O Desolation, thy mission is blest :
Fold thy calm wings o'er my spirit's unrest;
And help me to learn a great lesson of thee—
Before resurrection, the dying must be.

Faith, move the last doubt by thy heavenly art;
Roll, roll back the stone from the grave of my heart:
My soul waits in hope till a voice at the tomb
Shall proclaim that the heart's resurrection has come.

CHARLES DICKENS.

Struck like a towering English oak,
  Shivered with all its leaves unfurled;
And the sharp report of the lightning stroke
  Wakes an echo round the world.

From lip to lip, on the English coast,
  Flies the news of a nation's loss;
And, proud to think they love him most,
  They signal o'er the deep to us.

We catch their message o'er the wave,
  We see their half-mast banners play,
And pause to think how much the grave
  Has taken from the world to-day.

The heart that sleeps in calm repose,
  Sprung like an acorn from the soil,
A giant in the sunshine rose,
  Above the grimy ways of toil.

But deep in human nature's heart,
  His roots still found the vital springs
That form of all his leaves a part,
  Expanding into wondrous things.

And long he stood a verdant tree,
  With heart of solid English oak,
A champion for humanity
  Wherever Saxon words are spoke.

And in the future still he stands;
  Words are immortal — good or ill —
And he upon Time's drifted sands
  Leaves the impressions of his will.

A heart that loved his age and race
  Too well to shun the noble strife,
And fossilize, for men to trace,
  Unrighted wrongs and trampled life.

Around the world a murmur flies,
  And leaflets from the giant tree
Are gathered — now the hero dies —
  Mementoes for Humanity.

O BRIGHT AND SILENT SUN!

O bright and silent sun!
What are the memories of sad days to thee,
When o'er the path thy golden feet have run?
The shadows were for me.

How can thy radiant eye
Conceive the picture of a world in night,
When amber couriers, like a vanguard fly,
To make thy pathway bright!

A long horizon line,
Like a grand army with its flags unfurled,
Blazes with glory as thy dazzling shine
Goes round and round the world.

O gleaming waves of light,
Whose daily tides through seas of ether roll,
Ye sweep o'er worlds of chaos and of night,
And break upon my soul.

Upon this soul of mine
Ye scatter pearls of wisdom, and I see
Lives that have light within them still must shine
Through hours that darkest be.

With them no shadows frown;
They die like sunset as they lived like day;
And after them the solemn night comes down,
And earth grows cold and gray.

But just beyond the hills,
Whose summits rise upon the edge of Time,
Their soul's eternal sunrise breaks — and thrills
To-morrow's fairer clime.

O bright and silent sun!
Like thee I journey to the distant west,
And when my mission and my toil are done,
Like thee I sink to rest.

But when I rise again,
God's Heaven city shall be builded on
Thy broken orbit — shall I miss thee then?
"There shall be no more sun!"

THE BRIDGE.

How far, far away from us Heaven must lie,
When the light from some stars in the measureless
  sky .
Traveled millions on millions of miles in its flight,
And was thousands of years ere it burst on our sight.

If we set out for heaven to-day, and could fly
On the wings of the wind through the path of the
  sky —
If we never grew weary, and never grew old,
How long it would take us could never be told.

We should flash by the planets, and Venus and Mars
Would be lost to our sight in the field of the stars;
We should flash by the sun and pass out of his light,
And the gateway of Heaven be still out of sight.

For farther from us than the stars, we are told,
Is the city of God, with its pavements of gold —
A world might be born and grow old in the time
That a spirit could pass to that beautiful clime.

It might be a wonderful journey, I know,
With the azure above us, the planets below;
But, oh! how impatient at last I should be,
Lest the angels should weary of waiting for me —

Lest I should be lost when I parted from you,
And never be found in that desert of blue,
And my heart would grow sick with such terrible
    fears
That I could not endure it for *thousands of years.*

Ah! poor little dreamer, you are not alone
In dreading the way that leads up to the throne;
'T was a journey of ages, but shortened since then
By a *bridge* that was built for the children of men.

And over the bridge pass the good and the true;
And the rest are all lost in that desert of blue.
'T is wide as the world is, and firm as the sod;
For this bridge is the *love* and the PROMISE of God.

LOST.

Lost in the morning, and wandered away,
    Gone with the day that is ending,
A beautiful child; and the incoming night
    Finds a shadow already impending.
Eyes have grown weary, and cheeks have been wet;
Prayers have been offered in agony; yet,
Did you pass by it, and could you forget
                It was lost, lost?

You knew when you passed it alone, on the street,
    That you passed it forever and ever.

Gone, you, and the child, and the spot, and the hour,
  With the need that had brought you together,
Converging one moment, diverging again,
Yet, crossing your heart, left a burden of pain
That sometime and somewhere will meet you again,
      Not be lost, lost.

Lost in the midnight to you and the world,
  Down into infamy sinking;
'T was yours, but your love had forgotten, and now—
  God pity the dregs you are drinking.
You pray, but you think where the guilty one trod,
And you know that the love and the promise of God
Will never reach under the earth and the sod
      For the lost, lost.

Lost in the morning, at noon and at eve,
  Things that the angels are finding,
Bits of self-sacrifice, tangles of love
  That angels are patiently winding.
Exalted ideals, that might have been true
Had we been stronger to will and to do,
Are silently gathered and hidden from view,
      But not lost, lost.

Lost in the dark, on the edge of the grave,
  A deed to a mansion in heaven,
Paid for in gold that was wrung from the poor—
  And then to a charity given;
Souls that forgive not—a life that was grand,
A love and a purpose—all built on the sand,
With a prayer that went up with no deed in its hand:
      These are lost, lost.

LINES ON THE DEATH OF A THEOLOGICAL STUDENT.

J. T. KIRBY died at his residence near Germantown, N. C., December, 1869, of disease contracted while struggling to get the means to prepare himself to "preach the word."

INSCRIBED TO HIS CLASS IN THE BIBLE COLLEGE OF KENTUCKY UNIVERSITY.

Ah! think not he died ere his labor was done,
  Though he died ere he tasted its sweetness,
For result is the *crown* of a victory won,
  That descends on its perfect completeness.

Some lead the "advance" in the battle of Life,
  And fall 'neath the flag they fight under,
And some through the heat and the smoke of the
    strife,
  Reach the *Patmos* of age, where they wonder

Why they should have lived till the angels came
    down,
  And lift, with unpalpable fingers,
The veil that must fall 'tween the cross and the crown,
  While the soul with mortality lingers.

But not unto us as we toil in our day
  Is given this glorified vision,
And some never toil through the heat of the day,
  Who bear the divinest commission.

The " *Voice in the Wilderness* " hushed in its prime,
  Completed its grandest idea,
And lives in the measureless echoes of Time,
  That float out from the plains of Judæa.

And yet *he* went out ere the heroes came on —
Died ere the " *Commission* " was given ;
And before he was crowned with a victory won,
  He sat down in the kingdom of heaven.

You weep for the one who has gone from your sight,
  Has fall'n from the ranks, and you number
One less to go forth where the harvest is white,
  And one more to lie passive in slumber.

Like Paul, in the " *excellent glory* " *he* stands,
  While *you,* " in the ranks," are believing,
His faith into knowledge divinely expands,
  And calls you to grander achieving.

Think not you have lost what you silently weep ;
  But look up through the clouds that hang o'er you.
The brother you thought had *gone early to sleep,*
  Is made an apostle * before *you.*

LOVE'S CROSSES.

TO ISAAC AND HARRIET ERRETT.

WICKLIFFE CAMPBELL ERRETT—Fallen asleep, March 18th, 1872.
" His short record was all honorable."

The life that you loved into being has fled —
The lips that you kissed into sweetness are dead.

* " I also am an apostle, an eye-witness to his glory."

The heart in whose pulses you counted your own,
And molded for years with a look or a tone,
Untouched by your sighing,
Unmoved by your crying,
Has tasted the pain and the sweetness of dying.

You were watching, and saw when the curtain was
    drawn,
And the soul that awoke in the Heavenly dawn,
And the arm you stretched out, as he passed from
    your sight,
Was caught by a ray of the Heavenly light.
    Very near to the door
    Do we stand, in the hour
When our children pass by us and enter before.

Ah! we may be purer—but think of the years
When we shaped them with love and baptized them
    in tears—
They who should live after to conquer our pain,
And recover our losses by aid of our gain,
    And wiser and younger,
    And better and stronger,
Take the burden of life when we bear it no longer:

To wear all our virtues like jewels reset,
To redeem all our failures, our errors forget;
And step from our shoulders to heights more sub-
    lime
Than ever our feet have been able to climb:
    What sorrows we wear,
    What crosses we bear,
When they leave us alone in the valley of prayer!

But his soul was unstained, and his record all pure:
Would you lay your cross on him to do and endure?
Though he stood "in the line of promotion" *un-
scarred,*
Would you *stay "his commission"* that came from the
Lord?
  With nothing for fears,
  Is there matter for tears
That for him is bridged over the anguish of years?

You only can hope, when an angel is sent
To unbuckle your armor and fold up your tent,
At the foot of the ladder he mounted, to stand
And touch in the dark an omnipotent hand :
  You weaker and sadder,
  He wiser and gladder —
Between you the rounds of Death's mystical ladder.

We are glad when our babes have come safely to earth
Through the perils and pangs and the rapture of
  birth.
As we felt in the hour when they opened their eyes,
Let us feel when again they are born in the skies;
  And year after year
  Draw near and more near,
Till Heaven may be seen through the lens of a tear.

Oh! stretch out your arms o'er the grave and the sod,
And lay what you have on the bosom of God.
Draw nearer and nearer; the veil is so thin,
Love makes it transparent and gazes within.
  Love hath no denials;
  Its crosses and trials
Mark ages of bliss on its Heavenly dials.

MY PRAYER.

"Lord, who shall abide in thy tabernacle? who shall dwell in thy holy hill? He that walketh uprightly, and worketh righteousness, and speaketh the truth in his heart. . . . He that doeth those things shall never be moved."—Psalm xv.

O Father, when I lift my eyes
    Above the grime around,
And steadfast hold my empty cup
    Where naught but peace is found;

Although my faith may only seem
    An atom lost in space,
O Father, give it strength of wing
    And it will find thy face.

My heart is like the ark of old,
    Filled with its teeming things;
My faith its slow-winged dove, sent out
    To fly on weary wings.

It halts beside thine altar, Lord,
    And sees uplifted there
Hands that are false and hearts where hate
    Has left no room for prayer—

Sees souls ignobly bow to sense,
    And Truth weep over them,
While even in thy "Holy Place"
    Is stained her garment's hem.

So up and down the world it goes,
    Above the floods of sin—

My trembling faith — Lord, stretch thy hand
And take the wanderer in.

Though but an atom lost in space,
My faith but dreams of rest;
Lord, wing it with thy promises
And guide it to thy breast.

But as of old the mountains raised
Their summits from the flood,
In this broad world of evil, still
I know there must be good.

And still my soul and purblind faith
Are clinging to thy hand;
Amid the wreck of truth I see,
But can not understand.

My faith expectant looks to Thee;
My will and purpose wait,
Or mingle in thy hollow hand,
To weave the threads of fate.

Lord, let my strong foundation be
My everlasting trust,
And help me that I build thereon
With all things true and just.

My slender fingers, Lord, I know,
Sufficient are to do;
If we would be omnipotent,
We only need be true.

On truth, where angels rest their feet,
Lord, let me stand, and know,
By loving him, how much like God
A human soul may grow.

THE LITTLE SOWER'S PRIZE POEM.

Sixty-seven manuscripts were received as competitors for the prize offered by the *Little Sower* for the best poem received before December 1, 1869. On that day the manuscripts were submitted to a committee consisting of Rev. Edward P. Ingersoll, Pastor of the Plymouth Congregational Church, and Elder William F. Black, Pastor of the Christian Church. On the 18th day of December they submitted the following

REPORT:

The undersigned, selected as a committee to pass our judgment upon the poems competing for the prize of $25 offered by W. W. Dowling, Editor of the *Little Sower*, beg leave to report that we have carefully examined the manuscripts submitted, and have decided that the prize should be awarded to the writer of the poem entitled "The Golden Ladder."

EDWARD P. INGERSOLL,
WILLIAM F. BLACK.

INDIANAPOLIS, Dec. 18th, 1869.

THE GOLDEN LADDER.

The children watched the sun go down,
And in its gleaming changes,
The west seemed first a sea of fire,
Then golden mountain ranges.

And Fannie asked, "What are the clouds?
They look like hills of glory."
"The steps of heaven," Frank replied;
"It is a sweet, old story:

"A guardian angel every day,
    To each of us is given;
And everything we do or say
    They carry up to Heaven.

"When we do wrong they write with tears;
    When good, their hearts are gladder;
And every night they climb to Heaven
    Up o'er that golden ladder.

"And then the gates of pearl swing back
    Upon their gleaming hinges,
And all the sky seems melted gold,
    With red and purple fringes.

"But when the doors are closed again,
    The guardian angels gather
In solemn silence, with their books,
    Around our Heavenly Father.

"And then I close my eyes and think
    How, in that sinless dwelling,
Will sound the story of the life
    My angel must be telling.

"Some days, I know, my angel takes
    The record of my sinning;
But then I always try to make
    The next a new beginning.

"So, when at night our Father calls,
    My angel may be gladder,
And be the first to climb to Heaven
    Up o'er the golden ladder."

LITTLE QUARRELS.

The children had come home from school,
  And played an hour or more;
And now the hour had come to look
  To-morrow's lesson o'er.
But still the mirthful spirit ruled,
  And wished a longer sway;
For all the children were too tired
  For anything but play.

They sat around the merry hearth,
  The fire was burning bright;
And some one said, "Oh! let us ask
  A holi*day* to-*night.*"
"A holi*day!* why this is *night,*"
  Cried out a voice in fun;
As if she thought a world of mirth
  ' Was in the little pun.

"Well, day is night, and night is day,"
  A harsher voice replied,
With just a little tinge of wrath,
  And just a little pride.
"Well, I have heard that black is white,
  But never thought it so;
'T is painful to be ignorant
  Of things we ought to know.

"And I propose that we should sit
  And learn of Lady May,

Till we are wise enough, at least,
  To prove that night is day.''
The little joker's fun was gone,
  Her laugh to tears was turned;
As if, in picking up a joke,
  She found her fingers burned.

Then in the circle round the fire
  The mother's chair was set;
And in those little angry eyes
  She looked with deep regret:
''My children, men have *fought* for words—
  A God of love to please,
By breaking hearts and taking lives
  For idle words like these.

''For, standing by, I heard it all,
  And think you both were right;
For in the measurement of Time,
  We do not speak of night.
And yet we call the dark hours night;
  But such a slight mistake
Was hardly worth the angry words
  And aching hearts you make.

''And even jokes are sometimes wrong,
  Unless the wit is kind;
The merriest laughs may sever hearts
  Repentance can not bind.
If God should send a judgment on
  Each error that we make,
The best of all our lives would be
  One terrible mistake.''

OUR CHILDREN.

When they come in helpless beauty
  From the home of God afar,
With His seal upon their foreheads,
  Oh, how sweet the children are!
There 's a softer air about them,
  And a hush around them lies,
And the secret of creation
  In their deep, unshadowed eyes;
In their forms so sweetly moulded,
God's eternal life is folded.

Looking through those radiant lenses,
  Down converging aisles of Time,
We can see the first creation,
  And its miracles sublime.
We can see the great All-Father
  On Creation's threshold stand,
All the shining spheres uplifting
  With the lever of His hand;
Breath of His eternal Spirit
Is the life that we inherit.

Through the doorway of creation,
  On the threshold of our birth,
Come these pure and sinless spirits,
  Down the azure stairs to earth.
There 's a softer air about them,
  And a glory round them lies,
And the secret of creation
  In their deep, unshadowed eyes;

For the soul, unconscious seeming,
Of its heavenly birth is dreaming.

Never higher than the fountain
    Can the limpid waters flow;
But the restless waves forever
    Seek a level as they go.
Naught can bind resistless water,
    Naught can stay the restless tide,
Rising ever to the fountain
    In the channel's rocky side;
So our spirit's restless river
    Seeks the level of its Giver.

Radiant Children! they are linking
    God's eternal life with man's;
And this "silver cord" upholdeth
    All his everlasting plans.
May the restless waves of being,
    In their tidal ebb and flow,
Reach their fountain when the golden
    Bowl is broken here below.
May their calm eyes be the token
When the wheel of life is broken.

GRANDFATHER.

Grandfather's old, and his children said
That seventy winters have whitened his head;
But we think that seventy summers' skies
Have left their sunshine in grandfather's eyes;
And the sunny light of them all appears
When grandfather speaks of his seventy years.

While his form is withered and bent and thin,
His dear old heart is all warm within ;
And you see where the smiles have left their trace,
In the lines that wrinkle his dear old face ;
Could you only hear the tales he has told,
You would think it was grand to be growing old.

Grandfather's life has not always been
Free from sorrow and toil and sin ;
He had his troubles, and bore them too,
And the One helped him who is helping you ;
He toiled for knowledge, and fought for truth,
And kept for his age the heart of his youth.

We love his tales of the long-ago,
For grandfather's stories are true, we know.
We shout when he tells how, in sorest need,
He fought the giant of selfish greed,
And on through his boyhood and youth and prime,
Ran wonderful races with Life and Time.

Grandfather 's happy and wise and good,
Yet he 's not done all that he thought he would
When he dreamed and planned what his life should be,
Before he was grandpa, and we were we ;
But life is not made of such wonderful things,
And the best men of earth are not heroes and kings.

Grandfather never was rich, but you see
He divided with friends who were poorer than he ;
When you ask about money, he 'll tell you he 's lent
A fortune so large it can never be spent.
He means it is lent to the Lord, but I 'm sure
It was used to buy Bibles and food for the poor.

Grandfather says that his old eyes are dim,
And we know that the angels are waiting for him;
But the children will cry with their bitterest pain
When he leaves his arm-chair and his hat and his
  cane,
And starts out to seek, with an angel to guide,
His mansion that 's built where his treasures abide.

And we know he will find it; but oh, if he should!
With no grandpa to help us, how can we be good?
But he tells us he learned, through his seventy years,
We only grow better with striving and tears;
We shall not reach heaven with wishes or wings,
But climb up on stairs of the commonest things.

GRANDMOTHER.

The old lady sat in her easy chair,
  With her head leaning back and her feet in the sun;
And you knew by the shine of her snow-white hair
  That grandmother's work was almost done.

In her lap lay a stocking of white and red,
  Grandmother's knitting, but now complete;
And its mate on the floor was the kitten's bed,
  Where puss in the sunshine lay curled at her feet.

She loved the kittens and loved the sun,
  And smiled when the kitten unwound her ball;
Yet she counted the minutes one by one,
  Till the children came running along the hall.

Then she gathered the stockings from off her lap,
  And smiled to welcome the children home;
And even the kitten forgot her nap,
  For she knew that the kissing-time had come.

They are grandmother's children—she told us so—
  Grandmother's children to love and to teach;
And I think she is right, for years ago
  She gave a place in her heart to each.

When they came to earth like the flowers in May,
  Grandmother's love, like the sun that warms,
Tended and watched them from day to day,
  Till they burst into blossom in grandmother's arms.

And grandmother loves the children well—
  I can tell by the tremble that stirs her cap
When they are naughty, or cross, or ill,
  And come to the shelter of grandmother's lap.

I can tell by the throb of her patient heart,
  And the paper of candy she lays aside,
And the row of apples she counts apart,
  And the faults she is striving to mend or hide.

They are not always as "good as bread,"
  And as "true as steel," but they will be so;
For *love* is the golden road they tread,
  Grandmother says—and she ought to know.

She says we shall never grow better here
  By learning rules, and I think it true,
Unless in our hearts we hold them dear—
  What we learn to love, we shall love to do.

And they love grandmother, I can tell.
  She is their fairy with snow-white hair;
And an angel would never be loved so well,
  If it sat there in grandmother's easy-chair.

If grandmother's cap were a golden crown,
  She could never be more of a queen than now;
For she rules them all with a smile or frown,
  And a single shade of her snow-white brow.

For grandmother must be always right;
  If she is not perfect, who ever was?
For her heart is so pure, and her head is so white,
  And then, too, she loves them—of course she does.

But this is a secret I never tell;
  For more than one grandma we can 't obey;
And if all were so good, and loved so well,
  They would rule us, like grandmother, every day.

OUR BABY.

Oh! somebody kissed the baby,
  And somebody loves him too;
And somebody always watches
  To see what he will do.

He unwinds the spools of cotton
  With a very serious air;
And washes the face of dolly,
  And tangles its yellow hair.

And then he preaches sermons,—
And that 's the funniest thing—
With the kittens for congregation;
But the kittens will not sing.

And then he tries to teach them,
With a face so grave and stern;
And the kittens are attentive,
Yet they never seem to learn.

Then he writes papa a letter,
And he tells about his horse;
How his broken head "gets worser"—
'T was the *mending* made it worse.

If you read it, he 'll be happy,
If you laugh, you 'll see him frown;
But whichever way you turn it,
It is written upside down.

Baby never reads his Bible,
And he never says his prayers;
But he listens every evening
To the children saying theirs.

But if you try to teach him,
Such a chatter he will keep,
That you never can get farther
Than "I lay me down to sleep."

When at last you get him quiet,
He 's forgotten all you 've said;
Mouth and eyes are shut together
In his sleepy little head.

He 's a very naughty baby:
　Well, perhaps so; but, you see,
If our Heavenly Father has not
　Made him better, how can we?

Three long years we 've loved and taught him,
　Just as well as we could do;
We are not to blame, if loving
　Is the only thing he knew.

We are trying still to teach him
　All his little brain will hold;
Yet he still is but a baby,
　For he 's only three years old.

Lay him down—you see he 's going
　To the pleasant land of Nod;
Ah! there's some One loves the baby,
　And I think it must be God.

Love is all he knows of duty,
　And religion too, I guess;
But I think Our Father knows it
　Without loving him the less.

ROBED IN WHITE.

(Written for The Children's Friend.)

One who loved the Saviour best,
　Told a story strange and true,

Of a "City of the Blest,"
Out of mortal reach or view,
Where God's children, robed in white,
Wander in His loving sight.

On, through "shining streets of gold,"
Into jeweled palace homes,
Where no darkness, storm, or cold,
And no sunlight ever comes;
But "the Father giveth light"
Where His children walk in white.

But if here our spirits are
Soiled or stained by earth and sin,
Though the gates of pearl unbar,
We shall never enter in;
Never, never walk in white
Through the shining streets of light.

Only hands as pure as snow,
Only feet that stainless trod,
Only sinless spirits go,
To the "City of our God,"
Where sweet children walk in white
In the Father's loving sight.

SONG OF THE CHRISTMAS EVE.

'T is almost nineteen hundred years
Since Time renewed his age,
And turned the leaves of Providence
To date a fairer page.

Then first he wrote the anthem down
  That angels chanted then ;
And still we sing the Christmas song
  Of "Peace, good-will to men."

Above the din of daily life,
  Above its pain and soil,
Its silent melody of love,
  Its hammer-strokes of toil,
The gates of Heaven still fall ajar,
  And angels sing again,
On each returning Christmas eve,
  Still, "Peace, good-will to men."

To council hall of Church and State
  The wise men crowd afar ;
But we, like "wise men of the East,"
  See but one sacred star.
Sing! for millennial years shall dawn
  O'er Shinar's valley, when
The latest Christmas eve of time
  Brings "Peace, good-will to men."

THE EVENING STORY.

"No, we are not sleepy, mother,
  See how wide-awake we seem ;
Tell us something sweet to think of,
  Tell us something sweet to dream.

"Tell the very sweetest story
  That you ever heard or read,

And you 'll see that we 'll remember
Every single word you 've said."

Then I told them of a midnight
In the very long ago,
When the sky was full of angels,
And from every shining row,

In a voice of heavenly music,
Came a loving message, given
For the sake of one sweet baby
That had come that night from Heaven.

"Now, please tell us just another;
Tell the saddest one you know:"
And I told of one who suffered,
As he wandered to and fro;

Doing good to all around him,
Without fear, or sin, or pride;
Blessing those who most ill-used him,
For whose sake at last he died.

"Now, please, just one more, dear mother,
Tell us now the strangest one:"
So I told them of a journey
On a mountain-top begun:

Through the azure, in a body,
Just as here on earth he trod,
Up through shining ranks of angels
To the very throne of God.

Four blue eyes and two sweet voices
Waited till my tale was done;
Then they cried: "WHY THAT WAS JESUS!
Those THREE stories ARE BUT ONE."

A LETTER TO THE CHILDREN.

"AND HE SAID UNTO ME, WRITE."

Write for the children? How can I
Write of a time so long gone by?
I have no dollies and toys and things,
Beautiful buttons on wonderful strings;

And when my feet with the daylight fail,
Nobody tells me a wonderful tale;
And all the giants and fairies seem
To have passed away like a story dream.

Nobody takes me upon his knee,
And lovingly tells me how good I should be;
Yet deep in my heart I wish they would,
For still, like a child, I want to be good.

I think, and hope, and resolve, and try,
And believe I shall do it by and by;
I believe I shall one day set my feet
Firm on the beautiful "Golden Street."

But, oh! if somebody only knew
How hard it is to be good and true,
And how I slip as I mount and climb
Up the wonderful stairs of time.

Somebody does, and day by day
Somebody leads me all the way;
Somebody calls me a child, and waits
Just inside of the "Heavenly Gates."

Somebody tells me how and when
I shall become a child again,
And walk in the beautiful "Streets of Gold,"
With feet that never grow tired and old,

A child in my "Father's House;" and I
Forget the time when I toil and cry,
And only think what I shall do
When I am again a child like you—

When I live in a house with jeweled wall,
With angels flitting from hall to hall;
Where no darkness comes nor candle burns,
And no rising or setting sun returns;

And where I shall only care to rest,
Because I shall lean on the Saviour's breast;
Where I shall grow old for ever and ever,
Yet still be a child. and wonder whether

The fairies of Heaven (the angels) see
A happier child than I shall be.
I shall always be growing, and never be grown,
Always be nearing the "Great White Throne."

And all the poets that fill the earth
With tales of fairies and songs of mirth—
Ah! you may forget them all, and yet
The songs I sing you will never forget.

When I "enter the palace and live with the King,"
You shall hear the beautiful songs I 'll sing,
And learn how immortal children dwell;
But the "end of it"—only God can tell.

WHERE JESUS IS.

The olden prophets walked with God,
   And little children found him;
And Jesus on the mountain stood
   With angels all around him.

Yet I have watched the changing sky
   All day, and longed to find him;
I saw the curtained clouds draw back,
   But God was not behind them.

The angels poured the sunshine through
   Wherever clouds were riven;
It fell like heaps of golden sand
   Swept down the stairs of heaven.

But down the golden roads of air
   No angel's feet are stealing;
And still the clouds in joy sail on,
   No face of God revealing.

We can not hear the Saviour call
   From out the cloudy splendor,
But where sweet children sing his praise
   In voices low and tender;

Wherever patient hearts endure;
  Where souls grow tired of sinning;
Wherever love toils bravely on
  For something worth the winning;

Wherever bodies sigh with pain;
  Wherever hearts are broken;
Wherever some one might be won
  If loving words were spoken;

Where we make others happy, with
  Some good that God has lent us—
There Christ is walking by our side,
  And God himself has sent us.

His footsteps are around the door
  Where love to want is giving;
And where for His sake we forgive,
  There Christ with us is living.

MY LETTER FROM THE KING.

One day, a long, long time ago,
  As little children do,
I read a story o'er and o'er,
  And longed to find it true.

'T was of a great and mighty King,
  Who ruled a famous land;
And on a fairy hill-top built
  A palace vast and grand.

Then, by an order from the King,
    The gates wide open stood;
And messengers went far and wide
    To call the brave and good.

But somewhere on the winding way
    A giant lived in state,
And fought the pilgrims day by day,
    Who passed his castle gate.

He conquered some, and some were killed,
    And some, with many a sting
Of cruel arrows, reached at length
    The palace of the King.

And there at last, the story said,
    They all are living still,
With fairies flitting in and out
    The palace on the hill.

I lived to find my story true,
    To know the "famous land;"
And here 's my letter from the King,
    Whose gates wide open stand.

His palace is beyond the clouds,
    And all the stars on high
Are only golden lamps hung round
    His palace in the sky.

So I go on, and day by day
    Grow gladder while I sing,
Nearing the "city on the hill"—
    The "palace of the King."

I often meet the giant too—
My giant's name is Sin—
I fight him at his castle gates,
And will not enter in.

And I shall meet him yet again,
But angels help me still—
These are the fairies of my King,
The servants of his will.

My King is called the "Wonderful,"
The "Mighty" and the "Fair"—
His names are in your Bible;
My letter too is there.

When I am sad I read again
My letter from the King,
And looking toward the open gates,
Grow gladder while I sing.

OUR NATION'S DESTINY.

The years of the past in a sorrowful train
Come up from the grave, where they long have lain,
To tell of the nations that rose and fell
On the billows of time as they sink and swell;
And the sound of their footsteps gliding by
Echoes, "Nations like men are born to die."
The worm is ever about the root,
And the seeds of decay in the ripened fruit—

Thus the glory of Rome in its great renown
Has sunk in the night of the ages down.

But thy records tell that the crimson tide
Was poured to flatter a monarch's pride,
And the pillars of State are *never* strong
That are built o'er the grave of a terrible wrong.
So, sorrowful years, in your records old,
No words prophetic of time ye hold;
For the world of to-day is wiser, we know,
Than the world of a thousand years ago,
And the earth is purer for all the tears
That have flowed for the sins of a thousand years.

From the misty shadows of glory fled—
From the ashes of empires cold and dead—
From the chaos of error and pomp and sin
And splendor, and where their thrones have been,
A nation has risen whose youthful prime
Will forever defy the storms of time.
Oh! gaze, ye prophets of pitiless fate,
O'er the sun's broad path to his western gate,
Where, lapped on the earth in its emerald dyes,
The youngest-born of the nations lies.

'T was after the night of the middle years—
That sleep so troubled with doubts and fears—
As the eyes of the East in their westward way,
Followed the sun through the weary day,
They saw on the shore of the far-off land
A kneeling group, an unlifted hand:
"''T is a goodly home we have found to-day;
But the earth is the Lord's—give thanks and pray."
And the prayer that was offered on Plymouth shore
Is recorded in Heaven for evermore.

The solemn winds were the priests of God
That scattered the spray o'er the frozen sod;
The altar the rock, and the font the bay—
And this was our nation's baptismal day.
The sun on his journey paused and smiled
On the Earth as she folded her new-born child;
So the *royal mantle* of purple dyes
Was cast on the child from the crimson skies;
And day by day at his western gate
He lingers to smile on the fair young State.

Go back, ye ghostly prophet of doom,
To the temple of fate amid ashes and gloom,
Where the priests of Ruin are waiting for thee
To preside at their terrible mystery.
Go back and tell that a *higher* power
Controls *our* fate till the final hour;
For the youngest child of the earth shall be
The brightest one in her destiny;
And God shall speak her time to die,
When the earth shall be laid in oblivion by.

THE ANGELS.

One day at sunset, or the hour
  When day in Heaven grows old;
Just when the heavenly evening filled
  The city paved with gold,

Long ranks of shining angels stood
  Around the Saviour's throne,
And told of all the wondrous things
  That one bright day had known.

One said a thousand angels stood
  Before the Father's face,
Forever singing, "God is good,
  And this his dwelling-place."

And one said, all the shining stars
  That traveled round the sun,
Were only great and mighty worlds,
  In which God's will was done.

Another said 't was summer-time
  Down in this world of ours,
And streams of sunshine filled the earth
  With grass, and birds, and flowers;

And happy children laughed and played,
  And only hushed their mirth
At evening, when they thought of Him
  Who made this green old earth.

At last a brighter angel spoke,
  And all the rest were still:
"God sent me to the earth to see
  Who *did his holy will.*

"I watched the children all day long,
  Through all their work and play,
And when they slept, *I kissed the one*
  Who did God's will to-day."

And then the thousand angels sang
  Loud songs of joy and mirth
That overflowed the walls of Heaven,
  And drifted down to earth.

LINES, WITH A BIBLE PRESENTED.

"Thy word is a lamp unto my feet, and a light unto my path."
Psalm cxix. 105.

We met and we parted,
And now at your feet
I hold out this lamp
O'er the way we shall meet.
My heart must remember,
And lovingly still
I fain would rule over
Your heart and your will.
I watch and I wait, for, early or late,
You are ruler of destiny, lord over fate.

By the past I adjure,
By the present implore,
By the future entreat;
At the wide-open door
Where Love bears his chosen
Triumphantly through,
I shall leave my lamp burning,
And waiting for you.
I shall watch, I shall wait, for, early or late,
You are lord if you will o'er the kingdom of fate.

MY LIFE AND I.

How long I shall live, not the angels can tell;
When and where be the place of my dying;

Whose hands shall ungirdle a travel-stained robe
From a bosom that 's done with its sighing;
  Whose hands shall caress me,
  And whose lips shall kiss me—
The sweetest and last that go with me to Heaven.

In some hour that 's Eternity's centre to me,
  To my soul both an end and beginning,
My heart shall not beat for my passionate brain,
  And my hands shall not care for the winning;
    And a wonderful thing,
    Without visible wing,
Shall rise and soar up to the Kingdom of Heaven.

But what of the things that are left—shall I care
  What others shall say of my yearning,
And how they shall light up my weakness and pain
  With the eyes of their quiet discerning?
    What I shall have won,
    And what left undone,
And what taken with me unfinished to Heaven?

'T is a very small place in the world that I fill—
  Could I have enlarged it, I wonder,
With my strength and my weakness combining to
    keep
  My life and ideal asunder?
    Will my powers be stronger,
    Where life shall be longer?
Shall we dream and not do in the Kingdom of Heaven?

When some one shall quietly cover my face,
  And say, "All her labor is ended,"
'T will only mean this, that my failures are o'er,
  And my time and my task are extended.

O world of success
And infinite bliss,
Whose shadows fall over and glorify this !

MY THEORY.

Step like a child on the threshold of being,
  Into the future, forgetting the past;
Our vision is dim and our farthest foreseeing
  Is bounded by mist and by darkness at last.

Out of the range of our limited vision,
  Out of the reach of our toiling and strife,
Calm-browed with a sense of their holy commission,
  The angels are solving the problems of life.

They weigh our deserts with our power of endurance,
  And temper it all with the mercy of God;
Then send with their verdict the blessed assurance
  That only His children pass under the rod.

Our surest foundations may crumble in sorrow,
  Our air-builded castles in tears may dissolve;
Omniscience alone can decide for the morrow,
  And leave not a doubt for the morrow to solve.

Here in the twilight of weak indecision,
  Groping through mist of our gathering tears,
We longingly strive for that purified vision
  That comes with the sorrow and patience of years.

Then look up to God in His wonderful patience,
  And, hopelessly measuring our stature by His,
The possible life of divine expectations
  Is lost to our view through the failures of this.

Earth's story goes on like the change of the seasons.
  God turns a new leaf for each oncoming age,
And each with its failures, successes and reasons,
  Contributes an ill or a well-written page.

And those generations least willing to borrow
  The lights that were trimmed in the ages gone by,
Most eagerly look for a grander to-morrow,
  And catch the first glimpse of its dawn in the sky.

O infidel hearts, that o'er errors and losses
  In dust of eternal repentance lie down,
Accepting life's trials and bearing its crosses,
  Why, why not press on where He holdeth the crown?

God is not the poorer for all our wrong-doing,
  Or richer for lives that are wasted in tears;
'T is not an avenger our footsteps pursuing,
  But angels of mercy encompass our years.

Let us not be wreckers to toil o'er disaster,
  And weep o'er the fragments cast up by the sea,
But sail on like ships with a heavenly Master,
  From the life that now is to the life yet to be.

MY CREED.

I believe in God the Father, father of all human souls,
Not a ruler watching Nature while her wondrous plan unrolls,

But the Father of our spirits and the Moulder of our frames,
Loving each as one begotten, calling each by separate names—
  In the Father of our spirits I believe.

I believe the Holy Jesus loved divinely, suffered much,
That our God might reach His children with a close and human touch,
Drawing us with love so tender up the pathway where He trod,
Till we fall, like weeping children, in the yearning arms of God—
  In our King and Priest and Prophet I believe.

I believe the Holy Spirit fills the earth from shore to shore,
Round about, above, within us, bearing witness evermore;
Where the Holy Guest abideth, if He tarry but a night,
Even sordid eyes beholding, see the wondrous love and light—
  In the Paraclete of promise I believe.

I believe the holy angels hover round us all the way,
Each commissioned by the Father—clouds of witnesses are they;
To the throne they bear our sorrows, then return on tireless wing,
Bringing to each heart dispatches from the palace of our King—
  In the ministering angels I believe.

I believe in life eternal—trees and flowers and drops of rain
Live and die, and, decomposing, live and die and live again;
Doubting still what wondrous changes shall complete the perfect
  sphere,
Life I know is greater, grander than the segment pictured here—
  In the coming life eternal I believe.

I believe the holy message as infallible and true,
What therein the Lord commandeth, He will strengthen us to do;
Not in churches, saints or prophets, nor in wise men can I trust,
If they teach me words of wisdom, where they learned them, there
  I must—
  In the Word of inspiration I believe.

I believe that human loving is a lesson taught above,
I believe the cup of blessing is a brimming cup of love;
Loving, when the flesh is willing, is the sweetest drop of bliss;
Loving on through pain and evil is diviner still than this—
  In love, the law of love fulfilling, I believe.

I believe in sweet communion with the saints in praise and prayer;
I believe that in forgiving we rise upward stair by stair;

I believe in godly strivings, I believe in contrite tears;
I believe that in believing we shall live through endless years;
For the key of life is only—*I believe.*

NEARER GOD.

Sometimes when silence grows intense,
And viewless hands restrain
Within the close-bound gates of sense
The pris'ner of the brain,

When soul defiant yieldeth not,
And all its vassals keep
The wondrous sentry gates of thought
Against the power of sleep,

No longer doubt and pain and sin
My will and purpose mar,
And grapple with their might-have-been,
Across the things that are.

There seems no haste for things to be,
No error to undo,
No doubtful poise of victory,
No struggle to be true.

God underlies the solemn past,
The future far and dim;
All evil things that live and last,
Must live and last for Him.

Across the plains of human sense
The floods of evil run;
The mountain-tops of Providence
Are always in the sun.

Perhaps all souls a moment drop
The sins and ills they bear;
Each spirit hath its mountain-top,
And meets its Maker there.

So when the silence grows intense,
With darkness overrun,
I touch the hand of Providence
One moment in the sun;

One moment where no sin has trod,
High over human ill,
I lean upon the heart of God,
And find it kindred still—

Kindred through all our sins and woes,
Through all our pain and blight.
Evil like water downward flows;
Soul, upward to the light.

AFTER A WHILE.

After a while is a beautiful day—
The storm will be ended and brighter the sun,
The weariness over, the task will be done,
Some sweet thing is coming to every one,
                    After a while.

After a while is a prosperous day;
Then we shall have all the wisdom we need;
Our earnest endeavors shall always succeed,
Till every ideal expand to a deed,
    After a while.

After a while is an affluent day,
When our fugitive treasure shall all be secure,
And we shall forget that we ever were poor,
When patience shall blossom and friendship endure,
    After a while.

After a while is a halcyon day,
When the love we have lavished our bosoms shall
  bless;
Then shall be true every hand that we press,
The hearts we confide in, the lips we caress,
    After a while.

After a while, 't is a merciful day,
Filled with all comfort and free from all fear,
And thrilled with all love.   Ah! if only 't was clear
What the day of the month and the month of the
  year,
    After a while.

After a while!   'T is a far-away time;
For now, while impatiently counting, I see
'T is not in the calendar open to me,
So it must be in God's, in the life that 's to be,
    After a while.

DR. L. L. PINKERTON.

O life that has passed from our vision away,
  To the hearts that shall seek and not find thee,
The light shall grow dim in the face of the day,
  And the shadows shall lengthen behind thee.
And yet we are glad thou hast entered thy rest
Ere the sun of thy life had sunk low in the west.

Thy lot has been weary, thy pathway was hard;
  Dear heart! can we weep for the ending,
When thy beautiful dreams were all broken and
    marred,
  In the van of the battle contending?
But 't is always the same with the heroes that wage
A war with the errors and sins of an age.

We think with regret of the life that is spent,
  But the soul never dies, and the arrow
Death leaves in the bow of a purpose still bent,
  Speedeth on to its mission to-morrow.
And thy thought shall not die, but live on and ex-
    pand
Into deeds that are noble and lives that are grand.

Thou hast fought through the evil, still holding the
    right;
  Thou hast finished the task that was grandest—
Toiled on through the darkness and entered the light,
  And now in the glory thou standest.
Though tears stain the way where in pain thou hast
    trod,
'T was in parallel lines with the purpose of God.

We weep for the bowl that is broken; but think:
   The wine is not spilled; and forever
At the crystallized cup of thy purpose we drink,
   And grow strong by thy earnest endeavor.
Not so hard 't is to die as to live and be true;
Let us drink and grow stronger to will and to do.

O feet that now walk in a beautiful place,
   Thy errands of mercy are over;
O beautiful soul in a toil-hardened face,
   Humanity weeps for a lover.
But now looking up through our tears, we can see
'T is a glory-lined cloud that encompasseth thee.

We think of thy lips that are frozen and dumb,
   And sigh for their closed revelation;
But now in the land of the kingdom to come,
   They are touched with a new inspiration;
An apostle to witness His glory to-day,
Thy soul is not dumb, though thy lips are but clay.

MY VESPER SONG.

Filled with weariness and pain,
   Scarcely strong enough to pray,
In this twilight hour I sit—
   Sit and sing my doubt away.

O'er my broken purposes,
   Ere the coming shadows roll,
Let me build a bridge of song:
   "Jesus, lover of my soul,

"Let me to thy bosom fly"—
How the words my thoughts repeat!
To thy bosom, Lord, I come,
Though unfit to kiss thy feet.

Once I gathered sheaves for thee,
Dreaming I could hold them fast;
Now I can but idly sing:
"Oh! receive my soul at last."

I am weary of my fears;
Like a child when night comes on,
In the shadow, Lord, I sing:
"Leave, oh! leave me alone."

Through the tears I still must shed,
Through the evil yet to be,
Though I falter while I sing,
"Still support and comfort me."

"All my trust on thee is stayed"—
Does the rhythm of the song,
Softly falling on my heart,
Make its pulses firm and strong?

Or is this thy perfect peace
Now descending while I sing,
That my soul may sleep to-night
"'Neath the shadow of thy wing"?

"Thou of life the fountain art."
If I slumber on thy breast,
If I sing myself to sleep—
Sleep and death alike are rest.

Through the shadows overpast,
  Through the shadows yet to be,
Let the ladder of my song
  "Rise to all eternity."

Note by note, its silver bars
  May my soul in love ascend,
Till I reach the highest round
  In thy kingdom without end.

Not impatiently I sing,
  Though I stretch my hands and cry,
"Jesus, lover of my soul,
  Let me to thy bosom fly."

WOMEN—MISSION WORKERS.

That work hath the Lord for His daughter to do,
  The pillar of cloud is hung o'er us;
The field of the world stretches wide to our view,
  And the cross is uplifted before us.

Shall we pray that his kingdom shall cover the earth,
  The way to whose feet is so narrow;
And yet standing idly look up to our God,
  Waiting still for a fairer to-morrow?

No brighter to-morrow shall dawn on our sight;
  The age of our bondage is over;

No grander commission than ours of to-day
  Can the eye of a prophet discover.

Shall we talk of our spheres, and forever divide
  On opinions all erring and human;
And idly gainsaying fall out of the ranks,
  When a half of the army is woman?

It was at Creation, is now and shall be,
  Despite of our puny opinion;
God made us together to conquer the earth,
  And gave us with our brothers dominion.

Then He from the throne of his glory came down,
  The Redeemer was born of a woman;
The curse was dissolved in the shade of the cross,
  In a love that was tender and human.

While humanity stretches her sorrowful hands,
  Repeating her pitiful story,
At the foot of the ladder, like Jacob asleep,
  Shall we dream of the infinite glory,

When the ladder of love stretches up into Heaven,
  And we, like the angels descending,
May bear up a soul from the sin-burdened earth,
  From trial to triumph ascending?

The ages have blossomed for us, and we stand
  Where the field to our vision is given;
Let us rally to-day at the foot of the cross,
  And march on to the kingdom of heaven.

MY SUNSET WINDOW.

I saw the golden sunset overleaping
  The dark horizon with its flaming wings,
But only felt the long-armed shadows creeping
  Behind the substance of material things.

They clung about me, and each moment longer,
  Fleeing from nothing and pursuing naught,
Communing with the darkness, growing stronger,
  Grappled more firmly with the feet of thought.

I sighed and shuddered, and, the text forgetting,
  I read no sermon in the day's decline;
No golden poem where the sun was setting,
  And no hand-writing in the blazing sign.

And like the day, I wished I too was dying;
  Blinder than he who pressed the stony sod,
I, at the foot of Jacob's ladder lying,
  Saw not the angels that descend from God.

I wished that I too, like the day, was dying—
  Strange, thoughtless words; and yet why not, dear
    Lord?
From every vale of darkness, sin and crying,
  Some path of love must lead us gloryward.

To die like this fair day, would be to find it,
  To cross the hills of doubt that hem me in,
And see the golden city just behind it,
  Where there is no more darkness, pain or sin.

Why not, dear Lord? The only clouds that harm me
    Are those that shut Thee from my eager sight;
Down through thy blessed sunset look and warm me,
    Till death shall seem but entrance into light.

The clouds were parted, and a sweet inviting
    Came like a telegram of peace from heaven
Down wires invisible, and this hand-writing
    Was the transcription of the message given:

" There is no night in the Eternal City,
    And no night here to those who seek His face.
O'er the horizon of His love and pity—
    The road to heaven is straight from every place."

Ah ! what are tears to those whom angels visit?
    And what is darkness in a world like this?
When angels lower the lights of life, then is it
    To show us pictures of a world of bliss.

Eyes dim with tears may catch the glowing vision,
    Weak hands may clasp the angels as they fly
Up Jacob's ladder to the life elysian,
    Whose far perspective is the sunset sky.

Life grows exalted, and the things that grieve me
    Seem but lost atoms of a grander whole;
My greedy senses drink their fill, and leave me
    Here, at this sunset window, with my soul.

A PRAYER.

O Christ that loved me more than men,
    Upon whose faithful breast

I lean my weary spirit, when
I find no human rest,

Into thy listening ear I pour
My sorrows sore and long,
And learn the lesson o'er and o'er,
To suffer and be strong.

A thousand eyes look unto Thee—
A thousand hands implore,
A thousand weary hearts like mine,
Beseech Thee o'er and o'er.

For all the earth is filled with prayer;
Though voiceless, strange and dumb,
Its pulses thrill the conscious air,
And through the silence come

To throb upon that listening ear
That needs no sound, nor speech
Of man, and yet divines the thought
That fills the heart of each.

Thy love and patience are as vast
And soundless as the sea,
And there our frailest anchor cast,
Holds on eternity.

And yet how often while we think
Our treasures are above,
The plummet of our hearts we sink
In many a hopeless love.

They come, dear Christ, to seek Thy face
   When every light is gone,
As pilgrims seek a resting-place,
   Before the night comes on.

Just as the babe upon my breast
   Fears naught of human ill,
So hold me on Thy heart at rest,
   As helpless, loving, still.

Why do I leave Thy outstretched arms,
   And tempt the dark alone?
Why do I fear all human harms
   When I should fear but one—

Fear only that I grieve too much
   Thy patient heart, until
I slip from out Thy loving touch,
   To work my wayward will?

O Christ, by human love unblest,
   Through darkness, pain and care,
Like some tired child I seek Thy breast,
   And lay my sorrow there.

ACROSS THE SEA.

All I know of love is this:
It is something that we miss,
Never something we forget;
For a golden hour is set
Evermore in memory
When you went across the sea.

What we said I can not tell;
What we thought I know full well.
Hope was fair and speech was true,
Life was golden through and through,
When you told me, tenderly,
You were going across the sea.

I remember how your eyes
Dimmed with tears of strange surprise
When my trembling hand was laid
On the shoulder God had made
For my rest, though it should be
Going from me o'er the sea.

When the parting came, at last,
How your dear eyes held me fast,
While my quivering heart was pressed
Close and closer to your breast!
'T was a blissful dream to me;
But you went across the sea.

Ah! I should not tell a dream.
Love is not a woman's theme;
She should only patient wait,
Take or lose the gift of fate;
Weep, if must be, silently,
For a love across the sea.

This is long ago; and now,
With no kisses on my brow,
Love its solemn fast will keep
Through my waking and my sleep.
When I dream again, 't will be
I that go across the sea.

RETICENCE.

Sitting, dear one, all alone,
Let me catch the undertone
Of your thoughts, and softly glide
Into musing at your side.

Would you care if I should know
All the thoughts that come and go
Through your gentle heart and brain?
Darling, would it give you pain?

Would a sudden, swift eclipse
Darken o'er your eyes and lips
If I read the secret there,
Trembling in your waving hair?

All the thoughts are pure, I know,
Flitting trackless o'er the snow
Of your bosom, that to-night
Lures me with its stainless white.

I have told you all, my sweet.
Is a woman more discreet?
Must she always something hold,
Lest her love be overbold?

Gentle hands in mine you lay,
Though you have your willful way;
Tender lips and thrilling eyes
Full of love and sacrifice—

From my breast you look and plead,
Yet your thoughts I can not read.
See, I kiss your lips and brow:
Darling, can you keep it now?

So you think my love would fail
If your heart should rend its veil;
If I read you through and through,
That I should not care to woo.

So your bridal veil must be
Symbol of your life with me:
Always something sweet revealed,
Always something half-concealed.

Do I think it best?   Ah! well,
Loving you, I can not tell.
You will keep your secret still,
Pris'ner of your wayward will.

JOHN THE BAPTIST.

A SONG.

Into the wilderness round about Jordan,
    Went out the wonderful prophet of yore,
Preaching a kingdom that should be eternal—
    Preaching of wrath that should slumber no more.

Into the wilderness round about Jordan,
    Went out the Saviour untouched by a sin;
King of a kingdom that should be eternal—
    Pure as the dewdrop the flowers shut in.

Out of the waves of the swift flowing Jordan
Jesus emerging, the heavens divide;
Down from the throne comes a message, repeating:
"This is my Son" while the ages abide.

THE GREATEST PROPHET.

(John i. 34.)

Then came the blessed One, and John, beholding,
    Cried, "This is He who came,
The ancient prophecies of God unfolding,
    Before I knew His name.

"The Lamb of God, whose heart so pure and lowly.
    The sins of men shall bear,
The Lord's Anointed, for whose feet so holy
    A pathway I prepare.

"I knew Him not till, by the Jordan standing,
    I saw the sacred sign—
The Holy Spirit like a dove descending
    To crown the Lord divine.

"Before the brightness of His dawning glory
    My footsteps shall grow dim:
I but bear record of the wondrous story,
    And hide myself in Him."

THE SECOND MIRACLE.

A SONG.

(John ii.)

One moment water, then 't was wine,
Transformed by Him whose power divine
In loving kindness deigns to heed
The whisper of our smallest need.
Oh! all unworthy as I am,
Lord, at the marriage of the Lamb,
May I but drink, as guest of thine,
Thy blood transformed to heavenly wine.

O Giver of an endless good,
Who, spite of our ingratitude,
Sustains through earth and air and sea,
The life that is, and is to be!
Oh! all unworthy as I am,
Lord, at the marriage of the Lamb,
May I but drink as guest of thine,
Thy blood transformed to heavenly wine.

GOD.

God is the power sublime
That filled eternity and boundless space,
Before Creation, at the birth of Time,
Beheld His radiant face.

God is the power supreme
That o'er the chaos of eternal night
All smiling looked; and, like a glorious dream,
Creation woke to light.

God is the wondrous power
That breathed His soul-light into forms of clay,
To shine forever, from that glorious hour,
Lamps of immortal ray.

His loving, watchful eye
Looked down in pity, while the angels wept,
When man—God's image—taught by sin to die,
In earth's dark bosom slept.

But when the earth grew dim—
Dark with the shadow of its many graves—
While souls went hopeless through the shadows grim
O'er Death's unsounded waves,

His was the soul of love
That stooped in pity from His shining throne,
Left the bright angels and the bliss above
To suffer here alone—

To suffer and to die,
Meekly descending to the shrouded tomb,
Where generations of the years gone by
Slept in mysterious gloom.

His was the mighty hand
That swept the shadows from the grave away,
And lit the doorway of the spirit-land
With Hope's undying ray.

And many a tear-dimmed eye
Grows bright and brighter with each graveward view,
While souls their burdens at the door lay by
And pass with angels through.

But when the spirit's sight
Is dim, or blinded by earth's gath'ring dust,
The soul perceiveth not that heavenly light,
Feels not that heavenly trust.

God loves and pities all,
And His great heart shall cease to woo thee—never,
Till Death enfolds thee in his gloomy pall
Forever and forever.

Far in the future lies
A final hour, when suns shall cease to burn,
And when the tear-stained earth and smiling skies
To chaos shall return.

But when the hour shall be
When Time and all, all earthly things, a wreck,
Float darkly out upon Eternity,
A dim, dim fading speck;

When suns and stars are fled,
And all the universe waits dark and lone,
When stern old Death at last lies shrouded—dead—
Beside his crumbled throne;

The veil shall fall away,
And night's dark curtain be forever furled
Back from the brow of universe, while day
Springs from the spirit-world.

The souls, with Christ, who trod
Through weary suffering to perfection on,
Shall shine forever round the throne of God
Like stars around the sun.

A RESPONSE.

(Read before the General Convention, Thursday afternoon, October
22nd, by Miss Ida Hood, of Cincinnati.)

Sister Caroline Neville Pearre and other sisters of the Christian
Church, in Convention assembled at Cincinnati, O., October 20th,
1874:

'T is not because I loved my pen
I chose it from the tasks that lie
Around a busy woman's life,
Where cares expand and multiply;

It is not that I vainly hoped
My feeble hands could reach beyond
Life's common chords to touch the one
To which all human souls respond.

Although my little song may lull
Some sad, unquiet heart to sleep,
The world's calm pulses still flow on,
And he who sleeps may wake to weep.

But all that 's great or grand or good
Appeals to womanhood and me;
All that my faith hath understood
My purpose and my work must be.

Like one beside Bethsaida's pool,
In passive weakness, day by day,
I saw the angel's sacred feet
Disturb the pool and pass away.

Yet still I waited patiently,
And told my little dreams in song;
Content if some should say, Her voice
Was feeble, but her soul was strong.

And so in spirit I rejoice,
And, standing in the ranks, I view
Across the hills of Providence,
The dawning light that beckons you.

We know the age has bloomed for us;
For, when the Lord of Glory died,
Between the Manger and the Cross,
Our womanhood was dignified.

Shall woman still, from age to age—
Despite the wondrous sacrifice—
Still weep beneath the olden curse
That closed the gates of Paradise?

We stand upon a higher plane,
And God himself, who came to bless,
Still walks beside us day by day
In guise of human helplessness.

And those are God's who toil for Him,
Their purpose, not their powers in view,
Ordained in spirit for the work
He whispers to their hearts to do.

So in our hearts a voice is stirred
To wond'rous depths we knew not of,
A purpose and a work is born,
And all our souls are filled with love.

Now let us never doubting say,
I wonder if it is in vain;
But what is whispered to our hearts
We 'll dare to tell the world again.

No more beside Bethsaida's pool,
In passive weakness, day by day,
We watch the angel's sacred feet
Disturb the pool and pass away.

And you, whose tasks diverge from ours,
Toil you so well that you should dare
To tell us that we often mar
Work that should be divinely fair?

We know it; but a purpose bent
By such a puny human strain,
Could never half evolve the power
Concentered in an earnest brain.

Warmed by a patient human heart
That learned through many a doubting year
That what He bids us do or say
Is all we know of duty here,

We labor with our hands, and see
Exact results from effort grow;
But what our words accomplish here
On *earth*, we do not care to know.

The world is wide, and few are heard
Above its din of toil and strife;
But each may leave the world at last
The better for her rounded life.

So ever when He bids us work,
 Or speak His praise with tongue or pen,
Shall blows of truth, or words of love,
 Fall somewhere on our fellow-men.

Ah! tell us not our blows are weak—
 Our words of love in silence die;
God's balances are turned by hairs,
 And all our efforts in them lie.

While thus I think, my soul expands,
 And, for a moment grand and strong,
All things seem near and possible,
 And all my soul breaks forth in song.

THE CROSS OF CHRIST.

The Cross of Christ! I do not know
Its place in heaven or here below.
It flings across our human sense
The sign of His omnipotence;
Not borne aloft or hung in air,
Untouched, unseen, yet everywhere—
 The Cross of Christ.

The Cross of Christ—of old it stood
A cruel cross of iron and wood
That touched the earth and heaven and hell,
While round about it darkness fell,
When Truth was mocked and power defied,
And Love and Mercy drooped and died,
 O Cross of Christ!

The Cross of Christ for ages stood
The symbol of all human good,
The key of worldly fame and power;
The light upon the light-house tower,
That o'er the Middle Ages swung,
Before the bells of morning rung
The better day, when once again
The blessed Christ should speak to men,
    O Cross of Christ!

The Cross of Christ! For years it stood
The symbol of my solitude;
A daily milestone, where I'd find
How far I'd left the world behind,
And how much farther I must press
To find the final blessedness.
I missed the fact—the blessed Cross;
But grasped its shadow—pain and loss—
    The Cross of Christ.

The Cross of Christ! It came at last
To mean a struggle overpast;
A fellowship of scourge and rod,
And afterward the peace of God.
And in this peace—so wide and deep,
It fills my waking and my sleep—
My patient lamp of love I trim
As I lie down or walk with Him,
    O Cross of Christ!

The Cross of Christ! I do not know
Its place in heaven or here below.
It flings across our human sense
The sign of His omnipotence;

And I may see without surprise
Upon the hills of Paradise,
The Cross of Christ.

PENTECOSTAL VOICES.

On the rock my church is builded,
Far above the sands of time,
And those echoes still are rolling
Out through every land and clime.

In the grand wide-open doorway
See the great Apostle stand;
But the keys of life are given
Not to any human hand.

Evermore, like holy echoes,
Pentecostal voices ring
All adown the true succession,
Christ our Prophet, Priest and King.

Back within the solemn ages,
Underneath the upas shade,
Where on moss-grown trunks of error
Luther's sturdy axe was laid;

Where the forest of oppression
Waved the branches of its pride,
Shutting out the light of heaven
Where the holy martyrs died,

Wickliffe towered above the ages,
    Like a light-house on the shore;
Voices crying in the darkness
    Echoed from the Lollard's tower.

Tongues of men were tongues of angels,
    Touched by fire and winged by fame;
Lat'mer lit a broad horizon
    With his winding-sheet of flame.

AS OUR DAY SHALL OUR STRENGTH BE.

As our day shall our strength be:
    Whatever betide,
    His ear is not sleeping,
    He heareth our weeping,
    His infinite keeping
        Sufficient shall be.

As our day shall our strength be:
    The Lord will provide.
    If the load be not lightened,
    The way be not brightened,
    Still heaven is in sight, and
        Our God is the Lord.

As our day shall our strength be:
    He knoweth our frame.
    While faith, even, slumbered,
    By darkness encumbered,
    Our hairs were all numbered
        By angels of God.

As our day shall our strength be :
The promise is sure.
Mid toiling and yearning,
Still may we be learning,
With Him is no turning,
Nor shadow of change.

As our day shall our strength be :
The rest is with God.
His bosom shall cover
Our weakness, and hover
In tenderness over
The work of His hands.

As our day shall our strength be :
O Lover and Friend,
In rapture or sighing,
Still may I be lying,
In living or dying,
Close, close to Thy breast.

CHRISTMAS POEMS.

WHEN SHILOH CAME.

(Luke ii. 7.)

A light in the darkness—a wonderful thing—
A babe in the manger, the heir of a King.
From the palace of God came a guest in the night
To a manger and darkness, and sorrow and blight.
The seed of a woman, the brightest and best,
The blossom of ages, the promise of rest.

THF ANGELS' SONG.

(Luke ii. 13, 14.)

Down the shining ranks of angels
  Bursts an anthem loud and long:
Christ is born, and love eternal
  Melteth into joy and song.

CHORUS.

Hark! the angels sing together
Songs that echo on forever;
Still the sweet and blissful story,
Lord of love and life and glory.

Since the morning stars together
  Sang the anthem of their birth,
Only once the songs of Heaven
  Have come floating down to earth.
  CHORUS.—*Hark! etc.*

Then they sang a world created—
  Now, a world redeemed by love:
Glory unto God the highest,
  Peace on earth, good-will and love.
  CHORUS.—*Hark! etc.*

———

THE WISE MEN'S SONG OF WORSHIP.

(Matt. ii. 2.)

Led by the Star of Bethlehem,
  Before Thy feet we bow;

We knew Thee as the Lord of Hosts—
As Love we know Thee now.
Through all Thy prophets, Lord, we trace
Thy wondrous truth and power;
Thou art the Shiloh of our race,
The One whom we adore.

Thou shalt redeem our race from death:
Thy triumphs who can tell?
Sent by the Lord Omnipotent,
The Christ of Israel,
O Royal Child of earth, to Thee
Our grateful praise we bring;
Thou art the end of prophecy,
Our Prophet, Priest and King.

FRAGMENTS.

BEYOND the ocean of the air,
Whose tidal waves expand,
Creep up the western coast, and there
Break on its golden sand ;

Beyond the dear unconscious dead,
Who lie like babes asleep,
Unmindful that above their head
We sin and toil and weep.

ABOVE the level of the plain,
Where mountains cleave the air,
We hail the treasure-ships of rain
That never anchor there.

I STAND upon the edge of bliss,
  Or on the brink of sorrow;
I know not what the future is,
  But I can trust to-morrow.

I look into your melting eyes,
  And feel their gentle wooing;
But other hearts in just such eyes
  Have found their sad undoing.

SISTER AND I.

IN THE spring-time, I remember—
  Both were young, and one was fair—
We were sitting, while the sunbeams
  Gleamed like arrows in thy hair;
Softly on thy brow there rested
  Rays the sunlight can not bring—
Rays that only fall upon us
  In life's golden days of spring.

A FACE IN A CROWD.

The face was silent, cold and calm,
  Unmoved by thought or passion;
As undisturbed I scanned it o'er
  In strange familiar fashion.

What was the firm-closed mouth to me;
  The dark, bright hair, I wonder;
The tranquil breadth of brow serene;
  The eyes so restful, under?

I never moved their silentness
Where Providence shall use them;
I neither know, nor think, nor guess,
I only look and love them.

Their key-note is not mine to touch,
And yet my idle fingers
Construct a chord wherein a note
Of wondrous beauty lingers.

Ah! now 't is passed beyond my sight—
The visible and real—
Out through the gates of sight and sense,
Into the wide ideal.

And there, despite my consciousness,
It lives and moves without me,
Beyond the walls of commonplace
I daily build about me.

Could one more note have made for me
Life's march more grand and solemn,
And bid my straggling virtues close,
And march in solid column?

Perhaps; and yet perhaps withheld,
And for a better reason,
Let us believe whate'er we need
Shall meet us in due season.

Life is too grand to fail at last,
And we, or soon or later,
Grasp all we hope to find or be
'Twixt creature and Creator.

We needs must have some gath'ring-place,
Where what we ask is given,
Or want and loss would reign with God,
And blight the airs of Heaven.

THE ONLY DAUGHTER.

Child of my dreams, through all the years
When girlhood womanhood overlaps,
Thy face, the crown of them all appears
Since I was a child myself perhaps—
Child of my dreams thou **art.**

Child of my hope, a promise given—
No earthly fate too sweet could be;
And thou must have died and grown up in Heaven,
To have half the virtues I hoped for thee.
Child of my hope thou art.

Child of my prayers, I have kept the wires
That bear our petitions up to the King,
Untiringly burdened with my desires,
And now, as I wait for His answering,
Child of my prayers thou **art.**

Child of my love, I never knew
How Christ loves us till I saw thy face.
There was nothing too great for me to do,
As I looked at its sweet, unconscious grace.
Child of my love thou art.

Child of my own, in my heart and brain
  Has warmed the blood that now throbs in thine;
Perhaps—do I wish it?—who can explain?
Is thy soul, dear child, a part of mine?
     For child of my own thou art.

Child of my faith, thy face to-night
  In the halo around the cross I see;
And there may I see it with failing sight,
 When I look my last on the cross and thee.
     Child of my faith thou art.

And all the things I have done so ill,
  Thou wilt do them better in better ways;
And the things I did well, thou wilt do them still,
  And paint thy mother in robes of praise
     To a child of thine own dear heart.

GOING ON A JOURNEY.

All the house is full of bustle,
  Up and down the hall and stairs
Busy people rush and rustle
  Here and there and everywhere.

Some one's going on a journey,
  So a thousand things are done;
Opportunity is over
  When the journey is begun.

Here are books and there is paper,
  Here are clothes for some one, too,

So much and more to do, and only
   One short day in which to do.

For to-morrow, though we listen,
   Up and down the hall and stairs
There 'll be silence, no one calling,
   Wanting something anywhere.

Then shall I sit down and ponder
   How like death these journeys are: .
We are always getting ready
   For a journey long and far,

To the great, eternal Kingdom,
   Where beside a jasper sea
Travelers reach a golden city
   Where the many mansions be.

All the earth is full of bustle,
   Up and down the world we go;
But at last, if we 're not ready
   For the journey, God will know.

In a mansion built of jewels,
   And a city paved with gold,
We shall need such spotless dresses
   That will not grow soiled or old.

WHEN SHALL I SEE THEE, MOTHER MINE?

I sit in the porch, with the mother away,
   With the day wearing on to its ending;

And the shadows that slant in the wake of the day
With my thoughts are unconsciously blending,
As dark on my sight breaks the tide of the night,
In the porch at the close of the day.

And yet I am sure it is best as it is,
Or at least it is just as I will it;
But this evening I only am thinking of this:
Here 's a chair, and there 's no one to fill it.
The last of the sunbeams have flickered about,
And, missing your face, crept silently out
• Of the porch at the close of the day.

As I know that the sun seeks its children afar,
Who long and have need for its shining,
So in fancy I trace every spot where you are,
With a sweet, subtle sense of divining;
So I whisper good-night, without sorrow or pain,
To you and the sun till I see thee again
In the porch at the close of the day.

And when shall I see thee, dear mother of mine?
I fancy the leaves as they flutter
The secret are whispering up to the vine—
If I knew but the language they utter;
When they speak of the past I know all they would
say,
When they whisper together at close of the day
In the porch at the close of the day.

SATISFACTION.

The rugged path at length was trod,
 The topmost summit was my rest;
And circling through my soul there went
 A consciousness of being blest—

A sense of victory and joy,
 A calm that cometh after strife,
A peace that only waiteth on
 The winner in the race of life.

But joy and sorrow still are twins,
 And life and death walk side by side;
The misty plain that intervenes
 Is narrow when we deem it wide.

And so across my sunlit way
 There fell a shadow of the past;
And all the heights my soul had won,
 Were only barren hills at last.

A REVERIE.

Misty dreams of the past arise,
And youth returns to my faded eyes.

Under the maples' crimson sheen,
Under the beeches' gold and green,

Forms that went out through the world's wide ways,
Still walk in the light of other days.

Some drifted away, I know not how;
Some of them never met below,

Some silent wait till the angels come
To unclasp their frozen hands, and some

With frozen hearts and iron will
And averted eyes, are living still.

And yet when here I stand alone,
Across the gulf a bridge is thrown

That wrath and change and death redeems,
Although 't is but a bridge of dreams.

Here where the grasses taller grew
To catch the sunlight sifting through,

I 've often watched the branches spread
Their dark green tents above my head.

When I shall walk through Paradise,
Will something like this vision rise,

And all the loved and lost redeem
In sweet fulfillment of this dream?

MADALINE.

Madaline may bid the world good-night,
Drop the curtain, put out the light,
Kneel by thy pillow soft and white.

Purest spirits have need of prayer;
Happiest hearts, a cross to bear;
All of us need a Father's care.

All of us weave in a mystic loom,
Webs of duty or blight or bloom,
Bridal garments or shrouds of gloom;

But ever and ever, from youth to prime,
The Master-Weaver, with skill sublime,
Controls the woof in the warp of time.

He fills the shuttles of grand events,
And hands them down to feeble sense
With the golden threads of Providence.

And day by day, when we weave therein
Life's wondrous tissue so fine and thin,
There 's a golden spot where a prayer has been.

ONE DAY WITH GOD.

There 's something sweet that touches
    The key-note of my life,
And something strong that clutches
    The arm of toil and strife.

The care and toil still linger—
    I feel the burden now;
The soil is on my fingers,
    The lines are on my brow.

When in the early morning
　My heart wept bitter rain,
I could not bear the scorning,
　The sorrow, toil and pain.

Yet now, if one should ask me
　If changed is all the woe,
If different may the task be,
　My lips would answer, No.

And in my strong temptation,
　I sought where Christ had trod,
The way was smoothed with patience—
　I 've walked one day with God.

To-night he undergirdeth
　My life and labor too;
His Holy Spirit wordeth
　My psalm of life anew.

So while with patient blindness
　I walk with God apart,
He wraps with loving kindness
　His peace around my heart.

SOMETHING MORE.

Adrift on a wide, wide sea, my love—
A ship on a wide, wide sea,
Whose helm is faith and whose sails are prayer,
And whose port is destiny.

Sometimes when the sun of life is high,
  I can see its glories play
On the mountain ranges of Heaven, and break
  On the summits far away.

But my hands are weak, my eyes are dim,
  And the tide is dark and slow;
And the counter-currents of life set in
  To hinder me as I go.

I know I fall in the measureless arms
  Of an infinite love to sleep,
Upheld by the hand that holds the space
  Where the silent planets sweep.

But I long for earthly arms to-night,
  And a human voice and hand;
My heart goes out like a wounded bird,
  O'er a desert waste of sand.

GUESSING AT THE UNKNOWN.

Down the grand ladder of the sacred pages
  Whose-long drawn length is time, whose rounds
    are years,
Up which man climbs from far historic ages,
  And in the mystic future disappears,

Men peer and wonder, but see no foundation;
  The last round rests upon a new-born earth,
And underneath—ah! nothing but creation
  And chaos struggling into form and birth.

Howe'er we paint that far-off age of wonder,
This grand old earth once had a natal day,
Sometime and somewhere, in the heavens or under,
In the vast womb of power divine it lay.

Perhaps the universe stood still to witness
The ceremonial of a regal birth ;
Or vapory atoms with a perfect fitness
Formed silent, slow into the solid earth.

And when a thing moves on, it must have started :
So force existed before motion grew ;
And force without the motion it imparted
Is power, and without matter spirit too.

So power existed without minds to view it ;
Or reason backward from the great First Cause,
And Nature first was born when no one knew it—
Ordained by fiat or evolved by laws.

The power was first—the Power that planned and
waited,
And we as after atoms understand
That like to like can only be related :
He calls us children, and we take His hand.

And so we leave Creation where we found it,
Upon the shoulders of a Power that knew ;
And the light that inspiration throws around it
Brings us no nearer sight or clearer view.

THE IRON-HORSE.

'T is only a great, insensate thing,
 With many a lever and valve and wheel;
But the strength of a thousand lives is held
 In its muscles of iron and nerves of steel.

It walks the earth like a conqueror:
 Behind it civilization streams;
With every stroke of its iron-arms,
 It utilizes an age of dreams.

It strides across a mountain chain,
 Or delves the earth as a giant would;
Finds in her deep maternal heart
 The mystic hoard of primeval food.

AT REST.

Fallen asleep till the storm is over;
 Anchored where all the waves are still;
A happy voyage in sunny weather,
 Out of the shadow·of human ill.

A record opened where angels gather;
 A heart all pure and a life unstained,
Unscarred, gone up to the great All-Father—
 Ah! nothing is lost, but all is gained.

You strive in the conflict of many sorrows,·
 And dream of a rest that can never be,

Till over the hills of the dark to-morrows,
  You reach the edge of the crystal sea.

And ye only hope, when your toil is ended,
  To shake the dust from your weary feet,
And that heart and brain, with its pulse suspended,
  Shall enter a rest like His—complete.

FROM SUN TO SUN.

When we rise at early morning,
  While the dew is on the sod,
By our side there stands an angel
  With a message sent from God,
    Telling us what must be done
    Ere the setting of the sun.

Never shall we rise so early,
  Never can we rise so late,
But our hands may find the angels,
  And our hearts may feel them wait,
    Telling us from sun to sun
    All the things that must be done.

If we disobey or heed them,
  Still the message-bringers come ;
We can never drown their voices,
  And their lips are never dumb :
    One by one from sun to sun
    Still they tell what must be done.

Jesus planned our lives to make them
  Happy lives, and good and true ;

Jesus lived and died to teach us
   How the will of God to do.
   Evermore from sun to sun
   God hath something to be done.

Sometime we shall sink to slumber,
   And our busy feet grow still;
Shall we then be glad to waken
   Where the angels do His will?
   Help us, Lord, from sun to sun
   Till thy perfect will is done.

MY FRIEND AND CHRIST'S.

While others by thy pulseless clay
   Are dropping tears of woe,
It is not meet that I to-day
   Am glad to have thee go.

I could not tell to flesh and sense
   The strange, unerring thought
That in this silence speaks intense:
   "God took him; he was not."

Leaf after leaf of commonplace
   That memory reads to-night,
Grows dim beside that world-worn face
   Lit by a soul so white—

A soul that loved all tender things
   The dear sun shone upon,
And down in life's deep-hidden springs
   Found truth and love were one;

A soul that looked and found the Christ
  Before him day by day,
Some truth in prison sacrificed,
  Some stranger by the way.

And so I close thy life's pure page—
  Forgetting God knows when—
And wish thou in a purer age
  Had lived and walked with men.

WHAT OF THE DAY?

Sometimes when the day is over,
  And its pleasant tasks are done,
And this spinning world, revolving,
  Turns its back upon the sun,

When the shadows stretch their fingers,
  From the corners where they stay,
To my little open window,
  As if shaking hands with day,

Then I sit and think it over—
  Think of where the day has gone,
Gone to tell our heavenly Father
  What the world and I have done.

LIFE'S SERVICE.

Somebody said I was growing old—
  'T was only a whisper soft and low;

But unless you heard it over again,
 You would never believe who told me so.

Just think of them telling me such a thing,
 When my eyes are bright and my hair is brown,
And I have not reached the top of the hill
 Which those who are old are going down!

I love whatever the children love,
 And I always wish I had time to play;
For the saddest thing of my ripening years
 Is to find that life has no holiday.

Of course I can laugh or read a book,
 Or visit my neighbor across the street;
But over and under it all, I must think
 Of the duties that wait for my coming feet.

You look with scorn at my patch—and yet,
 Can you write a line as Whittier does?
And what do you know that science tells
 Of the world that is, or the world that was?

And what do you do for your fellow-men?
 Ah! blush as you look at your dainty hand;
Your life at best is a narrow line
 Above the useful, below the grand.

Do n't smile because I am darning socks.
 In a darn like this there is skill and taste;
And besides, I 'm a little disturbed to-night,
 And not inclined for the mirth you waste.

'T is not that I love to stitch and darn,
 But I know that the task is dignified;

And the grandest woman would not be good,
If such simple duties she laid aside.

You 've broken the thread of my sermon now—
Do n't say it is only my stocking-yarn.
I mount a ladder which you can not climb,
Though you think my life is a series of darn.

'T is true, I share the common toil,
Make baby aprons, and mend them too;
But this is but *one* of the trades I know,
I 've a wider field in the world than you.

There 's nothing too common for me to do,
And nothing too high, if I only can.
I am proud of the distance that lies between
The wide extremes of my daily plan.

There 's a little corner of life for me
Where there 's always something for me to do.
You think it is narrow, but how do you know?
It is hid from all the world and you.

But God leans over the walls of Heaven,
And singles me out as the only one
Who can fill that little corner well;
And what I neglect is left undone.

And this is as much as you can say,
For you can not do more than God intends;
And the grandest things in the world are done
With the least intention of noble ends.

At least, the sermon I preach myself
Is something like I am preaching now;

And I grow more patient afterward,
And have grander dreams of the work I do.

RIVERS OF SONG.

Sing of the One who is blesséd forever,
Arm of the feeble and Help of the strong;
Love looketh up to the wonderful Giver—
Pour out your praises in rivers of song.

CHORUS.

Sing, for the heavens are full of His glory,
Praises are swelling in rivers of song;
Sing till the earth shall reëcho the story,
Pour out your praises in rivers of song.

Sing in the morning: the blesséd Redeemer
Waits for the tribute our voices shall bring.
Tarry no more in the land of the dreamer;
Learn the new song that the blesséd shall sing.
CHORUS.—*Sing, etc.*

Sing in the noontide, when bright and unclouded
Hope shineth fair in a beautiful sky;
Sing, by the shadows of evening enshrouded,
Jesus our rightousness shineth on high.
CHORUS.—*Sing, etc.*

Sing of the One who is strong to deliver;
Sing of the One who is mighty to save;
Sing, let your praises flow on like a river
Over the silence of death and the grave.
CHORUS.—*Sing, etc.*

MY IDEAL.

Often, when the day is passing
   Softly, silently away,
When the gentle shades of evening
   Mingle with the fading day,
Comes a vision full of beauty,
   Noble dignity and grace ;
And I often gaze in fancy
   On that sweet, ideal face.

Yet I see it but in vision,
   Naught on earth is half so fair,
And no other human features
   E'er that gentle smile will wear ;
That calm brow a bright throne seemeth,
   Where sits calm and holy thought,
High and noble aspiration,
   Deeds of daring yet unwrought.

But the sweet, blue eye, soul-lighted—
   Fire and eloquence combined—
Flashing with a light reflected
   From the jewels of the mind,
How I love to gaze and ponder
   In the spell that fancy's wrought,
Passing from this world external
   To an inner world of thought.

Then the lips are slowly parted,
   And a voice comes soft and low ;

And I think I 've heard its music
Falling softly long ago,
In some other sphere of beauty,
Where my soul has wandered free—
Free to revel where the sunbeams
Fell like starlight on the sea.

Thus I love to sit and revel
In the spell that binds me there,
Till the light has all departed
From the brow and waving hair,
And the eye has lost its brightness—
Softly fading into night;
Then my lovely vision passes
With the last faint gleam of light.

Starting up, I see the shadows
Brooding where my vision smiled;
While above the earth is hanging
Curtained darkness, deep and wild.
But that face that beamed before me—
Naught on earth is half so bright—
Nowhere on this earthly planet
Shine those eyes of living light.

Others look on manly beauty,
Say 't is nobleness and grace;
But I never see embodied
Beauty like that dear dream-face.
Others have the eye of brightness,
And the forehead high and fair,
But they lack the world-ideal
That my fancy pictures there.

A VOICE IN THE STORM.

Wild waves were dashing on the shore,
  And darkness frowned upon the deep,
And sweeping by was heard the while
  The voice of winds that would not sleep;
Yet, mid the gloom, and on the wave,
  A bark was reeling in the storm,
And at the helm the lightning gave
  The outline of a human form.

All vain were human hand to save,
  And hope went out in night and gloom:
Before him stretched a rocky shore;
  Beneath, the waves prepared his tomb.
But, mid the pauses of the storm,
  When waves roll back in scornful play,
A wind-swept voice has reached his ear:
  "Steer this way, father—steer this way."

He grasped the helm with steady hand;
  Hope veiled her face in gloom no more,
For, mid each pause of wind and storm,
  That voice kept floating from the shore.   *,*
Still death may sing its cradle song
  While billows rock their helpless prey—
Yet still that voice shall guide him on:
  "Steer this way, father—steer this way."

Across the broad horizon sweeps
  That dark-browed spirit of the storm,

Casting its shadow on the shore,
  Where stands a little human form.
Now, flashing o'er each crested wave,
  A beacon casts its starry ray;
And, floating from the welcome land,
  Comes: "Father, father, steer this way."

Ye sailors on the sea of life,
  Who watch with dread a darkening sky,
And shrink when shrouded in the gloom
  The angel of the storm sweeps by,
Oh! have ye heard no loving voice
  To soothe the spirit's wild dismay,
Repeating o'er and o'er again:
  "Steer this way, father—steer this way?"

Ye, who have watched the lights of earth
  Go out in darkness one by one,
Oh! drift not, weary, doubting souls,
  Down to the isle of Death alone;
But gaze, oh! gaze, with eye of faith,
  Where heavenly lights resplendent play,
And voices of the loved repeat:
  O father, father, steer this way.

LINES TO MY HUSBAND ON THE AT-
LANTIC—OUTWARD BOUND.

I am with thee—I am with thee,
  My beloved, evermore—
With thee on the swelling ocean;
  With thee on the smiling shore;

With thee in the holy midnight
When God only sees thy rest,
With thy dreams all wrapped about thee,
I am sleeping in thy breast.

Naught can e'er estrange or sever
Hearts that are forever one—
Lives our Father bound together
Till our earthly task is done.
In my heart thy voice forever
Sings a thrilling undertone:
I am with thee—I am with thee;
Thou art nevermore alone.

Human love is never sinful,
If 't is faithful, true and deep;
And I 've thought the heart is purer
Where some image lies asleep;
For the one we love, my darling,
Seems an angel in the heart;
So we keep the bosom purer,
Lest our angel should depart.

In my heart are many voices
Singing ever to my soul:
First of all I loved, *our mother*,
Gave the key-note to the whole.
Now my soul lies dreaming, listening
To thy thrilling undertone:
I am with thee, my beloved;
Thou art never more alone.

LINES

TO M. C. RAMSEY, WITH A BIBLE, PRESENTED BY HIS
CHOIR.

To him who plods his patient way,
And times his march with holy song,
Our kind remembrance and our love
With all God's promises belong.

Bound by the love these pages tell,
Still may our memories cling and cleave
Like wreaths of fadeless evergreen,
From New Year's day till New Year's eve

And when we go at last to swell
The music in a summer clime,
Still may you lead us in the song,
Though we have done with keeping time.

CHANGE.

My thoughts flitted over life's opening flowers
Like beautiful birds over tropical bowers,
Or the sunbeams of summer that sparkle and burn
With the heat that is born in their mystical urn.

But now o'er my passionless bosom they go
Like winter-chilled birds over deserts of snow ;
As coldly they gleam through the halls of my soul
As the lights of the North that are born at the Pole.

IS IT BEST?

We are married! Ah! yes; and each to his chosen
Is bound by a link that naught earthly can loosen;
Yet, instead of a feeling of infinite rest,
The question returns: Is it best?—is it best?

It seemed best to be loved, and go on and go on,
Loving all the world better for sake of the one;
And now standing here on the threshold of fate,
Love makes it seem easy to toil or to wait.

If love should go on without change or eclipse,
To thrill from the heart through the eye and the lips;
If our souls could be white and our lips could be true,
And the arm never fail till the journey were through.

Do I tremble? Ah! well; if the picture is sweet,
Then what were the dream could we live it complete?
Should we ever look upward for infinite rest?
But the question returns: Is it best?—is it best?

I was loved and am married; yet, looking within,
There's the trail of the serpent and touches of sin;
And faults I have strangled and buried with hate,
Like beggars still sit at my Beautiful Gate.

Just now I have nothing to yield them; but still
They are stronger to-day than my love or my will;
And the one who clasps me to his passionate breast
Must even take them. Is it best?—is it best?

But, ah! if the soul that enwraps me should prove
As weak as my own, would my pulses still move
To the rhythm of love in a holy endeavor
To reach up through the flesh and grow Godward
    together?

If one shall be patient and one shall be true,
When our souls in their shadows are turned up to
    view,
Shall both be heroic, and bridge with a kiss
A gulf that might yawn to a loveless abyss?

In that terrible nearness we covet to-day,
Shall our thoughts never weary, and wander away
After vanished ideals, and wake in the nest
With that deep, silent cry: Is it best?—is it best?

But, oh! if the nest that we dream of should be
The home of new souls that are purer than we,
Shall we live and grow better, and lovingly bear
Our balm of thanksgiving and burden of prayer?

Should we ever be worthy the wonderful trust,
Till our souls are redeemed and our bodies are dust?
Shall the love-angel always brood over the nest?
If not, is it pure?—is it right?—is it best?

When passion is over and patience is ended,
Shall our souls, so diverse, have grown nearer and
    blended?
Shall the love that now fills us, yet scarce is begun,
To a love that's diviner be leading us on?

Shall we learn the sweet lesson to love and forgive,
And how to die grandly by learning to live?

If so, then, dear eyes and dear heart, let us rest,
While the future is God's—it is best—it is best.

A REPLY.

You ask me why I shut the door
  Upon a heart that is not cold,
And let the curtains of reserve
  Fall o'er its windows fold on fold.

You know the chamber of my heart;
  A pleasant guest you long have been;
You thought the world would love me more
  If I would only let it in.

So now and then I welcome one,
  Yet guard the door with jealous care;
But when they pass my threshold o'er,
  They melt to nothingness and air.

Some look into my eyes with love,
  Yet lean so heavy on my trust
I can not hold them, and they sink
  Down to a heap of fragrant dust.

Some up and down my heart will glide,
  And scatter faint, sweet incense of
Some latent dream, with warm, white hands
  That garnish all they touch and love.

But when I stretch my arms and clasp
  A glowing shadow, and in pain

I see the sunlight sifting through
A hollow heart or vacant brain,

In one dim corner of my heart
A waiting, smiling face I see,
To all the world substantial, still
Her shadow side is turned to me.

But why, I do not ask to know;
I can accept it if I must:
And this at least is better than
A fine, transparent heap of dust.

I am content to wait, and while
I pass before her make no sign;
I can not clasp a shadow, and—
I know she is a guest of mine.

But while she listens to my song,
I move her heart to love or pain;
'T is not what I had wished, but still
I would not snap the cord in twain.

And still she keeps her seat secure—
I look, and smile to think it so;
What mists may rise our heart between,
I may not live or care to know.

YE HAVE NOT LIVED IN VAIN.

Look at the flower whose fragrant head
Is bending neath the autumn blast,

When downy leaves and graceful stem
Have yielded to the storm at last;
Yet from its silent, peaceful death
Full many a lesson we might gain
To teach us in our onward path,
"Thou hast not lived in vain."

The lovely child whose infant feet
Still trod upon the flowers of youth,
Cut down before its infant heart
Knew evil from the way of truth;
Yet, angel visitant of earth,
Thou 'st woven many a deathless chain
Around true hearts that fondly loved—
"Thou hast not lived in vain."

And thou who through life's shadowy path
Hast walked, with sorrow oft oppressed,
Yet with a ready hand hast wrought
Comfort to many an aching breast;
When death's dark billows round thee roll,
Heaved by that ever tossing main,
Then shalt thou taste the rest prepared
For those who have not lived in vain.

LINES TO MY MOTHER.

(Written in my early girlhood, just after her deepest affliction.)

WHAT I LIVE FOR.

I live to make thee happy, to soothe thy sorrowing heart,
To chase away thy sadness—so dear to me thou art—
To share thy calm enjoyment, if such a lot be thine;
But love, whate'er betide thee, shall round thy pathway shine.

In helpless infancy thy love was tender, strong and true;
In after years 't was deeper still—and mine shall be, for you;
Care shall not weigh thy spirit down, and Time shall softly trace
Upon thy saintly brow the lines that love can not efface.

Soft as the winter shades of e'en, beneath a cloudless sky,
Fall gently down upon the earth, upon her lap to lie,
So shall thy age come softly on, with loved ones by thy side,
Like birds around the full-blown flower that fades at eventide.

To me there 's beauty on thy brow and in thy waving hair—
There 's beauty in thy sunlit eye, for heaven-born thoughts are
    there;
No other form could ever be so dear to me as thine;
No other memory could seem so human, yet divine.

Thy living faith, thy constant hope, thy love so strong and true,
Through many a year of care and pain, have borne thee safely through ;
When thy tired spirit, freed from earth, to its calm rest has flown,
Thy memory shall safely guide thy children's spirits home.

LINES TO A STRANGER, WHOSE WRITINGS I HAD READ.

I have never known or seen thee,
    Save in fancy's pictured dreams,
When with bright and glorious visions
    My imagination teems.
I may see thee as a stranger;
    Meet thee with a careless eye;
Coldly scan thy unknown features,
    And as coldly pass thee by.

Yet I care not if I see thee
    Never in this world's cold light;
For I know thee by the flashes
    Of a spirit warm and bright. *

I have thought thee good and noble,
  With a proud and manly brow,
Where the rays of future glory
  Circle in their brilliance now.

And the eye is soft and gentle
  That is beaming on my sight,
Shedding o'er the noble features
  Flashes of a spirit's light.
May that light shine on thy pathway
  Brightly, through all coming time,
When the knell of buried pleasures
  Echoes forth a mournful chime.

Years will pass, and on their pinions
  Bear my happy youth away;
Lights and shadows, often blending,
  Bring at last life's fading day;
Yet will memory, oft returning,
  Bring the sunlight of the past,
Till the day of life is over,
  And its sunset comes at last.

With the long forgotten pictures
  Memory bringeth, there will be
One distinct and bright as ever,
  When I gave this wish to thee:
May thy life flow smoothly onward
  As a gentle rolling stream,
Till hereafter thou awakest
  From life's shadowy, mystic dream.

A WISH,

FOR A FRIEND, WHO REQUESTED IT.

If wish of mine to thee could prove
  A blessing or a prophecy,
Where'er thy onward steps should move,
  Earth's choicest gifts should wait for thee:
Love, truth and purity entwine
A holy wreath for thee and thine.

And should some transient sorrows glide,
  Thy future life to overcast,
Higher, sublimer, purified,
  Thy lamp of life should shine at last;
No darkening passions e'er should roll
Their midnight surges o'er thy soul.

Each passing year should bear the trace
  Of high resolves and thoughts sublime,
Outstretching through the realms of space,
  Beyond the mystic bounds of time—
Of hopes fulfilled and labor done,
Life's battles nobly fought and won.

Then calmly wait the angels' time
  To go serenely to thy rest;
To learn the mysteries sublime
  Within the kingdom of the blest;
To lay thy earth-born honors down,
And in their place accept a crown.

LINES ·TO MY SISTER.

(On the Eve of her Sixteenth Birthday.)

Sister, another year has passed—passed silently to-day—
To mingle with thy girlhood years that all are passed away.
Sister, while walking year by year thy happy girlhood hours,
I 've wished thou mightest ever find thy pathway strewn with flowers.

As we were sitting side by side, before you said " Good-night! "
I looked into your fresh young face, your well-like eye of light ;
A smile was playing on your lips ; and, Sister, do you know
I wished the weary years might have the power of smiling so.

Not much of time has passed for thee—thy life has just begun—
And many years may come and pass ere its last cycle 's run ;
But though thy feet may weary tread earth's dark and tangled wild,
Still keep thy spirit pure and fresh—at heart a little child.

I 'm thinking, Sister, of the years far in the distance now,
And hoping Time will softly write his record on thy brow ;
But oh! a dearer, sweeter wish can a sister's love impart :
May angels trace in living light their record on thy heart.

LINES

WRITTEN IN A FRIEND'S ALBUM.

Thy life 's a garden bright and fair,
Thy hopes, the roses blooming there ;
And softly in youth's morning sun
They ope their petals one by one.

But hopes, like roses, bloom and fade,
As years pass on in sun and shade;
The brightest ones may fall apart
To die upon thy withered heart.

But as the odor of the flowers
Is sweetest in their dying hours,
And as the perfume of the rose
Is sweetest at the evening's close,

So may thy hopes, though dying, shed
Divinest incense round thy head;
And may they at life's evening close,
Be sweeter than the faded rose.

LONELINESS.

Are there none on earth to love me,
When this world is all so fair,
Blue and bright the sky above me,
Sweet and soft the balmy air?

Sunshine on the lawn is straying,
Sunshine trembles in my hair,
And its golden beams are playing
All around me everywhere;

Yet my soul has vainly striven
One bright sunbeam e'er to win—
One to light my spirit's heaven,
Or the lonely heart within.

A DREAM OF THE PAST.

As the stars in their glory gem the night
    In the azure realms above,
As the roses brighten on pallid cheeks,
    Or a smile on the lips we love,
As the sunbeams come from their mystic urn
    To the dark earth and the sea,
Even so a vision of gladness came,
    A beautiful dream to me.

My heart grew still in the charmèd rest
    Of love's sweet mystery,
For thou, in thy beauty and love and pride,
    Wert all of life to me—
My star on the night of a loveless life;
    My sun on its cloudy dawn;
My smile on the tear-stained face of Fate,
    When blushes and smiles were gone.

I deemed thee pure, with a voice as sweet
    As the spell thy memory brings,
With a mind that soared from the earth afar
    To higher, holier things;
And a heart whose strings were as finely tuned
    As the angels' harps above,
That thrilled with a melody wild and sweet
    At the touch of human love.

In the night of sorrow my love-dream died
    As the sunbeams pale their light,

As the smile fades out on the lips we love,
   Or stars in the crown of night.
My spirit, through many a lonely year,
   Has wearily borne its pain,
For o'er life's barren desert sands
   Such flowers ne'er bloom again.

Yes, thou art gone with the weary past,
   And I sit in the twilight deep,
A mournful watcher above the dreams
   I would hush in my heart to sleep.
I think of the beautiful lights of life
   That are fading one by one,
And I wonder if darkness will cover all
   Ere the day of life is done.

Our early dreams are the flowers of life
   That bloom in our hearts to die,
For Time, stern reaper, cuts them down,
   Whether lowly or soaring high ;
He darkens our love-lamps, though their light
   Would brighten all the years,
But the lights of memory alone
   He can not quench in tears.

MY SECRET.

I know an eye, a true, deep eye,
   That never cares to rove,
But in its own light seems to be
Taking a miniature of me,
   A photograph of love.

Though every face that passes by
Is mirrored in that love-lit eye,
 They come and fade
 In light and shade,
Where mine shall dwell forever.

I know a bosom, pure and true,
 Whose bridal chamber's mine,
And there my image doth repose,
The heart within the folded rose,
 Love's idol in its shrine ; .
But should that bosom cease to keep
My image in its charméd sleep,
 And should the rose
 No more enclose
Its heart, 't would mourn forever.

I know a heart, a true, deep heart,
 Within whose inmost shrine
I reign all spotless, pure and calm,
Not the poor human thing I am,
 But glorified, divine ;
But should that heart e'er cease to be
The sacred throne of love and me,
 I 'd fling my crown
 Of earth-love down,
And trust no more forever.

A PRAYER.

Lord, let our strong foundation be
 Our everlasting trust,

And help us that we build thereon
With all things true and just.

Our little fingers, Lord, we know
Sufficient are to do;
If we would be omnipotent,
We only need be true.

On truth, where angels rest their feet,
Lord, let us stand, and know
How much like God, by loving Him,
A human soul may grow.

THE HALF–WAY HOUSE.

There is a half-way house to Heaven,
Where mortal feet have never trod;
Yet in our daily worship there,
In spirit we may walk with God.

And there no wailing undertone
Rings through each sweet and happy sound;
And where the palm-trees meet the sun,
They cast no shadow on the ground.

And where the nodding roses bloom
They hide no withered leaves away;
For summer here is endless June—
A thousand years are but a day.

The cross is lifted from our hearts;
A crown is laid on brow of care;

And in this half-way house we meet
Our Father at the hour of prayer.

THY WILL BE DONE.

'T was not in words God's will was done,
When Christ, in toil, and sweat, and blood,
His great eternal kingdom won,
And on the brink of glory stood.

CHORUS.

This world was made for labor,
And the next—the next for rest.

His prayers were echoes of His deeds—
Prophetic of their future yield:
God's blessings are the scattered seeds
Of an eternal harvest-field.
CHORUS.—*This world, etc.*

How dare we look to Heaven in prayer,
Unless we toil along the way,
And through our daily pain and care
Grow nearer God from day to day?
CHORUS.—*This world, etc.*

Ah! broken-winged are prayers that rise
Where idle feet the vineyard trod;
Poor stranger birds in Paradise,
And aliens in the home of God.
CHORUS.—*This world, etc.*

WAVES OF GALILEE.

There 's a step on the shore and a voice on the sea,
Where it breaks on the sands of the blue Galilee;
And age after age tells the story again,
Of Jesus, the Lover and Teacher of men:
He taught them of love as he sat by the sea—
Of a life to be lived and a kingdom to be.

CHORUS.

O footprints by the sea!
O waves of Galilee!
O winds that wander free!
Ye tell the story still
Of Jesus by the sea.

The multitudes shift like the sands of the shore,
But the Saviour loves us as he loved them of yore,
And his lesson of love will forever be true,
And the story of Jesus will always be new,
Till the Saviour shall come, in that wonderful day
When the sea and the shore shall have faded away.
CHORUS.—*O footprints, etc.*

PART II.

PROSE.

THE FIGHT OF PATIENCE.

Some one says: "Men will wrangle for religion; write for it; fight for it; die for it; anything but— live for it." True. One has only to look into a chapter of his own life to see how incomparably easier it is to oppose wrong than to quietly follow right.

Wrangling, and even fighting, for religion is extremely easy for most people. It is an opportunity for serving God and Satan both at once, which is too congenial to human nature to be easily resisted. To speak of religion as a "battle," is to put it in its most attractive light to many. They may be really good people, but combativeness craves something to oppose, and destructiveness something to destroy. The church is fuller of Peters with drawn swords ready to cut off high priests' servants' ears, than of Maries to

wash Christ's feet with tears. Very often, too, like
Peter, these bellicose disciples come out of a *battle for
the Lord*, and then—deny their Master; and yet, at
last, like Peter, they would willingly be crucified
head downward for the Master's sake. Then, too,
there is something glorious in dying for the Lord.
We must all die; but it is grand to choose it.
There is something mighty in clasping death, and
with a kiss bribing it to sweeten dissolution. This,
in the conception of many, is the highest triumph of
spirit over dust, the nearest approach to a divine
impulse.

Men will write for religion; and this is very easy,
for, aside from any inspiring influence of the Holy
Spirit, religion appeals strongly to the æsthetic part
of our nature; ideality, sublimity and veneration,
here find their widest field of happy exercise.
Whether men deal sledge-hammer blows at vice and
error—blows which, to the ecstatic sense of the hour,
resound like echoes from Sinai; or follow the divine
Thought through the written poetry of revelation, or
the unwritten poetry of nature, they have a sense of
growing up into something grander than themselves,
of thinking the thoughts of God, and clothing themselves in garments that all men know came from the
looms of heaven.

Men will fight like Peter, and die like Paul; write
visions like the Evangelist, or valedictories like the

apostle to the Gentiles, and yet be too weak to transcribe into their lives Christ's Sermon on the Mount, and altogether too weak and cowardly to endure the severe drill of Peter and the long marches of Paul as soldiers of the cross. The reason of all this is plain. There is an inertia about human nature, as in the material world; all forces spend themselves.

Given a life to which the Holy Spirit has given a momentum and started it heavenward; first, the temptations of the "world," like the attraction of gravitation, draw it downward; then comes the friction of the air, or the devil—"the prince of the power of the air"—and lastly, the inertia of human flesh.

No wonder, then, that the Christian, with these three powerful and subtile agencies arrayed against him, finds an hour's enthusiasm, or a moment of supreme self-sacrifice, easier than a life of simple patience.

A spiritual impulse potent enough, for an hour, to make a hero or a martyr, will ebb away and be lost in a life-time. There are lives recorded for the triumph of a day—the lives of men who died in the flush of an immortal victory, or lived afterward, as a Frenchman said of Lamartine, to survive themselves. And there are lives unrecorded, in whose quiet, uneventful flow, there was heroism enough to have led the forlorn-hope of an army, or have opposed a Spanish Inquisition. There is nothing so sublime as patience, and nothing so commonplace. There is nothing of which men take so little note, and perhaps nothing which the angels so carefully record. From page to page the holy writings are sprinkled with exhortations to this crowning virtue of the life that *is;* and on the very edge of the life *to be,* the dying Christ illustrated the glory of the patience that "endureth to the end."

Patience is the golden string upon which every other virtue may be threaded. It is the bridge over which we may walk from the sin and confusion and peril of Time to the calm of Eternity. Bishop Doane wrote :

"Stand like an anvil: noise and heat
Are born of Earth and die with Time;
The soul,like God, its source and seat,
Is solemn, still, serene, sublime."

THE BIBLE STAGE OF CHRISTIANITY.

As soon as the Roman Catholic power departed from the capital of Spain, in the person of Queen Isabella, a London Bible Society made an appropriation for three millions of Bibles to be scattered in Spain. Then, without delay, the cause was taken up by the American Bible Union, and now there has long been a printing-press in Madrid, working day and night, printing Bibles, Bibles, only Bibles.

As soon as Pius IX. went out as chief mourner at the funeral of the Catholic power in Italy, colporteurs went with Bibles into Rome. And wherever the Bibles go, Sunday-schools are opened, and faithful men and women, "beginning at the same Scriptures, preach unto them Jesus."

It is a very suggestive fact, that men do not think of pulpits and pulpit preaching, except in connection with somewhat educated and enlightened sinners. And when we see them very much educated and enlightened, the pulpit teaching gradually divorces itself from any element of Bible teaching, and, as a result, we have "magnificent sermons,"—sermons that, with telling effect, go straight to the mark and convert the *imagination* of every hearer. But when, before the eyes of men, there opens a really great, untrodden field, where sin and ignorance have slept together for ages, they send only Bibles, and the simplest men and women, as mediums to bring their great truths into contact with the masses.

In Italy there are some seventy Sunday-schools, and a Sunday-school paper, which has a large circulation.

On the Island of Madagascar a printing-house, with its staff of twenty-five printers, is taxed to its utmost, and is unable to supply reading matter for the converts learning to read. Two thousand imported copies of the New Testament were sold at once, and ten times as many were in demand.

About twenty years ago, the Rev. Mr. Snow, of the Micronesian Mission, went among the savages with no written language. He civilized and educated them, caught and fixed the sounds of their words, and to-day is busy superintending the printing of his own translation of Mathew and Luke, in a dialect known to no other white person on the globe but himself and his wife.

The Sandwich Islanders are a Bible-reading people ; Chinese Bibles are printed in Pekin; copies of the Holy Scriptures are now sold in Constantinople and in Rome; in the royal palace of Antananarivo, the Queen of Madagascar, like another Queen of

Sheba, listens to the words of One greater than Solomon.

On the Island of Madagascar there are five millions of people who are so much interested in the new movement, that in many places they are actually erecting church-buildings in advance, to await the missionaries who are coming to tell them of the great "new God"; yet—with all the simplicity and strength of those two great men—no one wishes that Spurgeon or Beecher could be sent among them: we only think of Bibles, Bibles, battalions of Bibles. We learn that an "English 'bishop,' with a full staff," is to be sent out to the island, upon which the *Independent* observes: "Offenses must come, but woe to him by whom the offense cometh."

Ah! why, when we have carried our Bibles to the end of the earth, must we follow them up with our theology? All primitive churches are a sort of Sunday-schools, or, if we like the name better, Bible-classes, and the missionaries are simply Bible-readers and teachers. The Word of God is considered, among Protestant people, as the center and circumference of all we are to know among the heathen. No dust gathers upon its leaves. But, this foundation once laid, "evangelical religion," "orthodoxy" and theology in its hundred shapes, come in to "perfect" the work; and, that the "man of God may be pefect, thoroughly furnished unto all good works," the Bible is overlaid with a prayer-book, a creed, a confession of faith, a discipline, and all manner of codicils to the last "will and testament," until it is well nigh buried out of sight. Then, like the transformations of a dream, the "*little children*" of all ages grow up out of the Bible-class stage of Christianity, into the full stature of men and women in— *theology*, and the missionaries, the Bible-readers, "decrease," like John the Baptist, "having made straight ways for the "—great preachers who preach "magnificent sermons," and the bishops who muster in, according to the "apostolic rite of confirmation," the troops of the King Eternal that are led by the "Prince of Peace."

THESE TEMPLES.

It is said that in China a doctor's fee is limited by law to eight cents. Let us be thankful that no such a law obtains here. While doctors' fees are large, society is preserved from the consequences of an inclination to be overdosed. We do all manner of violence to our bodies, and then attempt to obtain absolution from these reckless sins, by doing penance in swallowing drugs. Poor bodies, how sadly we deface these beautiful "temples"! Sometime and somewhere, shall not even these rise up in judgment against us?

Over nothing, not even our thoughts, have we a more absolute dominion than over our own bodies, and yet upon nothing do we commit such outrages. What a story the stomachs of some men could tell, of long fasts, that were not for *their* benefit or the glory of God, but enforced in the interests of Mammon; and then feasts, against which the stomachs themselves entered protests of disgust and pain, which in due time were followed by the penalty of disease. And then what a witness the brain will be, telling of our undue use of its beautiful machinery, that at last has worn "the wheels of life away," before the Father's hand has stayed them; or else, of disuse and rust and degradation, which has impaired them for this life and the life to come, and set the purely physical, animal man to reign over the spiritual and immortal to the debasement of both.

Some one has said that it takes one life-time to learn how to live. This is as true in a physical as in any other sense. Sins committed against our bodies are sins committed against God; and in taking care of our bodies we are taking care of what God has made very beautiful and considered very precious.

This should even be a part of our religion. When we conscientiously apportion air, exercise, rest and food to our physical uses, we shall certainly be in a condition to live nearer to God. By a closer adherence to His natural laws, shall we not rise to a higher appreciation of the spiritual and divine, and some day be all the better prepared to give an "account of the deeds *done in the body*"?

It is a false religion which ignores the physical man. These bodies are not tents, to be patched up for our temporal uses only; but temples, where the Holy Spirit should be our guest to-day—temples to be raised, and dwelt in forever.

A SERMON FROM THE PEW.

One night not very long ago we sat in the corner of a comfortable pew in a comfortable church, thinking what a good prayer-meeting it was. As the alternate prayer and praise rose from the lips of earnest worshipers, a great and wonderful calm fell over the cares and toils and weary striving of the day. They were not forgotten, for even religion can not make vexations and trials seem other than they are; but they were like discordant music heard a long way off, softened by distance and sweetened by indistinctness.

Then one preacher rose and commending those who were there, exhorted them to a continuance in well-doing. "These meetings," said he, "are the life of the Church—here our duty lies. Let us not forsake it, but stand up nobly to the work like soldiers of the cross." This exhortation was good and effective, and fell through attentive ears into earnest hearts. But in one instance, at least, it awakened a train of thought quite on a tangent to the speaker's purpose, and yet not wholly unprofitable.

Not many years ago it was customary among a class of good people to speak of church-going as "attending the means of grace." Aside from an old-fashioned beauty in this phrase, it contains the essence of a truth. Christ did not die to make church-goers of us; church-going is not so much a duty to be performed, still less a labor to be done; it is not an end, only a means—a "means of grace"—a draught of a spiritual tonic; at best a glimpse by faith into the kingdom of heaven, and the mystery of God's wonderful love.

After the spiritual birth, the Christian is fed—if fed judiciously—first upon milk, then upon meat; is this all? If so, then he is like the man who lived to eat and ate to live. But this is not all. Feeling our hearts grow warm at the weekly prayer-meeting, and our souls expand when we partake of the emblems of Christ's body broken for us, is not *serving* God; it is only getting ready to serve Him, a partaking of spiritual food—a "means of grace"—but the *end*, the "grace" itself, must blossom in our lives, when, daily developing the Christ within us, we exercise it for the benefit of the world. Yet there are those who spend all their lives applying the means for an end which they never reach and never consider—an end which they die tranquilly without accomplishing. But they went to church—death found them within the fortress of the walls of Zion, and the church and the world write them down among the "blessed dead," and Christians speak of an "irreparable loss." This is true ; for since their religion consisted mainly in "going to church," when they no longer go and fill the accustomed seats, the church indeed sustains an *"irreparable loss"*—this was *all they did*, and now they are gone. But when a shining Christian dies, there is a vacancy. but no real *"loss;"* and even the vacancy is like a mount of transfiguration, where the Holy Spirit hovers, saying: "Blessed are the dead that die in the Lord, for they rest from their *labors, and their works do follow them."*

Religion itself is not an *end:* it is only a *means*—God's appointed stairway into heaven ; but we shall never reach the top, unless, step by step, we leave some sin and weakness behind.

The apostle speaks of those who are ever learning, but never come to a knowledge of the truth: is not this true of *us*, when we attend regularly the services of the Lord's house, and return home to live over again all the sins and follies of yesterday, neglecting the same duties, and indulging in the same vague dreams of a mansion in Heaven—a mansion in Heaven, which may prove to us but a castle in the air?

Let us regard religion as a means, and the end, everlasting life ; but between there must intervene the lever of our unbroken effort, if even the power of God saves us. There must be a beginning of the end; there must be a spiritual life here, to blossom into the life eternal.

Our religion, then, as a means, should make us patient, cheerful and laborious; are we not told that "all things shall work together for good for them that love Him"? It should make us content; "all things are ours;" we only wait for the day of our inheritance. We should be happy, very, very happy, for "eye hath not seen, ear hath not heard" what only waits *our coming.* There is no virtue which men call beautiful which should not shine in the life of the humblest Christian.

A religion which is not false, a mere ritualistic observance of church-going, will make us manifestly better citizens, husbands, wives, parents and children. "It can not be hid."

Last, and perhaps most difficult of all to do, the daily exercise of our religion should finally wear away the last remnant of that practical infidelity which most of all retards our growth in the divine life. We all think we are stockholders in that company whose treasures are laid up in heaven, and yet our faith so slowly grasps the fact that, dollar by dollar, by the divine alchemy of *giving*, we may transmute our earthly possessions into heavenly treasures—literally change our earthly coin into currency of the eternal kingdom. We Christians, with weak, half-infidel lips, say: "We know if this, our earthly tabernacle, is dissolved, we have a house, not made with hands, eternal in the heavens;" and yet, when such a Christian falls asleep, we shroud ourselves in a kind of modern sackcloth and ashes called "mourning," and write obituaries about "*inconsolable* grief." We pray for strength to overcome the world, and pray sincerely, too, and then go forth into the wilderness—not led, but walking complacently on—to be tempted of the world, the flesh, and the devil, just in the hope of climbing the "high mountain," or standing for one dizzy, thrilling moment on the "pinnacle" of the world's esteem.

These are some of the sins which so easily beset us—the dross in the gold of our religion.

This is the practical infidelity which makes our prayers heavy, wingless; and when they do not rise, we too often conclude that we have asked for something which it is not the Lord's will to grant us, and thus beget a habit of prayer in which the soul only half expects its petition, and then we call this "*resignation,*" which is truly infidelity.

Ah! if we only lived our religion in the small details of our daily life at home and in the world, preachers would not need to exhort us to assemble at the church. Christians would all flow together, as the rivers to the sea, and every Lord's day would be a new inspiration, and every prayer-meeting a half-way house to heaven. The holy vestments of our religion, worn through all our hard and dusty work-day toil, would make it easier for us to keep ourselves "unspotted from the world;" and, borne up in the invisible arms of angels, we should grow "in grace," daily more like the apostle John—not John, the poor exiled slave on the barren Island of Patmos—but John the Evangelist, looking upward into heaven.

THE LEVER OF ARCHIMEDES.

Archimedes, the ancient philosopher of Syracuse, once said: "I could move the earth, could I but find outside of it a fulcrum for my lever." This certainly was true. What would have been gained by it, is not so clear. It is a dizzy thought to imagine one disturbing the two accurately balanced forces that hold our planet in its orbit, and sending it off making and suffering uncalculated eclipses among its sister worlds.

But Archimedes toiled on and was killed at last among his problems, but had never thought of doing it. And he bequeathed to the world his wisdom and his lever, yet the world has never been moved, for never was the fulcrum found; and this enthusiastic declaration of the ancient philosopher and mathematician has come down to us only as a curiosity of gigantic thought.

The Philosopher's stone, the Elixir of Life, and Archimedes' fulcrum, have long ago been labeled "impossible things"—and pigeon-holed together in the curious brain of the antiquarian.

Yet this heathen philosopher was a heathen

prophet, and spoke a grand truth destined to be fulfilled.

Two hundred and sixty-four years after the death of Archimedes, there was born the inventor of a system that made his words not only vast and sublime, but actual, possible and practical.

But this great inventor, by a singular reversal of our human modes of thought, contemplated first the moral world, and moved it, not by arbitrary power, as he one day proposes to move the physical earth, but by a more beautiful and perfect machinery; not indeed the lever of Archimedes, but the lever of Christ, a living faith, on the fulcrum of divine inspiration.

In every age inventions have been regarded in the light of inspirations of genius, and always entitled to a careful consideration of their claims, which were to be decided not by reason or logic, but by their practical adaptation to the end in view, and their ability to accomplish it.

When James Watt, sitting beside his sister's boiling teakettle, evolved from his strange brain the perfect idea of a steam-engine, men first looked on and doubted the power of the giant that had laid for ages coiled up in steam. But when once satisfied, they went on building them over and over and over again, until their combined power might, if gathered in one single force, be adequate to move a planet from its orbit.

It is so with all human institutions and systems; once perfected, they stand as great models for a world to copy. But when even from the low stand-point of doubt and infidelity, we consider Christianity as a human invention, we tangle ourselves in a mystery unsolved and insolvable. We see it, though without precedent in the past, yet simple and easy of comprehension, a system of moral machinery adapted to the humblest human uses, yet even with the grand model before us, as impossible of reproduction or even variation, as the solar system or the change of seasons. We might indeed in some new system reënact every law, but where find an inspiration to enforce it? We might build every axle, wheel and lever, adjust their fulcrums with a perfect nicety, and connect the whole by a strong belting of human faith; but the impelling power of the Holy Spirit men could never reproduce; and the vast machine, though never so perfect in each polished shaft and wheel, would be powerless to move the world from the low grounds of selfishness and sin up the steep way of self-denial for the sake of virtue and the hope of heaven, were there no inspired visions of the "many mansions" beyond.

Yet, day by day, unconscious of the absurdity, men are trying to move the moral world by levers of human philosophy on the fulcrum of human reason. Humanity, unaided, would lift itself. This is the moralist; whether we consider him as a man or a community, it is the same; he girds himself with human philosophy, inspires himself with human wisdom, and then seizing hold of his own girdle, believes that he lifts himself upon the upward inclined plane of morality, utterly forgetting that even there human nature, unsupported, gravitates downward. It is so with all things. By a law of the universe, everything tends to its own center, physical, moral and eternal; it is always "earth to earth." The superstructure may be beautiful, the foundation grand; but underneath, if there is no eternal corner-stone, there are still at work the everlasting forces of change and decay, and dust sinks down to dust, despite all human leverage.

Some minds who have thought just enough to realize this last truth, and not enough to know that human hands and brains are the levers and wheels of God, when used by his authority, only stand and wait for a miraculous interposition of divine power to move them up the ascending way to heaven—some power, vague, arbitrary and irresistible; and failing this, die at last, dreaming of some spiritual Darwinian theory of development in a future, higher sphere.

And still Christianity stands waiting for us with the calm assertion of demonstrated power, secure in the wisdom of ages, and the strength of God. And

still men doubt because it is simple, and reject it because it is consistent with its divine origin and purpose; and, with an arrogance worthy only of pity,
refusing to work in partnership with Him, seek with
human machinery to compass divine ends.

The will and the effort are human, but the conditions of Archimedes are met; and on that fulcrum
beyond the earth, invisible, divine, eternal, the wondrous lever of human faith may raise the world by the
puny force of human will. When we can compute
the measureless power necessary to overcome the inertia of the solar system in the beginning of time, and
start the planets in their courses, "To weave the
dance that measures the years," we may conceive
the immensity of that moral impulse which is sufficient to impel the children of men over all the friction of the life that is, into the golden track of promise for the life to come.

In vain men doubt and calculate and wait. All
power is lost without the fulcrum of the word of God.
No human machinery will ever move the world. Man
will never know the secrets of the power of God. But
when we shall all place our faithful hand across the
sacred pages, we shall, in that day, see the world over-
coming the inertia of ages and the friction of ignorance and sin, slowly rising into the perfect day, and,
like Archimedes, we may cry, *Eureka! Eureka!* The
world is waiting, and above us arches the grand orbit

of eternal life, whose center is the "Sun of Righteousness," the unfathomable love that redeemed what it might have crushed, and left no stain on the universe of God.

PILATE'S WASH-BASIN.

Ever since Pontius Pilate, the Roman Governor of Judæa, performed his historic ablution in the presence of the multitude, wash-basins have been a popular institution—a means of grace under trying circumstances.

When the spirit of truth becomes a disturber of the peace by its uncompromising and inconsiderate cries for just words and just deeds, we may indeed pass on with composure. The outcry is simply for a theory. But there come times when this spirit of truth makes grave and awkward entanglements in human affairs, and then something must be done.

Perhaps in a future age an ethical Darwin may discover that, after all its assumption and outcry, truth was not truth originally, but ascended from some vague half-formed notions through all the "monkey stages" of opinion up to what it is now, a little more than human, according to the average specimen of the latter. Such a Darwin in ethics would undoubtedly bring relief to a large class of men in the world and the church, the press and the pulpit.

But, alas! that day is not yet come, and truth
walks the earth with a supreme disregard of all
human interests, and yet, with a regal assumption, embraces and meddles with all human plans at
will.

Truth is inconsiderate and arbitrary, even to its
friends; but to one who dares to make an issue with
it, or even question its authority, it reveals itself a
spirit strong and terrible, with the features of Deity,
and behind it the twelve legions of angels. Such an
one begins with making war upon truth in the shape
of a theory or a fact, and in the end finds himself in
antagonism with God; with earth and heaven and
time and eternity pledged to destroy him, or drive
him from his position.

Ever since the first chapter of human affairs, truth
has always been believed in, yet never popular, and
no man has ever been able to find a verdict against it.

Truth came wearing a leathern girdle, and was be-
headed in prison; but Herod was eaten of worms,
and not Herod alone—to one who could read human
faces to-day, how many of them would reveal that
the heart beneath is eaten of worms, the penalty of
some truth willfully dishonored.

The "voice in the wilderness" may be silenced in
prison, but the Christ is always just behind, walking
steadily on to the judgment-seat of Pilate. We know
the chief-priests and Pharisees—they live and walk

among us to-day; we know them by this, that they
love their church better than the Christ. We know
the unreasoning multitude they rule. All these were
there confronting Pilate, and nothing withstood them
but a frail human body in which, to Pilate's eyes,
centered the truth. Pilate's informal verdict was:
"This just man;" and then "he took water and
washed his hands." O wonderful basin! what white
fingers have been dipped into thy historic water; what
priestly hands have been laved, and what red hands
have been made pure in the eyes of more than fifty
generations of the children of Pilate.

The cruel multitude, blind because they will not
see, still shout and go shouting to their graves, and
there is never wanting the central figure of truth; in
the robes of a king or the rags of a beggar, it is
always there, and the children of Pilate are always
troubled. With their physical eyes they see the
chief priests and Pharisees, and the clamoring multitude; with their spiritual eyes they discover the
"twelve legions of angels;" and when their human
responsibility becomes greater than they can bear,
they reach forth their trembling hands and bury their
dismay and confusion, their human weakness and
their divine opportunity, their cross and their crown
in the time-honored basin of Pilate.

O blessed basin! for eighteen centuries, in thy capacious depths, men have found consolation in that

hardest of all earthly trials, when they saw the truth, but "feared the people." .

O marvelous basin! large enough to drown the human responsibility of a race, and yet too small to cleanse a single human soul.

O treacherous basin! rivaling in its promises the blood of the Redeemer, and yet unable to wash away a single human sin—saving Pilate from the vengeance of a single mob of eighteen hundred years ago, and exposing him to the malediction of all Christendom since then. Till Christ shall come again, men will go on saying in every language under heaven: "He was crucified under Pontius Pilate."

Of the mob who nailed their Redeemer to the cross, it is written: "Father, forgive them, for they know not what they do." But of the Roman governor it is written: "Pilate and Herod were made friends that same day." And Pilate and Herod went down into history together, and the wash-basin of Pilate remaineth with us until this day.

THE LEAVEN OF THE PHARISEES.

In the Querists' Drawer of the *Standard* a reader asks for and receives some instructions for making the bread used in Communion.

While no institution which God has ordained should be observed carelessly, this is right. But, after all, does it not strike us how much easier it is to be careful in detail than sound and unprejudiced in the general—how much easier it is to observe the letter than the spirit of the law? In nothing relative to Christianity is this more clearly illustrated than in the ordinance of the Lord's table.

As there is no precept, there is, we may suppose, no invariable use concerning communion bread. Yet, as that which our Saviour used—being prepared for the Passover—was certainly *unleavened* bread, it has become at least a very general practice to prepare unleavened bread for the Lord's table. This is usually made in a flat cake, as it would not rise well in a loaf. One church, of which we know, objects to it on this account; and as Jesus—we are told—took a *loaf*, they also take one of ordinary bread, and carefully slicing off the crust all around it, use what remains. Still, if they are very particular about it, it would seem that a loaf that has been *cut* is not even then an *unbroken* loaf, in accordance with the type, for the idea is not contained in the difference between breaking and cutting, but in that it must be *undivided*, an emblem of the one unbroken body of Christ, which in turn is the type of the Church.

Those who are desirous of having a *loaf*, and that loaf *unleavened*, because it is so described in the New Testament, can not be more exact than by using a loaf of aerated bread, leaving the crust on; and yet there was no aerated bread in the days of the apostles. But it is certain that unleavened bread made at home by ordinary means and skill must be thin, or very heavy and unpalatable.

But it is probable that the whole idea is preserved if we use a loaf, thick or thin, and made in any manner, since it is then a perfect emblem of the body of Christ broken for sin. It is a unity. It is life-giving.

The Jews' shewbread, more beautifully called the "loaves of the presence," was always twelve loaves, which God intended to be, in many things, distinct, separate and individual. It is in contradistinction to these that the *one* loaf of the Christian's banquet stands out in beautiful significance of the unity of the Body of Christ.

Even in the observance of the Lord's Supper we see continually illustrations of the payment of

"tithes of mint, anise and cumin," and a neglect of
"the weightier matters of the law." There are professed Christian churches, which observe with religious
care to use the *one unleavened loaf*, and let us suppose,
with a full knowledge of its deep significance; and
yet draw sectarian lines through the living body of
Christ, dividing it asunder. Their *one loaf* thus becoming a type, not of a body broken *for the sins of
the world*, but *by* the *sins of the Church*.

Unleavened bread indeed it may be, to them; but
in the eyes of reason and the sight of God, is it not
permeated with another leaven—"the leaven of the
Pharisees"?

THE WONDERFUL WILL.

When Christ departed to that "far country," and left his last will in the hands of twelve personally appointed executors, they were divinely commissioned and miraculously authorized and instructed for the work. For this labor they were to put away even the hope of all things earthly, and be fed and clothed by divine providence; and, borne up in the invisible arms of God's absolute protection, they were invulnerable to all the powers of earth and hell. They walk the earth superior to misfortune, accident, death, ignorance or misconception of the divine truth of their mission. But when their work is done, the mantle of their miraculous power falls from their human shoulders—they step from the rostrum of divine inspiration, and through violent and ignoble deaths fall into the arms of waiting angels.

One indeed, St. John, lives to see on the island of Patmos a grand but uncomprehended vision of the future; but when a dimness spread over the scene, and the spirit of the beloved apostle seemed exhaled into the glories of heaven, with him departed the last representative of infallible wisdom on the earth.

But the work was done. The executors had administered upon the estate of Christ's immeasurable love, and laid down with ineffaceable clearness the changeless conditions upon which humanity may inherit the broad lands on the river of life and the many mansions of the Holy City. There was nothing more for inspiration to do, and a silence fell from heaven, unbroken for eighteen centuries, to be unbroken still until the second coming.

What need have we of apostolic succession, when the voice of Peter and the flaming tongues of Pentecost still startle, teach and warn? Is he not still with us? Not Peter in the flesh, who denied his Master; nor him crucified head downward for his Master's sake; but Peter clothed with inspiration, holding in his hand the keys of the kingdom.

Generation after generation, Athens changes, but Paul ascended Mars' Hill, to stand there forever, speaking words of truth and soberness; and still we hear the words of the beloved apostle, walking the streets of Jerusalem, saying: "Little children, love one another." They never die. There they remain—sufficient unto their day and all days to come. But when we have gathered up the scattered words of wisdom of Christ and his executors, we find them bound together between an unspeakable blessing and a withering curse, inexorable, authoritative and changeless.

And here we might stop, for it is useless to beat the poor wings of reason against the will of God. And yet it is not always impossible to see the reasons that may underlie divine legislation, and not always unprofitable to trace them.

If we mass the testimony of the apostles, cancel all the details of incident, figures of speech, repetitions, and arguments used to enforce their doctrines, we have from all the same story of the Cross, crystallized into the same "form of doctrine," without variation of fact, faith or practice; and yet these men all spoke at different times and places without reference to each other, and in perfect fulfillment of the prophecies, dating back through a dim twilight age to the beginning of time.

We have then a wonderful estate to be inherited by an inspired will, and administered upon by infallible executors, and witnessed by prophets and holy men, all down in an unbroken line ever since "Abraham saw Christ's day and was glad." Is not this sufficient for human reason, enough for human hope? When divine wisdom deigns to make us partners in the work of our own redemption, shall we attempt by our own vain cavils to lock the wheels of boundless love? When we review every system of ethics or religion which the world has conceived, we fail to find a parallel to the unity of the provisions and the administration of this wonderful will. When we think of the complications of time and place, and the varied skill of the many workmen, reverence is forgotten in a vast surprise that even in the room of God's providence human hands could have woven so perfect a fabric, "a garment without seam" from top to bottom.

LATEST FROM PARIS.

"The very latest from Paris," whether a bulletin, a bombshell, or a bonnet, becomes at once an object of paramount interest, a sort of center for the earnest and intense regard of this young Republic.

With all our American independence and boastful self-assertion, it is marvelous to behold the humility with which we lay our convenience, our morals and our taste, at the feet of Paris.

"The very latest from Paris" is an argument against which neither wit, wisdom nor religion can prevail. The most they can hope to do is, to effect a respectful compromise.

Impressed with this solemn conviction, we turn over the morning paper to learn what the "latest from Paris" really is. First, in large, bold type, we learn that it is a most elegant little hat, to be worn *en costume*, with an overskirt which is "perfectly elegant," and has but one drawback—it is just of that distressing length which makes it impossible to decide whether it can, should, or ought to be, looped up or not. These articles, we are assured, are "*direct from Paris*, and the very latest style."

How astonishing! and here all this while we have been thinking of Paris as enduring all the isolation and horrors of a siege. We had supposed that the latest Paris fashions would be, not hats and ribbons, but mourning veils and sackcloth and ashes.

A little bewildered, we turn the paper, and under the head of "Latest from Paris," we read of the terrible progress of the siege, and come to the following sentence:

"It is strange and painful to see groups of well-dressed women looking in the windows of pork butchers and tripe shops with the same eager curiosity with which they gaze at ribbons and bonnets."

The latest Paris fashion! Is it, then, to be hungry? Again we turn, eager to fulfill our manifest destiny, by learning every detail of the latest Paris fashions. This time we come to a description of some of the beautiful suburbs of Paris, where the grand old trees, that have waved their green banners for a century, to-day are cut down, to make straight the way of a bombshell. We could weep over the beautiful woods of Boulogne—weep for the weary, and the little children that will miss their shade for half a century to come. But, poor trees, could they see, or hear, or feel, they would long ago have grown tired of holding out their cool green hands in benediction over mad, hot, bloody Paris, that would not be blessed.

Trees are the friends of a great city, and Paris has slain her guardian angels. But this, we are told, was done in accordance with a military order, "the very latest from Paris."

But, lest we become sentimental over the old trees, which some one suggests will make excellent lumber by the time they are duly seasoned by French and Prussian fire, we turn again to something more from Paris. It is a fine engraving of the interior of the grand palace of the Hotel de Ville, filled with hospital-beds and wounded men, and silent, patient, tearless women. This is a Parish fashion-plate, but we have seen it before on American soil, which is often true of other fashions that a credulous public are entirely willing to accept as "Paris fashions." So, to-day, we are selfish enough to *say*, and rejoice, that this is *not* America. By the memory of the prayers on Plymouth Rock, and bloody foot-prints of Valley Forge, and bloodier pathway of our later years, we are constrained to pray, that never in all time to come shall this fashion be reproduced on the soil of our great Republic.

Again our eyes wander up and down the columns— they rest on a paragraph which says:

"In Paris many hundreds of the little children are dying every week for want of suitable food—starved, in fact, because they have no milk."

Still the *Herods are slaying the innocents*, and yet

American women and American mothers look over to this *Rama*, full of weeping *Rachels*, and ask for the "latest Paris fashions."

Is it not time this folly was ended? Must the farce and the tragedy still be played on together? Have American women no higher inspirations than this? When French fashions *really came* to us breathing the perfume of elegant Paris, they were a *real* temptation, and often a snare, into which economy, piety, and even virtue, fell, and were lost. But now that the spell is broken, shall we not rejoice that we are free from the bondage and tyranny of " Paris fashions "?

When American women, with all their beauty, culture and purity, clad themselves in servile imitation of perhaps the "frailest" women in the world, it was bad enough; but when they only *pretend* to, it is contemptible.

Paris fashions—we have worshipped them so long we can not afford to abuse them now, but may thank God that their imperial reign and our serfdom is over. Henceforth, they must be but the ghost of a by-gone folly that went down in the maelstrom of war.

In Paris beleaguered yesterday, or Paris surrendered to-day, fashion finds no votaries, no gods, no altars; all are swept away in the great agony, which, in love and sympathy, let us hope, will bring forth a purer life for France.

Women of America, let *us* not rebuild these broken altars, but turn from the ashes and mourning, where the old idol has fallen, to our younger and healthier American society, resolving to erect a purer and higher standard of taste for the "coming woman" of a better age.

Perhaps, in time, it may not be for this Republic alone; for when the women of America learn to appreciate the grand possibilities that lie in their culture and their unfettered freedom, they may be the social law-givers of the world. They may inaugurate a social millennium, wherein culture and labor may shake hands, and taste and religion kneel down together.

A SOCIAL "RAMPAGE."

A writer in the *Gospel Advocate,* growing very indignant over fashion-books, says:

" I believe I would consent to subscribe for Mr. Godey, Harper or Peterson's books of filth and corruption, if they would give us old fashion-plates of the worthy mothers now in their graves, and at the same time accompany these with a stated contrast between their habits of useful industry and the fruitless indolence of their daughters; the economy of one, the thriftless waste of the other; the humility, shame-facedness and modesty of the former, and the daring, boldness and pride of the latter."

While we can not but see that there is some just ground for this righteous indignation against fashions, we see, too, with half an eye, that its expression is far more fervent than original. It has become a *fashion* for a class of pious people to cry down all fashion and taste; and the "fashion" of crying down is followed quite as assiduously as other fashions are. Yet these very criers, as a rule, do not *live* them down. If men, we see them wear just the length of coat and width of pantaloons, that, if absurd yesterday and to-morrow, they will rest in tranquil assurance, is just the thing to-day. If it is women who deliver this moral and religious lecture, they do it in bonnets of the regulation size, and hoops of the right dimensions. Their very over-skirts are looped up just right, or they think so, which is just as well, since it gives them the vantage-ground of *perfect propriety*, from which to lecture their fellow-sinners. Nor is this inconsistent. If these lectures are delivered at all, they must be delivered from a stand-point that will be respected. Instinctively every one feels this. Wo to the bold reformer who dares to harangue his fellow-men, attired in sackcloth and ashes of a by-gone style; his bodily presence will be contemptible, and the absurdity of his appearance will creep in and mingle with his speech, in the comprehension of his hearers. Why? Who can tell? yet so it is! Still there is a reason. A soul that is really in harmony with all that is good, is also in harmony with all that is beautiful, and would clothe even its body to delight its eye as God hath clothed the earth. Now comes the difficulty. Our ideas of beauty are all changed and molded, and marred by habit. Nothing seems grotesque when it has grown familar to the eye. But we must wear something, and surely the fashions of to-day are quite as good as the old ones. It does seem to a candid observer that no amount of modesty, prudence or religion, could suffice to reconcile us to a toilet like that of Queen Elizabeth or Anne of Flanders; and even turning from them to a later age, we

are confronted by our grandmothers, and fall back
in consternation and despair before coal-scuttle
bonnets and sleeves which have assumed wild
dimensions, after being filled with half the contents
of a feather bed. Do we want to imitate these?
Heaven forbid! The truth is, the world has not
gone wild all at once; it has been showing symp-
toms of insanity for thousands of years, and the
freaks of to-day are no more than the freaks of yesterday.

But through all these is a gleam of reason which
is a hopeful sign for the future. Fashion can not be
cried down, and *will not* be ignored; why should we
wish it to? Let us rather mold it to our will, and make
it serve some purpose. In other words, let us not
serve fashion, but make it serve us. Let us make
ourselves beautiful, that we may enlarge the sphere
of our influence, and do this that we may do good.
A beautiful soul—a beautiful life will make itself felt
in the hearts of men always, but it is possible to add
to this the subtle, silent influence of what is lovely
to the eyes. To do this we must dress not to astonish, but to please; not to dazzle, but to satisfy. To
some extent dress should even be matter for study.
We can not afford to throw away a means of personal influence over the world, which is at once so
silent and so wide. To say nothing of modesty,
economy, and a hundred other virtues which we may

illustrate in our dress; by the faultless elegance of a quiet harmony, may we not suggest in our outward selves the peace and order and quiet of an inward life, set in harmony with that standard whose beauty is holiness?

We have no inspiration concerning clothes, yet we must wear them, make them, and learn how they are to be made. It certainly can make but little difference whether, in order to do this, we buy a fashion-book or spend an afternoon watching from the window those who have reproduced its suggestions upon their backs. Many would decide well in favor of the former. That this is *all* wrong we know, but it never will be better while one-half of society is engaged in a mad gallop after the follies of fashion, and the other half in a wild crusade against them. What society wants is, men and women wise and patient, and sensible enough to make a friend of fashion, tame it down, put a bit in its mouth, and then harness it to do the will and bidding of its tamers.

PENS AND PATIENCE.

Once when Lyman Beecher descended from his pulpit, after preaching his remarkable sermon on the "Government of God," he was asked how long he was preparing it, to which the distinguished preacher replied: "About forty years, sir." When we think of this sermon as being the concentrated essence of the wisdom of forty years, cast into a mold by deliberate and patient labor, we do not wonder that Dr. Skinner said of it: "It was the most tremendous discourse I ever listened to." Gray's Elegy was written in a little less than half that time; and the line of the Scotch Poet—"And coming events cast their shadows before,"—was the golden product of a sleepless night, spent in coaxing thought by cups of tea. Dickens, who is said to have been such a rapid writer, says of himself that when he wrote "Chimes," his Christmas story, he took a little cottage in the suburbs of London, and shut himself up for a month; by which time his story was completed, but he himself was as haggard as a murderer.

From Dickens' posthumous papers we learn that much which an unthinking world attributed to the miracle of genius, is attributable rather to the miracle of labor.

Genius, says one of that exalted brotherhood, is only a great patience; another says it is only an unusual power of concentration, which is much the same thing; and this too is the verdict of Sir Isaac Newton, who, from the great scope of his mental powers, ought to be a good authority. Certainly this was true of Newton himself and a vast number of others, and it would be matter for curious and not unprofitable research to compare the solid fame of a large number of great men with the relative time and labor spent in acquiring it. It is probable that we should find, generally, that those whose fame outlived their day and generation, had built it with patient toil, carefully and painfully polishing every gem of thought with a great faith that it would be set in the crown which the world waited to bestow.

This is especially true in literature; and yet in no other department of labor, that is not professional, is there so much looseness, inaccuracy and lack of patient and careful attention to detail, and nowhere is it so unpardonable. The man who builds or invents a machine pays the penalty of carelessness and inexactness by its failure in his own hands. A bad picture claims only a single glance of indifference. But a careless, tautological and verbose writer, compels us to give him our time for no adequate value received.

When we consider the number of books already in the world, and endeavor to estimate the number that is yearly thrown into the capacious lap of a long-suffering reading public, and think how few of them have both the virtue of well digested thought, and the grace of accurate and concise expression, we are ready to groan that such a vast mob of ragged, unkempt thoughts, should be admitted into the republic of letters. Our only hope and comfort is, that life is too short to read them all.

But when we come to newspapers, it is worse; an editor's sanctum is like a forest in autumn, "nothing but leaves." A correspondent conceives an idea, and forthwith he proceeds to develop—or dilute it— on half a quire of paper; and, after all, the chief merit of the production lies in the truthfulness of the personal postscript: "I have just dashed off an article for you"; and what this obliging writer has spent an hour in "dashing off," he modestly expects ten thousand people to spend a half hour each in reading, making an aggregate of five thousand hours or nearly two-thirds of a year; and all this to be spent on one article which he "dashed off."

Daniel Webster once excused a long speech by saying, "Had I had more time my speech would not have been so long." For a man of Webster's gigantic labors, this excuse may suffice; but he who writes simply because he thinks he has something to say, and will not take time to condense his thoughts, has no right to expect his readers to wade through his unpruned verbiage. But, you say, the man is a genius. Even so; then if he is honest and conscientious he will see that a time of reckoning must come if he dares to neglect the cultivation of those fertile mental fields over which God has made him lord and master.

This vain and unreasoning reliance upon genius is akin to the old doctrine of the divine right of kings, and is a sort of intellectual "infallibility dogma," causing an incalculable amount of mischief, first, to the genius himself, who rises superior to logic, rhetoric or rhythm, as the case may be, discovering in himself a power which needs not to be cultivated by these; and, secondly, to his admirers, who, confounding his beauties with his blemishes, admire and vindicate them both.

A man of moderate talent will often write a better article than a genius, simply because he depends upon no intellectual scintillations, but thoroughly masters and classifies the thoughts in his own mind, and then expresses them in the simplest and most accurate language at his command. Having done this, he will find he has no need of ornament; exactness and strength themselves are beautiful.

Any one who can think connectedly, reason clearly, and talk sensibly, can, if he chooses, write well—
that is, with some reasonable hope of informing or
pleasing his readers. He may not astonish, but he
will not utterly disappoint. But, above all, is it necessary that he should have something to say, something which he believes implicitly.

Happy is he who, having written, has developed
one distinct living idea, something that is tangible
enough to be pigeon-holed in the brain for future reference. No matter if it is embryotic ; if it is an individual thought, it may grow up to maturity in the
mind that gives it lodgment. We all are conscious of holding ideas that were not born of ourselves, but are a kind of adopted children that have
grown up with us, and these are often the most
valuable ; for, standing upon the shoulders of another's thought, we reach where unassisted we could
not climb.

Lastly, when you speak or write, say something
true, something which you will one day like to remember, something upon which you can invoke a
blessing, something which will never be a stumbling-
block in the path of a brother, a sword in his heart
or a scourge in his hand ; and condemn your pen
and your tongue to silence rather than use them so
that their edge may be turned against truth and justice. "Whatsoever things are true, whatsoever things

---

are pure,'' these do, and these write ; and year by year your pages, like your thoughts, will grow with the grace of a truer rhetoric, the poetry of a higher life, and the strength of a diviner inspiration.

LIFE-WORK; OR, RAISED FROM THE DEPTHS.

CHAPTER I.—A LITTLE MYSTERY.

John B. Gough says that our judgments of persons are often utterly changed, simply by a knowledge of circumstances. This we know is true; and were we disposed to be witty at the expense of a very large and industrious class of society, we might suppose that it is because they so much desire to have all their judgments entirely just, that gossips take such infinite pains to discover all the circumstances connected with the affairs of their neighbors.

Could this be proved, it would at once not only remove an old prejudice, but place them in the front rank of philanthropists. But the evidence is not at all clear, and I neither believe them to be urged on by so good a motive, nor, on the other hand, to be as malicious as most people suppose. The fact probably is, they are, as a class, a little blinder and more zealous in their worship of that great deity, ''Something New;'' but then most of us worship this god, it is said.

I think it is true; if not, then I can not possibly
explain why, on a certain Lord's day in December,
when the sky was not particularly brilliant, nor the
pavement particularly dry, there was such an unusually large number gathered in the little Christian
chapel at Athens.   I said "little," but it really was
not so, but indeed too large for the very respectable
congregation that built it; but now that it was finished
and a new preacher engaged, no one doubted that
there would be additions to the flock until all the
seats were filled; at least, this was the remark made
by a quiet-eyed man in the front pew of what is
sometimes called the pious corner, to his neighbor,
Deacon Worthington.

"Oh! yes," replied the deacon, "no doubt of
that, if he is the right kind of a man—a man of influence, you know, who will draw outsiders in—a
man of talent—why, the house is nearly full already
—almost time for service; hope he is prompt.   They
say he is a fine preacher—ah!"

The deacon did not often talk so much before service, but the sight of the handsome house, filling
rapidly with well-dressed people, all eager to hear
the new preacher, excited the good deacon a little,
and he talked on in a quiet whisper for a full minute,
and finally brought himself up short with the word
"*ah!*" just as the new preacher walked quietly up
the aisle and entered the pulpit.

At once every eye was fastened upon him in such a respectful silence, that an attentive heathen, with ritualistic tendencies, might have supposed the laying aside of his overcoat and gloves to be a religious ceremony, instead of an observance for his own comfort.

The new preacher was a quiet, gentle man, with a manner so modest and appealing, that unconsciously the congregation settled themselves more noiselessly in their pews, and gave him that quiet attention which is the surest sign of sympathy. He read the fifty-third chapter of Isaiah, and then offered what seemed the shortest, yet most fervent opening prayer that they had ever heard from the pulpit. His voice was deep, musical and sonorous, and came like a surprise from the fair, quiet face and slender figure. There was, when he spoke, something unusually interesting about him. His manner appealed to their sympathy, his voice and words raised their expectations and commanded their attention. While in manner he seemed to look humbly up to them, he addressed them like one who was not afraid to lead them in and out among the green pastures of God.

His sermon was on the subject of the Word made flesh among us, and with glowing words he followed the "Hero of the Cross" through all his checkered life: the babe of Bethlehem, the refugee in Nazareth, the mysterious boy in the temple, the tempted in the wilderness, the feeder of the multitude, the scourged in the Sanhedrim, the transfigured Christ, the Christ of Calvary, and the giver of the new law. In all this there was absolutely nothing new, no reference to any other gospel ever preached among men, and yet the simple, thrilling story seemed to pour out from unexpected depths in the heart of the speaker, and shook every heart upon which it fell. And when he came to dwell particularly upon Him who went about doing good, and Him who bowed his head and wrote upon the sand before he said, "Neither do I condemn thee; go, and sin no more," a God and yet a man, human and yet too pure and modest to look even in sternness upon such guilt, which yet he could forgive: when he had repeated all this in glowing words, he had collected every scattered fragment of attention, and every heart, forgetting time, and place, and speaker, felt like holding up imploring hands to that arm which in human flesh had reached down in unmeasurable love from heaven.

The story—for this only it was, the story of the Cross—was ended, and after a moment's silence, he repeated slowly, "Come unto me, all ye that are weary and heavy laden, and I will give you rest; take my yoke upon you, and learn of me, for I am meek and lowly in heart, and you shall find rest for your souls; for my yoke is easy and my burden is light." During the song, after this invitation, two

Sunday-school children came forward to make the good confession, but after them no grown person, or "influential outsiders," as Deacon Worthington expressed it; but then, as a sister afterward said, "It was truly a gospel for children—a story of a hero, and a hero that may be worshiped."

After service the preacher seemed at once to subside again into the quiet, modest stranger, and not all the fervent greetings of his new people could do more than draw out a smile, or a sweet, low-voiced reply. Deacon Worthington stood apart, silent and thoughtful, now that the usual talking time had come; something in the sermon had touched a new chord, or an old one, and made it vibrate to an old memory; yet what, he could not tell, except that it was something sweet, sad, and long past. By this time, seeing that the hand-shakings were subsiding, and the pastor stood hesitating and helpless between a dozen invitations to dinner, the deacon rushed blindly to the rescue of the preacher and his own hospitality, saying quaintly, "Bro. Arden, as these good people are persuading you to eat a dozen dinners, I think it my duty to see that you eat but one;" and literally bore him off in triumph, with quite a number of the disappointed candidates for that honor.

Seated at his own table, the deacon grew fluent again; but in vain he strove to draw out that silent guest who sat at his wife's right hand, according to the deacon's stately ideas of courtesy.

Meek and grateful to all, the new pastor seemed willing to be familiar and confidential with none, and shortly after dinner took his departure for the house of the brother with whom was his present home, pleading as excuse the necessity of preparing himself for the evening service.

After conducting his guest to the door, the deacon returned to find his friends quietly discussing the departing preacher; and Mrs. Everett began, "Well, Deacon, how do you like our new pastor?"

"Quite a pleasant gentleman—quite so," replied the deacon, evidently wide of the point, as though he spoke courteously at random, while in his own mind he was giving the subject a far deeper consideration; but, undeterred by this, the doctor himself now filled up the conversational gap, with a remark more likely to draw the deacon out.

"I was away," he began, "when the church called Bro. Arden, and have never heard whence he came or who he is, except what I now perceive for myself, that he is a man of remarkable gifts, and evidently as good and earnest as he is talented; I was told you recommended him. Where did you make his acquaintance?"

"I did neither. Sister Ada Clifton, who visited New York last summer, spoke of him as a beautiful and earnest speaker; and this fall Bro. Wilson heard him in some little town there—I forget the name—and wrote to our committee recommending him, and of course I endorsed the recommendation, remembering what I had heard of him before. I learn from Ada that he has no relatives, and lost his parents in childhood. It's almost a pity he is not married; I think he would be more social and approachable."

"Quite a pity," sighed Mrs. Everett; "he would have been so much more useful, and we really need a pastor's wife, to—"

"To sit in the preacher's pew," interrupted her husband, "and put her feet on that nice little cushion." At this they all laughed a quiet, cheery laugh, all except Mrs. Everett, whose idea it had been to furnish one pew for the special use of the preacher's family. Not that it was carpeted or cushioned differently from the others, but a few items were added as a love-offering, for the pleasure and comfort of the anticipated new comer, such as a book-rack, with a small but elegant Bible and hymn-book, and a foot-cushion, just referred to. This latter article came near being a stone of stumbling to one or two sisters whose hearts were better than their reasoning powers, for they said, "Foot-cushions reminded every one of Catholic worship, and we certainly ought to keep out of our churches everything resembling that." But, after all, the question was pleasantly settled by a witty sister, who observed that as long as the Bible remained in the rack the cushion must be harmless. And now this little labor of love, like many a larger one, was in vain; there was no preacher's wife to enjoy it; and to good Mrs. Everett the subject appeared quite destitute of a single amusing feature.

"Don't laugh," said Miss Ada, who had not spoken a word before, and now broke her silence to visit on the doctor's bald head the whole enormity of a smile that had in truth gone around the circle; "don't laugh; if we were all more tender and unselfish to each other in body and soul, how very much more it would mean to be members of the family of Christ. It's absurd to call men and women 'brothers' and 'sisters,' and then concern yourself no more about their welfare or comfort than if they were strangers."

"That's true," said the doctor, musingly, with the air of a big boy in the class who has been prompted by a small boy below him, "that's true; and in the church we have no love to spare; and it does occur to me that while we meet so regularly on Lord's day for the service of God, we ought also to serve each other through the week; but, instead of that, with us men at least, the rule of life is, 'the race *is* to the swift, and the battle to the strong,' and no man helps his brother."

Soon after the guests all departed for church; and as Mrs. Worthington tied her bonnet-strings to follow, she turned to her husband, saying as she straightened the bow under her fair double chin, "Ada Clifton is *mistaken* about Bro. Arden's being an orphan from his boyhood. His mother, at least, died very lately; he wears crape on his hat *now* for her."

"How do you know it is for *her?*"

"I asked him who it was for, and he replied that it was for his mother, who died a few months ago."

"Well, my dear, I can not see that it affects *us* at all when she died. Are you ready?"

"No, it doesn't affect us at all, but it is rather strange. But I'll find out."

CHAPTER II.—LADIES OF CHARITY.

On the following Thursday there was a regular meeting of the Sewing Society at Dr. Everett's. Mrs. Worthington, herself a very active woman, was the president, and during the year, one by one, nearly all the sisters had dropped in, making the society quite a success. Their object was at first to furnish the new church, and after that was done they decided to continue their work and devote the proceeds to paying off a small debt upon it.

After a little business had been disposed of, Miss Ada Clifton rose and moved that the Society should devote a portion of their time and means to clothing poor children for Sunday-school, first appointing a committee to find them—a work which would not be very difficult—making it a kind of home missionary branch.

This proposition had been laid before the Society three months before, and seconded by Miss Ada, but was then postponed until the new church should be completed and opened; and now old Mrs. Webb, the original proposer, seconded it, but the vote was not carried, and the resolution fell. So Miss Ada, evidently disappointed, took up her patchwork and sewed on, and the conversation, at first general, narrowed down to gossip.

"It is a very good object, indeed," began Mrs. Everett; "but then our church has been a great draft upon us, it has to be finished and paid for, and I think we ought to pay the last dollar of our little debt before we do anything outside the church."

"Yes, indeed," replied Mrs. Worthington, "and in truth I have little faith in working outside. In the church we have very few really poor; the Deacon says in that we are greatly blessed. And among the poor outside, there are so few that are really worthy. And, Miss Ada," she went on, addressing her most conclusive remarks to that young lady, "if we dress these children of which you speak, and make them decent, we have no certainty that they will continue to attend Sunday-school and church; and if they did, it would be, as the Deacon says, more for the clothes we give them than the good we teach them."

"I know it, but it is precisely for the reason that they are so ignorant and unworthy, that I am anxious to gather them in and hold them by any means in our power, until we shall have had time to teach them of that wonderful love which crowds out selfishness in every heart which it fills." If in this reply Miss Ada intended any sarcasm, she did not show it by her manner, nor did Mrs. Worthington observe it, or, for reasons of her own, did not appear to, as she continued:

"Then so many among the very poor are Catholics; and, as the priest, who had heard of Miss Ada's plan, very insolently said, the religion we teach them will not outlive the clothes we furnish."

" *That* will be *our* fault," remarked Mrs. Webb.

" Well, perhaps so," said a very dressy lady, stopping to pick some threads off her flounces—"perhaps so, but I think, like Sister Worthington, that we can benefit the church far more by confining our efforts to our own class in society.".

" But 'the poor have the gospel preached to them,' says Holy Writ. The poor are the legacy of the church."

"Yes, Sister Webb," replied Mrs. Worthington,

"but the Bible says, 'The poor you have always with you;' and so as we have no fear of their departing from our midst, we can turn our attention to them at any time when our present charities are accomplished. They are at least a legacy which we stand in no danger of forfeiting." At this they laughed a pleasant, thoughtless little laugh, but a moment after old Mrs. Webb said, very gravely:

"Sister Worthington, you said 'when our present charities are accomplished.' I did not know we had any. What are they?"

"Why, furnishing and paying for the church."

"Is that a *charity?*"

"Well, it's *giving*, at any rate."

"Is it?"

"Don't you think so?"

"No!"

"What is it, then?"

"An *investment*, perhaps."

"Then you think this Society is not in any sense engaged in a charitable work? What do you think, Ada?"

"Like Sister Webb, I think this church is ours; we have furnished it for ourselves, to have and to use, to walk on the bright carpets, to sit on the soft cushions, and invite our friends. Certainly it is no charity to provide conveniences for ourselves. *It is*

an investment for our own comfort. If outsiders contribute, then it may be giving."

"That reminds me," said the dressy lady, "of
my husband saying that, as he was not a member of
the church, his contribution was an investment in *my*
religion; and Cousin Harris, who is a great tease,
was impertinent enough to ask him if he considered an
investment in my religion a good speculation. He
thinks I am worldly, you know." At this they all
laughed again, not unpleasantly, but the lady laughed herself, and seemed amiably unconscious that
many others shared the opinion of "Cousin Harris."

Mrs. Worthington was one of those ladies who run
exceedingly well in a narrow groove, but who do not
like to be convinced; and so when the conversation
took this unexpected turn, she was glad to let Miss
Ada's last remark pass without further comment; but
Mrs. Everett, who had dropped her sewing a few
minutes before, seemed to have picked up the new
idea, and sat silently turning it over in her mind,
while the dressy lady continued—

"But of course that is all talk; for husband is really
interested in the church, and he likes the new
preacher, and last Sunday"—

"Please say Lord's-day," interrupted old Sister
Downs.

"Thank you. Well, Lord's-day—but that word
always sounds so old-fashioned to me—last Lord's-

day—what was I saying?—oh! yes, husband said that story of the Cross was worth all the sermons we heard in New York last winter, and I am sure it had more effect upon me. I can not say I recollect the others, but I shall never forget that, even if I do grow worldly," and she laughed again, in a free, thoughtless way.

"Nor I," added Miss Ada, replying only to a part of the last sentence, "and, oh! how I wished that all the poor, ignorant people around us could have heard that sermon last Lord's-day. It was a sermon suited to the poor and ignorant."

"Well, I think it suited us, too, and "—

"Certainly, a gospel sermon suits *every one*, but debates and lectures on Christianity may be entirely beyond the comprehension of some, and uninteresting to others."

"Bro. Arden is certainly a gifted speaker or an earnest man; both, I think," observed a quiet young lady, "for when he told that old story in that grand way, it all seemed to start up strange, and new, and wonderful again."

"Well," observed another dressy lady, the wife of Deacon Storm, "I am somewhat tired of hearing of that wonderful sermon, but what was there original about it after all? Of course it was good, but "—

"Well, that is all any of us said," laughed the dressy lady again.

"What a pity, though," continued the other lady, paying no attention whatever to the interruption— "what a pity that Bro. Arden's manner is so uninteresting! He would be quite distinguished-looking in the pulpit if his manners were better. He has so little dignity."

"He appears like one who has contracted a silent habit from being alone, or in study," observed Mrs. Webb.

"Oh! it 's not that, but what some would call 'humility,' a kind of silent apology."

"Oh! it is only a peculiarity he would lose if he were married," said Mrs. Everett, reverting to her favorite topic. "He ought to marry; a preacher should always have a wife. Don't you think so, Ada?"

"He has had no parents from his boyhood," said Ada, replying very indirectly, "and I think mingled very little in society, having no relatives."

"Are you not mistaken," asked Mrs. Worthington, with great interest, "about his being an orphan from boyhood?"

"No; he told me last summer that he had lost his parents before he remembered."

"That *is* strange. I noticed crape on his hat, and he told *me* it was for his mother, who died a few months ago. Are you sure he told *you* that?"

"Yes, quite sure," replied Ada, rather nervously, "but probably we do not know all about it."

"I should think not," said Mrs. Storm, "but they can 't *both* be true, and it certainly looks very mysterious."

"Well," said the dressy lady, "perhaps there *is* some mystery about him. Would n't it be romantic if there was?"

"Not for a *preacher*," was the stern reply; "that and his manner together do look doubtful, and I shall ask Deacon Storm to make a few very quiet"—

Here they were interrupted by the entrance of the new pastor, convoyed by Deacon Worthington. In the confusion of the general introduction a great many threads were dropped, among them the thread of conversation, and the new mystery. But a great many curious eyes noted the band of crape on the preacher's hat, as Mrs. Everett politely relieved him of it.

"I find," began the Deacon, "that Bro. Arden is very much interested in benevolent societies, and so I brought him here to introduce him to the sisters, for I believe, except our annual missionary subscriptions, you ladies represent the active charities of the church."

This was intended as a compliment; but there was a puzzled, embarrassed look in Mrs. Worthington's face, and no one made the slightest response for a a moment, and then Mrs. Everett came to the rescue, saying, "We are glad you thought of us, for I can assure you we thought of you this afternoon, and spoke of you, too, Bro. Arden."

"Yes, indeed," began the dressy lady, "and Sister Everett has taken a wonderful interest in you, and—yes, I will tell you," she pursued, with a spice of malice in her eyes, as they encountered several anxious glances, "some of the ladies are very anxious about"—she paused—"the preacher's pew. They think there ought to be a pastor's wife to sit in it."

"Well, I am very sorry," began the pastor, with a tone and manner as humble as if he were making a genuine apology for misconduct, "I am very sorry, but perhaps in there being no preacher's wife, I lose as much as the ladies do. I often think so in my lonely hours; but then I am used to being alone—I have always been."

In these few words, spoken in that low, musical voice, there was something so touching that every heart felt a tender sympathy. They showed it in words of gentle courtesy, and by being very social as they gathered up their sewing as the twilight came on; all but Ada, who moved away to the window, saying she could see there to finish her seam. But Mrs. Everett noticed that she had left her work behind and forgotten it, and she herself folded it, making no remark. Looking up once, she saw the pastor's eyes fixed thoughtfully on Ada, and she thought from the flush on Ada's face that she knew it.

They all took tea and spent the evening, and by the time the party dispersed they were all quite conscious that whatever else the new pastor might prove to be, he was certainly a refined and cultivated Christian gentleman, although peculiar and reserved. They quite forgot "the mystery" about him until the sight of his hat recalled it at the door. Deacon Worthington said, at parting: "Now do n't forget, Bro. Arden, that we are anxious to have you fill that preacher's pew, dedicated to you with so many prayers and good wishes."

"I will do the best I can," he replied gravely. "Good-night."

CHAPTER III.—TRUE TO HIS TRUST—THE MOTHER OF
A SOUL.

On the following Lord's-day morning, the preacher's pew was not vacant, but in filling it the pastor committed an unpardonable sin. It happened in this wise: In making pastoral visits, the young preacher heard of a poor Sister Hill, who lived in some small rooms behind a dram-shop, in the meanest part of the town. Her husband, who had kept it, died several years before, and the widow made a little grocery of it; but liquor sold better than groceries there, and she was obliged to give it up, and in other hands it became a dram-shop again. Still she rented the little rooms, a quiet, inoffensive woman, with a heart above her surroundings, and when she joined the church, a few years before, might have occupied quite a respectable position in it, but for her children. Her sons had gone in the steps of their father and become drunkards; indeed, for that they had not far to go, only behind the "bar;" and her daughter had become—at least, so rumor said—even worse. Upon all these trials was heaped one more: the church treated her only with coldness and neglect, and after a year or two she came to church no more. She told her story very simply when the pastor called, and when he asked her to come to church she replied: "I should like to hear you, Bro. Arden, but I have been reading my Bible at home; and I do n't think the people would like to see me in the seats up in front, and I 'm a little deaf now."

"I have a seat to myself—that is, it was intended for my family, had I one; I should like you to sit there when you feel able to come. If you will come early next Lord's-day, I will show you into it myself." And this was how it happened that, when a few minutes before service, a shabby woman, just a little past middle age, walked up the aisle, the pastor gave her a quiet little hand-shake, and showed her into the preacher's pew, to the horror and indignation of the sisters who knew all the dark details of her *outside* family history, but nothing of the pitiful struggle of her *inner* life.

Again the young preacher filled every ear with the music of his wonderful voice, and every heart with the reflected glow of that love which, for Christ's sake, sees in every man a brother.

Again, when the service was over, he sank down from an inspired speaker to a timid, reticent man, while the members crowded up in groups to express their varied shades of delighted approval.

So, week after week, the pastor grew into his work, and thrilled them with his earnest, eloquent tongue; but week by week a small annoyance grew into a large one, and the pastor's pew was often filled with what the sisters called "the lowest kind of people." Still they were not all low; some of them were only very poor: but Mrs. Worthington said the effect was much the same, and the deacon added, "Very detrimental to the gathering in of influential outsiders." Still they came, and one after another a dozen of these people, among them two of Sister Hill's sons, made the good confession before three months had passed. The Sunday-school was similarly invaded, and the rows of ragged children made weekly encroachments upon the seats hitherto sacred to well-dressed little ones. But, in spite of all, the preacher did "draw influential outsiders," and the house was often crowded; yet, little by little, the poor young pastor felt that among his own congregation his popularity was surely waning. One or two, besides the two who assisted him, were in perfect sympathy with his work. Those two assistants were Mrs. Webb and Ada Clifton. Both had for years spent their time, the latter, who was wealthy, her money, in Christian work. But, next to God, whom he so faithfully served, the young pastor's eloquent, tongue was his most influential friend; yet he sadly felt that his whole idea of a Christian's work was opposed to that of the majority of the congregation, and, humble though he was, he appeared unwilling to yield an inch to these worldly prejudices. When, after some consultation, the deacons gave him a gentle hint that a pastor should endeavor to work as much as possible according to the idea of his people, he replied: "I claim no privileges because I am your preacher; I should do as I do were I only a member. I only seek the unfortunate because, with an exception or two, the rest do not. When I see the rich neglected, I shall seek them; but to all I preach alike that gospel which teaches that all men are my neighbors." From the first they had felt that there was something about this meek, quiet man that made it very difficult to confront or oppose him; notwithstanding his humility, he was not easily influenced. Perhaps they respected him the more for this, but still the dissatisfaction grew; the church, the Sunday-school, the prayer-meeting grew likewise, but still it did not heal the evil.

Six months had passed away, and the poor young pastor was still called a "great preacher," and crowds came to hear him ; but still many were poor or low, or in some way objectionable, to the great alarm of the deacons and influential members, who, in their grieved imagination, already saw the church filling up with what they termed common people. This state of things did not at all trouble the old elder ; but since he had been infirm, his office had become almost nominal, and in reality Deacon Worthington, on account of his wealth and position, and other reasons, wielded more influence than any other member of the church.

Deacon Worthington was at heart a good man, and in truth very zealous in the cause of religion, and it had been the brightest dream of his life to see his church rise grandly superior to worldliness, infidelity and sectarianism, and teach the community around him what a wonderful power is a church founded on the written Word of God alone. But, like the Jews in the time of Christ, his ideas of prosperity and power were founded too much upon worldly grandeur and worldly influence—as if God needed them ; or, needing them, would not have pointed to them in His Will. When the new church was completed and a fine speaker installed, the Deacon saw his dream in the way of rapid fulfillment; but now he almost groaned aloud to see the long rows of shabby people, some of them with shabby reputations, sitting before his insulted eyes. After a great deal of quiet consultation with the officers, a deacons' meeting was called for the purpose of seeing what could be done. They made a last vain appeal to the preacher, and his reply was: "I only go where duty calls me; when I invite hearers I *dare not omit* those whom my *Master* called. Send me where you will to invite sinners here, but send another to invite them away."

All this fell very heavily on the heart of the devoted young pastor; but still he went about doing good, following so closely in the steps of his Master that, like him, he was reproached for "eating with publicans and sinners."

In the midst of all this, a darker cloud fell and seemed for a time to lower between him and his few faithful friends in the congregation. Only *one* never forgot to pray for him with silent devotion, always believed in him, and always would; and that one was Ada Clifton. From week to week his face was her comfort, and her face was his inspiration amid discouragement and isolation. The cloud was a number of very vague, dark rumors, respecting the preacher's past life; and they all came from this: Accord-

---

ing to promise, Mrs. Storm and the Deacon had made some "very quiet inquiries" concerning the pastor's antecedents, for the purpose principally of settling the question of the date of his mother's death and learning of his family. They had made them very quietly indeed; but besides Deacon Storm and his wife and Mrs. Worthington, a dozen gossips, men as well as women (for gossips are of both sexes), had resolved themselves into a volunteer committee to push the inquiry. They learned that the young preacher had for some years been a faithful, earnest missionary in New York City, preaching in the Reform schools and Bethel churches, and when his health failed, visited western New York, preaching wherever he went. They learned all this and no more. Whether the congregation woke up some morning and told its dreams, or whether the gossips talked in their sleep, is not known; but this simple account at last expanded into vague, wonderful stories: according to one of them, the pastor had deserted his mother until she died of grief; another hinted that he was an impostor, wearing an assumed name. Fortunately these rumors had not gone far beyond the gossips themselves, and a few "*interested*" people in the church, but they had reached the pastor's ears and crushed him as nothing in life had ever done before; but still he plodded on, and told his sorrow only to God.

Of course, these stories reached the Deacon's ears, and at the next officers' meeting were referred to. None of them attached much importance to such vague trifles; but Deacon Worthington urged that as there were graver reasons why the pastor did not suit them in his work, it would be best, on every account, to sever the connection. Many objected. Some were really attached to the devoted and pious young pastor; others only saw in him two qualifications not always found together—wonderful eloquence and the zeal of an earnest, faithful-laborer in the vineyard of God. But Deacon Worthington prevailed, and at last they decided to remove the pastor. For the sake of appearances, they concluded to give him, instead of a formal dismissal, a recommendation to the Missionary Board, for which he was indeed well fitted; and the next annual meeting was the time appointed for laying the matter before the congregation.

As the time approached, Deacon Worthington felt very nervous about the matter, for his influence, operating strongly from the first, had finally carried the decision against the pastor. Not that he regretted it, yet he could not put away the thought that his responsibility in this affair would some day tell heavily for good or ill in his account with heaven.

On the appointed night there was a large attendance. A few came to say some strong words in favor of retaining their faithful pastor; a few, who had already done their worst, only to sit still and vote; but still a greater number came only intending to hear everything with that sublime indifference which does not speak unless questioned, and then replies: "Oh! whatever the rest do, I shall be quite satisfied."

On the night in question, immediately after the opening services, to the surprise of all, the pastor rose and requested permission to make the first remarks, and then said:

"Brethren, when six months ago you called me to be your preacher, I accepted with joy. I expected to be very happy among you if I pleased you, but I have failed. Yet before I go away to my old field again, I desire, for good reasons, to tell you my story. Some here," he added significantly, yet kindly, "will be interested in hearing it, a few may be happier or better; I will make it tedious to none.

"Where my eyes first opened to the light, I do not know, but I remember life as it appeared to me from the low door-stone of a small dram-shop in a squalid alley in New York. I never knew how it might have appeared from a mother's lap, and day by day I sat there in the sunshine and watched coarse drunken men and haggard women pass by, or listened to the din within doors behind me. I can not remember that any one ever cared for me, till one bright day"—and he clasped his hands, speaking

slowly—"it was bright then, and will be bright in
my memory forever—a beautiful lady who passed
almost every day, but hitherto always went by—to
me like an angel from another sphere—stopped and
spoke to me sweet, petting words which I scarcely
understood. Her eyes filled with tears, and she entered the dram-shop, but in a few moments came out
again, and, wiping my face with her handkerchief,
kissed me, and then without a word took me with
her just as I was, hatless, shoeless, friendless, from
my home on the door-stone.

"She went on first to a mission-school, and, watching her all that summer afternoon passing up and
down among rows of ragged little children, I caught
my first idea of love. But I was too young for this
place. She took me home and cared for me a few
days herself, then put me in an asylum, from there
to a school, then to an institution out of the city,
where she often visited me. In all these changes
she seemed to have but one purpose in view, that purpose centering in myself.

"So I grew up to boyhood, loving her with a devotion that I can not describe. For her sake, no
place was solitary or strange to me. Where her
hand placed me I was certain to stay, feeling always
that my real home was in her heart.

"When I was sixteen, my loving guardian died. I
was not with her, but she did not forget me. I re-

ceived a loving farewell letter, dated a few weeks before her death. In this letter she informed me that
I had been provided with a scholarship in one of our
best colleges, and means to support myself while I
finished my studies.

"Her concluding words were a solemn charge:
'Now, my son in Christ, who has so far rewarded
my watchful care, and never disappointed my love, I
have done all I can for you in this world, and in return
it is my wish—' for this purpose have I raised thee up'—
that you give yourself and all your life-long labor to
Christ, to whom I now commend you with my prayer
and my love.'" He paused. There were tears
around him, but his eyes were bright and happy as
he continued: "So far I have obeyed her, and with
God's help I shall try to walk in her footstsps to the
end.

"For years I labored in the mission-schools in
New York and preached in the mission-houses, and
there, through God who guided me, last autumn I
found my earthly mother. I did not know she lived
until I found her dying. She had heard me preach,
and after some difficulty discovered who I was. I
baptized her, and at last she died in my arms, and I
have been happy ever since; not happy because she
is dead, but because there is joy in heaven over one
sinner that repents." He paused again, amid a silence
breathless and profound, broken again by his voice

saying: "I have told you my history. I have no right to be a proud man, and I am not, or I should not have told you. Now my heart will not rest until I also tell you the name of her whom I shall call my patron saint, if so I dare call any earthly creature. Her name is Martha Worthington. I remember her as she looked in those years; I thought her beautiful then, I know she is beautiful now as she walks the Eternal City among the children she has gathered there, and listens to an everlasting echo of these words: '*Inasmuch as ye have done it unto the least of these, ye have done it unto me;* and I am happy, for as long as the New Jerusalem shall stand, I shall be what she first called me, her ' son in Christ.' Brethren, I have told you my story."

He sat down amid the profoundest silence, for tears are noiseless, and all eyes were turned upon Deacon Worthington, who sat as if turned to stone, with pale lips and startled eyes, looking as if struck by an arrow of Providence. Then he rose and said in an unsteady voice:

"Brethren, God has visited me in wrath and in mercy too. Martha Worthington was my mother. I am her unworthy son. Like Saul of Tarsus, I have been ' ignorantly kicking against the pricks,' or rather striving against the life-work of my mother. May God and my brethren forgive me. Brother Arden, pray for us all."

The young pastor did not leave them, after all ; and year by year he grew like his work, nobler and grander.

The church at Athens was filled, and if there were some "common people" among the number, the Spirit of God was there, and as it fell upon them, ennobled them all. This little church expanded, and became a power in the community, and men said, "They are a *grand people;*" some attributed it all to the preacher's wonderful eloquence, but those who knew best said, "No; it is because *they all work together with God.*" And still they gather in the lowly and poor, as well as "influential outsiders" who will come; and Deacon Worthington and his wife are happy. Year by year the dressy lady becomes less worldly, and Mrs. Everett is content, for Ada Clifton now sits in the preacher's pew, filling by the best of all rights the place of the pastor's wife.

Bro. Arden is not at all likely to leave Athens until he is called to the Heavenly City, and if he has any fear over his life now, it must have come from reading this scripture: "*Woe* unto you when all men shall speak well of you."

DEACONS AS EVANGELISTS.

A CHRISTMAS STORY.

There are two churches in Lanesboro, situated facing each other, on opposite corners. One of them has a very tall steeple, a bell, a clock, and an organ. Each and all of these ornaments have in turn been pronounced evidences of unsoundness, especially the bell and the organ; yet every Lord's-day their sound goes forth, and so do the people, who prosper in every good word and work, and some way the cause of Christ does not appear to be hindered. I say does not *appear* to be, because this I must admit; but I do not wish to be considered as defending anything so wicked and unscriptural as a steeple, a bell, or an organ.

The church across the street have never added any of these things to the simplicity of their house and worship, but the congregation has twenty-one deacons—which the other church considers just fourteen too many—and, still worse, they are guilty of the very questionable practice of observing Christmas. Every year they buy a load of turkeys and a number of loads of coal, and begin a protracted meeting on Christmas week.

The church with a steeple does not approve of it; yet the members attend the meetings of their brethren across the way, and even contribute toward the turkeys and the coal. How all this odd state of things came about is quite a story. It was really one of the most successful failures I ever knew.

Some years ago, when the church with a steeple was owned and used by the Methodists, the church across the way, on a certain Lord's day in December, began a protracted meeting. The pastor preached excellent sermons, though they were said to be a trifle too long. They were certainly earnest and sound, and intended to do a great deal more good than they succeeded in accomplishing. But the room was a little cold, and the congregation colder; the meeting did not belong to any one in particular, and, being an orphan, it died in about ten days, of neglect. The meeting closed on Friday evening. The pastor felt discouraged. Some members, who had only attended from a sense of duty, felt quietly relieved from both the exertion and the responsibility; others said the failure was a great shame. Among this latter class were the usual number of people who had done nothing whatever to advance the interests of the meeting or the church. A few of them were persons so unselfish that they had not

even once attended, to claim their share of the preaching. But these, nevertheless, thought the meetings
should have gone on, and, thinking only of the good
of others, pronounced the failure a "shame." The
people walked home in groups, talking it over; and
the next morning it was busily discussed in church
circles, with no abatement of interest. There was no
election just over, and none shortly expected, and at
the time of which I speak the mysteries of the Tam-
many Ring had not been flashed from end to end of
the Republic for the instruction of our admiring people; so, there being no rival subject, the unsuccessful
meeting was the topic in many a store and work-
shop, and on street corners, whenever two or three
had gathered together. Some laid the blame upon
the pastor; others, more merciful, divided it among
the whole twenty-one deacons. By Saturday evening
a great deal had been said which did not add to the
comfort of all concerned, and several went home to
tea with an oppressive sense of having talked too
much, and several more who ought to have felt so
did not.

With Saturday night came around the regular time
for deacons' meeting. The deacons were very slow
in gathering, and when at last eleven of them were
assembled, an outsider would have supposed that
they had met to talk over the unsuccessful meeting
again. Just as the discussion was once more pro-

gressing finely, and in a fair way to become personal and unpleasant, Deacon Headly came in with a heated look, which at once indicated him as the bearer of later news upon the distressing subject. Deacon Headly informed them that some one had told the pastor that the deacons said he was an utter failure, unfit to attempt any meeting, and not wise enough to see it. This information brought the discussion to an abrupt close, and in the silence which ensued, Deacon Headly remarked that a great deal too much had been said, considering that it was all said too late, and that it was wicked to wound the pastor's feelings, since, with all his failings, he had been quite as faithful as the deacons or the rest of the congregation. This speech met with a very hearty approval, and no one thought it worth while to remind Deacon Headly that he himself had contributed his full share of whatever talk there had been. After a few more remarks, Bro. Headly proposed that, without at all referring to the unpleasant matter, the deacons should show their kindly feelings to the pastor by making him a Christmas gift. This met with approval, and the collection was at once taken up by Deacon Headly himself. But when the money was counted, it proved to be only twenty-nine dollars. They talked over the absent deacons, but they were all poor men, not likely to increase the sum much—all except three, and these were not

over friendly to the pastor, having fallen out about
the singing, and so could not be made available.
Twenty-nine dollars! It was out of the question.
But suppose they could increase it to forty-nine, it
would still be a sum too small to express the kindly
feelings of *twenty-one* deacons. Some were in favor
of persisting in the effort; others of returning the
money to the respective deacons, lest they should
fail at last, and the story, getting out, draw down rid-
icule upon their defenseless heads. Neither party
wanted to give up, and the discussion grew hot, and
bade fair to continue, when Deacon Gray said:
"Brethren, we did not begin right; we should open
our meetings with prayer. Let us remedy the mistake at once, and see if things do not clear up. Let
us pray." Deacon Gray prayed—earnestly and devoutly, a very short prayer, not for the spread of the
gospel, nor for the Millennium, not even for sinners,
but rather for the saints. He implored wisdom to
correct all their mistakes, and love and faith enough
to guide them all into a happier future. When the
prayer was concluded, Deacon Scott proposed that,
as the money was insufficient to furnish a suitable
Christmas gift for the pastor, the deacons should seek
out all the poor connected with the church, and devote the money to providing each with a Christmas
dinner or a load of coal; also, that they should ask
the pastor's coöperation, and make him chairman of

their committee.   Never was there a more complete success.   The deacons all shook hands with Bro. Scott, and offered him a vote of thanks for his solution of the difficulty.

It was getting late, and some one spoke of adjourning; but as they all felt comfortable and friendly, they concluded to call up and dispose of the affair about the church repairs.   This was an old bone of contention.   The church had long gone without repairs, because they could not agree on the way they wanted to do it.   But to-night almost every one had a new idea, and they were soon unanimous again.   Even after this was over, they remained for a concluding prayer, and at last reached home so late that the wives of some of them thought if the church had so much business, they ought to appoint more deacons.

The next day there was a very good congregation, but the pastor looked gloomy and discouraged; and there was even bitterness in the way in which he commented on the text, "I have called, and ye have refused; I have stretched out my hand, and no man regarded."   It was plain that the preacher was "*put out*," and no one felt much better for the sermon. He concluded by reminding them that the next Wednesday was Christmas, and hoped that the folly of observing it would not make them forget that Wednesday was their prayer-meeting night.

As soon as the service was over, seventeen of the

deacons—the whole number present—led the pastor
into his study, and kept him there for half an hour.
When they came out there was a look of general
satisfaction upon the faces of the whole party, very
much as if each had proposed his favorite measure,
and carried it. The pastor's face had lost a part of
its gloom and all its bitterness, and though he found
his dinner cold, he ate it with a heartier relish than
he had eaten for a week. His wife watched him with
surprised pleasure until he went up-stairs and closed
his study door. She did not know he knelt down
and prayed over a sealed letter, and then rose up and
put it in the fire; but when he went into her room,
he stooped and kissed her, saying: "I've concluded,
after all, to decline that call; I don't think the
church here want me to leave, and some things look
a little brighter; I am not quite sure I have done my
best here yet, and I want to try it longer."

In the afternoon the pastor and the deacons all
met at the church door, and after five minutes' conversation went off in couples in different directions,
Deacon Scott closing up the rear, arm-in-arm with
the pastor.

"I do not suppose," said the former, "that we
have a very great undertaking before us; we are
blessed in not having many poor—I *think*, and I am
tolerably familiar with the church records." To this
view of the case the whole body of deacons had

practically subscribed. If they did not know of any
poor besides two or three regular pensioners, how
could there be any? But Deacon Scott knew better;
indeed, among his unsound crotchets he always held
to one—that "a loaf was a good missionary," and
that bitter poverty destroyed a great deal of piety;
hence he only replied, quietly, that a church record
was not a very good directory among the poor.

The back streets of Lanesboro were well canvassed
that Lord's day afternoon, and the committee all
went home to supper sadder and wiser men, and better, too. Deacon Gray told his wife of a poor widow
with three feeble children, who supported herself by
making nine hundred little tobacco bags for a dollar.
"Now, mother," said he, "I've promised that you
shall give them all a decent suit of things Christmas
morning, so that they can come to church—they
want to come. We divided out the work, and I selected this family as your share, for I know you will
like the poor sister."

Deacon Headly went home and told the story of a
poor woman whose husband was paralyzed. With
the aid of a consumptive daughter, this unfortunate
paid the rent of a rickety hovel and fed four children,
by making drawers at fifteen cents apiece. "Now,
my dear," he concluded, "let us take this family as
our share of this Christmas business." "But, Mr.
Headly," interrupted his wife, "I thought you set out

to find the poor *members,* and"—"Bother the poor
members!" broke in the Deacon; "so we did; but I
should feel as if we insulted the Lord Jesus himself,
if we passed by a case like this, and made a chalk-
mark on the door, ' *These are not Christians.*' There,
don't look hurt; I'm not cross, but a little—well,
tired, I suppose; and don't give me green tea to-
night."

The.pastor went home with traces of tears on his
face. He had no appetite for supper, and let his tea
get cold while he told his wife a long story. With
Bro. Scott, he had been all the afternoon on the track
of a young man who belonged to a family that
"nobody knew," *socially.* He was a recreant member, who at first had fought bravely against the disre-
pute of his family, but when the church figuratively
and literally let go his hand, had descended the
stairs of poverty and bad repute and recklessness
into sin.

They had at last found him and his mother and
four younger brothers in a miserable attic, and arrived
just in time to close the dying eyes of his father, that
old publican, who had gone to answer for the shame
and heartache which, from his own sins, he had flung
backward upon his family. He had gone where their
poverty would be considered as *his* crime, and his
drunken eldest son would be the most damning witness against him. There was nothing to be done for

the dead now—if anything could have been accomplished earlier; no one had a right to say so, since none had tried it.

There was very little comfort to offer this wretched mother; but this very, very little she had so much need of, that when she asked the pastor if he would pray for them, he kneeled down and poured out for this miserable family in one petition more fervent supplication than he had expended over the whole protracted meeting.

The preacher looked thoughtful, and, on entering his study, tore up his paper of heads for the evening discourse, and jotted down a less copious set of notes, beginning: "Define Religion—Hungry, and ye fed me—Cups of cold water—The poor saints."

The deacons persevered in their enterprise, and their work grew; their fund evaporated, and their purses grew thin. They had done so much in other directions that they fell short on the original proposition for turkeys and loads of coal. They met in groups, and talked it over; they had great faith in talking things over. Finally they agreed to approach *very carefully* the three deacons who had come to grief, and tarried there, on the singing question. The result was amazing. They found those three brethren in consultation, deciding to volunteer their assistance, having waited in vain for an invitation. Being thus reinforced, they proceeded in decorous squads to call upon all the members of that well-understood but not well-defined body called the *"influential members."* Even here they were moderately successful, and for three days Lanesboro was the center of an active missionary work, carried on strictly on the loaf-and-Bible-together principle. They went among all classes, saints and sinners. Seemingly their zeal had outgrown the original proposition. By Christmas noon a hundred homes were glad, and twenty-one deacons and one preacher were so happy and busy that their own Christmas dinner was a cold lunch, taken with their wives in the basement of the church. It was all they had time for; but dear old Sister Scott said it was the very best thing that could have happened, as it would save them all a fit of indigestion, and put them in good trim for the evening prayer-meeting. Then they drank the pastor's health, in a cup of tea made by the pastor's wife at the furnace-fire.

By this time Lanesboro began to hear of the matter, and, in accordance with the rules of gossip, the versions were interesting and various. In the evening, the editor of the Lanesboro *True Record* sent out a reporter to gather the facts, and embody them in a few spicy paragraphs.

The prayer-meeting was the most successful meeting of its kind in the annals of the church. Besides those whom Deacon Headly humorously called the "regular old guard," there were present the whole twenty-one deacons, a thing that had not occurred before since they were ordained. There were also present one or two from every family visited during the week. The widow who made tobacco-bags brought all her children. The widow whose husband was buried on Monday came with her five sons, and although she was not a Christian, she wept when her eldest son went forward, and, making his confession, renewed his broken faith to his Lord and Master.

Poor fellow! he looked so woe-begone, and in his face were marks of a bitter conflict. Deacon Scott rose, with a look as if a mountain could not have held him down, and said: "Brethren and sisters, let us too make our just confession to this brother; we forgot our brotherly love—we forgot to help him bear his burdens. Let us now pledge the united effort of this congregation to repair our error. Strong drink is his enemy; let us consider it the enemy of the church. We will fight his battles with him. Let us ask our Lord to forgive our past mistakes, and open our eyes and our hearts to the duty of bearing each other's burdens."

To the endorsement of this sentiment the whole congregation rose, and some brother, who was not the choir-leader, and therefore not authorized, began the song, "Come, let us anew." It was just at this moment that the reporter slipped in, and taking in with a rapid glance the crowded room, long rows of influential members and long rows of poor, with a plentiful sprinkling of those whom he knew to be outsiders, concluded to remain. At the conclusion, the pastor simply reminded them of the appointment to-morrow night. This appointment was already understood to be an invitation from the deacons to all interested members to discuss a revision of the poor fund.

The next morning the following item of news appeared in the Lanesboro *True Record:*

"A CHRISTMAS REVIVAL.—Our friends, the Disciples, have been carrying on a protracted meeting for the last two weeks, with great success. The strange part of it is that they have kept it so quiet; yet their meetings continue with unabated interest. They have so thoroughly converted *themselves*, that even their Methodist brethren ought to be satisfied. They have organized a relief committee, whose field embraces the whole city. We do n't know much about religion; we have n't time; but we like this kind; it looks substantial: something like the definition given by the apostle Luke or James—our readers will know which. The seats are free, and we shall drop in whenever our duties will permit."

Whether or not the reporter did "drop in," did not transpire; but so many others did, that the committee meeting was obliged to adjourn to the large room up-stairs. But five hundred people, with a liberal admixture of outsiders, was a very impracticable body for a committee. So the pastor, by common consent, filled the office of preacher instead of chairman. At the close there were three confessions and one baptism, one of them the widow whose son was reclaimed.

During the preparation for the baptism the officers held a hurried consultation. Deacon Headly was excited, Deacon Scott in tears, and the old elder could not speak for emotion. Whatever the movement was, it was evident that they were all unanimous and eager, and at the close of the services, the preacher said, without further explanation: "These meetings will be continued until further notice, and we hope the friends who have bid us God-speed, will continue to sit with us from night to night; and," he added, in a strangely earnest tone, "let not the brethren forget to pray, lest the Lord depart from our midst."

Again they went home in groups, with a new topic, of wonderful interest, to talk over. "*Bless me*," said dear old Sister Green, "I had no idea the meetings were so interesting, or I should have come last week, though my rheumatism was so bad."

So the meetings continued. At the end of a week the Methodists began to come over now and then. At the end of a month, a score of them had united with the church. They were charmed with a religion at once so simple and liberal, and yet so spiritual, and the *promoter of such good results;* this last was the keystone in the arch of perfection, and as long as the heavens are above the earth, it will be.

The Methodists acknowledged that they had never done the Disciples justice.

The Methodist preacher tried to stem the tide for a time, and then went to hear, then studied, prayed, hesitated, and at last went over the way, carrying with him the whole weight of his pious precept and godly life, and forty more of his membership.

By this time the Disciples were wise enough to set the full value upon this new element of full-grown zeal which came over like a tide of strength from the Methodists across the way. They did not reduce the preacher "to ranks," and consign him to a pew, but, being satisfied that he was "sound," they put him in the pulpit at once to assist their well-nigh exhausted pastor. They thought it only just to continue his salary; and so the wondering people of Lanesboro beheld a church of Disciples with two pastors in one congregation, *a thing very rare among that people, who do not always have one.* But as no one discovered that the practice was unsound or unscriptural, no trouble ensued, and things remained in this shape till the end of the year. During this time the congregation had nearly doubled, and they had established a large and separate poor fund, and a regular visiting committee. About the middle of December the deacons held a meeting with closed doors, inviting only two or three influential members who came from the Methodists, and that pastor.

The result was a request by the deacons that the congregation would celebrate the anniversary of their last year's success, by giving turkeys and coal to the poor, assuming the expense thereof. The church agreed willingly, and voted to do it every year.

On the following week the deacons and the Methodist element had a great many private conferences, on a subject kept entirely secret.

On the Lord's day before Christmas, a heavy looking document was laid on the communion table, which every one seemed to know contained something of importance. At the close of the service, the regular pastor opened it, and read as follows: "The twenty-one deacons of this congregation, being desirous of making this anniversary of a happy improvement in church affairs a landmark in this congregation, do hereby present, with our Christian love, and as our personal gift, a title deed to the meeting-house across the way, known as the 'Methodist Church,' for which we have paid the sum of six thousand dollars.

" We would further state that in this purchase we are indebted to the kind offices of our Methodist converts, through whom we obtained these liberal terms, as a compromise of their just claim on the church property.

" We also beg leave to recommend, when this large congregation shall divide, that the old pastor be called to fill his old pulpit across the way, with the assurance of our entire love and Christian confidence."

The proposition was put and carried, amid tears of rejoicing over all the crowded assembly ; and no one doubted that *" the Lord was in the thing."*

They made an equal division of everything, and the congregation divided, generally following the preacher they liked best. Most of the Methodists went back to their old house.

Some one proposed that the bell and the organ be taken out, but the Methodist converts requested of the united congregations that they might be retained. In a new house they would have done without them ; but old memories centered *there*, and they did not like to see their old home dismantled. The request was made in the spirit of brotherly love, and in the same spirit it was decided to retain them, stipulating, only, that they should *have only congregational singing, and that the organ should always be played by a member of the church, and the music be under the supervision of the eldership.* This met the views of all, and was the *nearest approach to a creed* that they ever made. Judging the tree by its fruit, the Lord of Hosts went with them into the church across the way —went with them, and tarried in their midst.

ORDINATION.

I have just witnessed what I believe to be a very unusual ceremony, a regular apostolic ordination, by the laying on of hands. As an ordinance to be observed at the present day by our brotherhood, it is almost new to me, for which reason I suppose it may be to some, if not many, of your readers.

To suppose any member of a Christian church ignorant respecting any public ordinance of that body, would seem to presuppose a very late induction into the kingdom, or a very great and culpable amount of ignorance; but this would be wrong, since in what is considered the largest, and certainly not the least intelligent and scriptural congregation in Kentucky, there has not been a ceremonial ordination, as I learn, for thirty years; yet, in one-third that length of time, one has seen in this church, officers elected and inducted, I will not say into office, but certainly into the grooves of official duty; and if any one noted a lack of ceremony, certainly it was not commented on, and I am forced to doubt if any, or many, did. And yet now that we have had a regular scriptural imposition of hands, all parties appear to be equally as well satisfied as before.

Early in the present year, the church at Fourth and Walnut streets, in this city, elected a number of new officers, to be added to the old body, which was considered insufficient for the needs of the church. After the election, the third Lord's-day in February was announced as the day for the scriptural ordination. On the preceding Lord's-day, the subject of discourse was the doctrine of fasting and prayer, and the laying on of hands. While nothing scriptural can be absolutely new, yet some points in this sermon left—at least upon the less informed among us—the impression of novelty. To read, '' And when they had fasted and prayed they laid their hands upon them," and ''They ordained them elders in every church,'' produces upon the mind a different effect from that of being exhorted to prepare for such an imposition of hands upon the brothers who sit before and behind you, and that, too, when the brother at your right has been an accepted officer for twenty-five years, without the fact or expectation of any such ceremony. To return to this sermon: the usual scripture selections preceded the usual arguments concerning fasting and prayer; and then followed a very careful comparison of texts, and some very clear, forcible arguments concerning the apostolic example, and the present duty and purpose of the laying on of hands, all tending to the conclusion that it is the only scriptural mode of induction into office. And certainly, while the argument stood in array before one, it seemed difficult to believe the fact that for a period of thirty years a large, intelligent and sincere body of Christians had allowed this ordinance to drop as entirely out of sight, or out of use, as if it died with the apostolic age. The address concluded with very careful, earnest and detailed instructions for a fast, to be observed on the next Lord's-day morning, throughout the membership, without exception, unless such exceptions decided to remain away from the ceremony of ordination and the house of God. The exhortation to this fast, as precedent to the prayers and imposition of hands, was made in the name of such authority, and with such earnest insistence, that if any member hesitated about observing it, such hesitation was not born of that hour, but afterward, when the echo of those sternly solemn words had died upon the ear.

The sermon and exhortation were certainly scriptural; and yet it is undeniable that a strong, forcible and authoritative attitude of speech has much to do with the strength of the impression made upon the hearers, the arguments remaining the same.

On the following Lord's-day, Bro. Milligan, who had been invited to officiate at the ceremony, delivered, as announced, instead of the usual sermon, a

short address concerning the occasion. After reading the Scripture referring to the selection and setting apart of officers, he made a little, very brief,
quiet and impressive comment thereon, treating the
subject as if it were, in the mind and conduct of the
church, a familiar and oft-practiced ceremony, and his
main object were only to concentrate the attention of
the congregation upon the solemn work before them.
I can not refrain from giving you, in substance,
his concluding remarks, hoping I may not seriously
mar them in quoting from memory. Though very
simple, they impressed me as containing the "golden
rule" of church organization and government.
"Brethren," he concluded, "this is no one-sided
covenant. If you have elected these officers, you
have committed yourselves to uphold and assist them
in all things, so far as they work according to divine
instruction. If it is their duty to teach, it is your
duty to be taught. If it is their duty to rule, it is
your duty to be ruled, as far as they teach and rule
according to the holy oracles. If it is their duty to
do works of charity, it is your duty to make all the
necessary provision for that work. They are not indeed appointed to do the work of the congregation,
but for the purpose of so organizing it, that it may
most efficiently do the work of the Lord. He is not
the greatest general who does the most fighting himself, but he who so organizes his men as to be able

to throw the whole strength of his army in any given
direction in the most effectual manner."

Bro. Milligan then stated, in substance, that as the
authority to appoint officers was by God invested in
the church as a body, only by that body could the
authority to ordain them be delegated to him. Then,
somewhat after the manner of a marriage ceremony,
he propounded two sets of impressive questions concerning their solemn, conscientious and prayerful in-
tentions, first to the church, who responded by rising ;
then to the body of officers elect, whose responses
were given verbally in concert. In the case of the
congregation, the question was repeated in the negative for the hearing of any conscientious objection.
Then followed prayer; after which the officers elect
remained kneeling in a half-circle around the speaker's
stand, Bro. Milligan, repeating, "And after they had
prayed they laid their hands upon them," laid his
hands upon each of the fifteen heads, repeating, "By
the authority of the Lord Jesus Christ, vested in the
church, and by them delegated to me, you are thus
ordained and set apart as Elder (or Deacon) of this
congregation, by the laying on of our hands. May
the Lord bless you, and make you a blessing to the
church over which you are appointed." With the
hand of Bro. Milligan was laid two others, those of
Bro. Hopson and another Elder, newly elected here,
but who had been ordained, and had endured long

years of service elsewhere; and, as the three hands were laid successively upon each bowed head, the solemn formula of words, almost without variation, repeated over and over again by Bro. Milligan. Then a blessing was implored upon all, collectively, and the ordination was over, and gave place to that royal banquet which is only served to priests and kings, and at whose head, sitting invisible, is the Lord of Hosts, and the transfigured Christ of Calvary.

In this account I have endeavored to be very exact in detail, for two reasons, which are indeed the two purposes for which this letter is written: First, because the simplest description would be the most interesting to those who have never witnessed a similar ceremony, but could not but fail to have heard endless opinions and arguments concerning it; secondly, I do not presume to have any comments to offer, or opinions to hold—for, ordination not being a matter which, strictly speaking, is connected with our daily Christian duty, the more humble are content to keep very close to shore, believing that He who gave inspired rules will give his Church and under-rulers wisdom to apprehend them. Still, as I have been taught that the straight road to knowledge is thickly set with interrogation points, I now wish, if you will allow me, to set up here on this subject, a number of those crooked little mile-stones. If I crowd them confusedly together, or put them in awkward con-

nection, please consider that I am seeking information only because I want it myself; yet boldly, in
the consciousness that any one holding out a light
upon this subject will flash it into many more eyes
than mine.

First, as I have said, the Scripture-reading will,
of course, satisfy any one that ordination, by the
foregoing ceremony, is scriptural. Then, why is it so
rare—some churches never practicing it at all, another resuming it after thirty years intermission,
without (so far as I can learn) any professions of new
light upon the subject, or confessions of neglect—
said church having, in the intervening time, made officers, and, within ten years, sent out two regular
preachers from among its private members, giving
each, instead of an ordination, a few words of solemn
charge, exhortation and advice, given informally by
the official speaker, who, on one of the occasions,
said substantially: We do not ordain this brother;
we have no authority so to do; but we simply pray
for him, and commend him to the work? Now, if
ordination was necessary thirty years ago, and was
necessary in the same church, on the third Lord's-
day in February, 1870, was it not also in the case of
those evangelists and officers coming between, and in
other churches which do not practice it at all? Was
it not a sin of commission thirty years, and this
week, or a sin of omission ten years ago?

It will be seen that these queries are chiefly confined to the practice of one church, not at all because they are personal to that church, but because the history of its practice is open to me, and fairly represents the subject of inquiry.

One brother replies: "It is not well to spend much time in endeavors to decide this matter, for ordination is a subject concerning which there has always been a difference of opinion." But this advice would lead one to approve and coöperate in ordination or its omission, or, in other words, to subscribe to the doctrine of non-essentials, in the matter of church ordinances, a doctrine against which the Christian Church has waged uncompromising warfare from the beginning.

If this ceremony is to be observed or not, opinion deciding the matter, then if we practice it at all we practice a ceremony in the name of Christ, yet resting professedly on the shifting basis of opinion; and though this opinion may, in turn, be based upon apostolic example, yet as long as opinion professedly underlies the ordinance, it becomes a sort of ritualistic addition to scripture text, and it is only yielding one step more to opinion, to lay hands upon children, adding, at discretion, a few drops of water. Of course, here we get entirely out of sight of a "thus saith the Lord," or thus did the apostles; and we are glad to return to the words, "And when they

had ordained them elders in every church," etc. But
here one of the most careful Bible-students, and, indeed, one of the most intelligent Christians in our
brotherhood at large, says that this is one of those
apostolic institutions which were given and intended
only for the safe conduct of the church in its infancy,
when there were no holy oracles to consult; and in
the absence of the apostles, who represented in person the inspiration of that age, every question which
arose would be liable to create division and anarchy.
For this there would seem to be the shadow of an
argument in Acts vi. 1, and the context.

Now, what is there to say against this brother's
view of things? If he is right, then we get back to
the dilemma of finding ourselves practicing not only
a non-essential, but an obsolete ordinance, and making for its observance a preparation throughout the
membership more solemn and general than is made
for any other ordinance of the church, scarcely ex-
cepting the Lord's Supper. If he is wrong, then
does not the neglect or non-practice of this ordinance
show that we are diluting the faith with opinion, or
stand divided upon an essential?

Of course, prefatory to anything else, you will first
reply, "Ordination is not a gospel to be preached,
or a cross to be taken up, and the lines of our daily
Christian duty do not cross it." I know it. Yet I
feel, in every case where there is a command involv-

ing the fulfillment of the smallest part of "all right-eousness," there must be a point of sight from which it stands revealed in incontrovertible distinctness. That point in this case I wish and wait to see. Not seeing clearly, I still believe, but in a very vague, unsatisfactory way, vainly endeavoring to reconcile ancient example with modern practice, and, mean-while, I stand in unarmed defensive against a whole battalion of sectarian ritualism, at whose head is that able tactician, non-essential.

LITTLE BY LITTLE.

Some one says: "There is no man suddenly excellently good, or extremely evil."

Practically, we all know this, and yet we are forever expecting to be, ourselves, an astonishing exception to this rule. If it were not a matter affecting our eternal interests, it would be matter for laughter —in fact, a gigantic joke—to observe the prayerful, tearful New Year's Eve and other resolutions which we make, perfectly sure that we *intend* to keep them, yet knowing in our inmost hearts that we are not likely to. And why not? Simply because we invariably set out with the intention of becoming angels, and at once devote ourselves to pluming our wings for heavenly flights of grace and self-denial.

But all at once life does not seem to answer our expectations at all; it is not a "far flight into the heavenly air," but a simple matter of climbing, for which our wings are ill-adapted; our plumage becomes draggled, and by the time we come seriously to consider the matter of giving up wings in favor of feet, we often find that we have fallen a little in the rear of those poor redeemed sinners who have never tried to do more than *march* on " to the prize of the high calling."

All this is a little disturbing, especially when some one who never made a failure, because he never made an effort, quietly recounting our shortcomings, says: " Do not even the publicans so ?"

There is a spice of malice in the way the world re- minds us of it, every time we set out to forestall the millennium, and succeed in—a failure. But, after all, this is a bitter tonic that may do us good.

We know by intuition that effort never ends in utter loss, and slowly we come to discern that Chris- tianity is not a matter of resolutions kept or unkept, not a matter of wings or of feet, but a matter of the daily growth of the soul—of the daily tension of spiritual bone and muscle—a daily bondage of our evil nature—a daily " keeping of our body under," and a daily crowning of the " holy guest," the Christ within us.

Christianity is not so much a journey heavenward as a preparation for a resurrection. Nor do we fail when we break these resolutions which we intend all along to keep. Not at all. To have succeeded in keeping them, might have destroyed us ; to succeed in *trying*, may give us heavenly strength. Does any one doubt this ? Then let him recall just how he felt when he failed, just a little short of his work. We can tell how he looked : he was gazing upward with such an earnest, longing, tearful gaze, that if God had deemed it for the best, a legion of angels might have come down to help him over that one inch of ground. But this was not the end in view. Yet he had grown better with the effort, a little stronger, a little less worldly, a little nearer God, a little better fitted for the infinite possibilities of an endless life, as well as "a day's march nearer home."

"PUT OUT THE LIGHT."

Between the following facts there exists a singularly perfect and consistent relation. We commend it to the prayerful thought of all those who have felt their hearts grow warmer under the pressure of little heads, and all those who have felt their hearts grow sadder with the coming of feet that have wandered into sin:

"The Board of Public Instruction, in the city of St. Louis, have passed a resolution providing 'that at all examinations, exhibitions and celebrations pertaining to the public schools, neither prayers nor benedictions shall be offered by any clergyman of any religious denomination, nor shall the singing of any religious hymns be permitted; because such acts impress upon examinations, exhibitions and celebrations a religious sectarian character;' and the Common Council of the city have adopted a statute providing for the licensing of houses of prostitution."

Thus have these "City Fathers," in whose hands lie the interests of a great and growing city, deliberately ignored and excluded the pure and good, and recognized and accepted the foul and evil.

Christianity aside, they have committed a crime. Even the brutal Robespierre once said: "If there were no God, a wise legislator would invent one, to restrain the license of the people." But these "wise legislators" have solved the problem in another way: instead of a *God to restrain* " the license of the people," they have decided to *provide*, by municipal law, for a people's *license unrestrained.*

From the contemplation of these *two facts,* and their relation to each other, even decent moral sentiment turns with indignation and disgust, discerning the filthy odor of "free Paris," in the days of Mirabeau, rather than the virtuous liberty of a sane republican commonwealth. To men who prostitute the powers of a sacred trust, and thus wantonly chase liberty through the gates of godless freedom into licensed crime and shame, the prayer and praise of little children must be—should be—*foreign things.*

If these men of St. Louis had not, by their own act, shut themselves out of the pale of Christianity, we might, in reference to their late decision, quote: "They love darkness rather than light, because their deeds are evil." But though they have swept the Scriptures out of their way, as did the heroes of the French Republic, like them they may still retain a taste for poetic truth, and so appreciate the following oft-quoted description of their own moral retrograde:

> "Vice is a monster of so frightful mien,
> As to be hated needs but to be seen;
> Yet seen too oft, familiar with her face,
> We first endure, then pity, then embrace."

They have insulted Christianity, stared virtue out of countenance, and outraged decency while *selling indulgences* to vice ; and then, what wonder—they have *put out the light.* There is no gospel to preach to *such* men, until they learn by the terrible logic of facts, and reap in the spiritual degradation and bodily defilement of their *own* children, what they have sown in this their godless seed-time to the foul demon of lust.

CHRISTMAS.

Christmas, or *Christ-mass*, as its name indicates, had its origin in the early history of the idolatrous Roman apostasy. As an institution, it is supposed to have been founded by Pope Telesphorus, who died A. D. 138.

It is recorded that three times the Roman Church discovered infallibly the date of our Saviour's birth, and each time fixed it on a different day. Finally, in the fourth century, the question was again disturbed, and at the urgent entreaty of St. Cyril, of Jerusalem, Pope Julius I. issued an order for another investigation concerning the day of Christ's nativity. At last, after due discussion and inquiry, directed by *infallible wisdom*, this migratory anniversary rested at the midnight hour of the twenty-fifth of December. The chief grounds for this decision were the tables of the censors in the archives of Rome, a testimony which, strangely enough, was considered as inadequate then as now, by the fathers themselves. Yet since that time the twenty-fifth of December has ruled by the "divine right" of Popes, and has been crowned throughout all Christendom as a very monarch of days, reigning alike in the heart of the church and the world.

Fifteen centuries ago the Roman peasants flocked into Rome to celebrate Christmas morning, and still the Swabian minstrels come down from the mountains around Rome and Naples, to sing carols at the shrines of the Virgin, and hear the three masses said, at midnight, dawn and morning.

Only a little later, the early Germans decorated their Christmas trees of yew, just as we do now; and bedizened a merry peasant with fur and finery, and loaded him with toys, a living, human Santa Claus.

The twining of the holly and the oak at Christmas, marks the blending of this festival with the pagan legends of the Druids, when the barbarous but noble old Britons kept the first Yuletides on the soil of Britain ; and the Yule-log was burned and the wassail-bowl went round among our Anglo-Saxon ancestors before the Norman Conquest.

Century after century Christmas changes a little with time and place, but never loses its character of hearty human sympathy, as a leveler of worldly distinctions, an exhortation to all human charity, and a gospel of peace and love.

From the time when Pope Julius I. fixed the date of the world's redemption, to the time when Pius IX., a bowed old man, bore out upon his shoulders from the Vatican forever the ark of the "mother

Church;" from the time of the Norman Conquest to
the fall of Napoleon III., Christmas bells have been
rung, and Christmas carols have been sung, and
Christmas greetings have gone down the centuries
and around the world.

In vain our wise men tell us that Christmas is a
myth, the merest ghost of a legend; still we point to
Christmas printed in capital letters in every almanac,
and like the words ANNO DOMINI placed before the
date on the title-page of an infidel book, we refute
them without an argument, and triumph over them
with our *Merry Christmas.*

We sit down conscientiously to teach our children
that, as a Christian festival, it is but adding unto sacred things an idol bearing the mark of the Beast, an
idol still preserved amid the debris of institutions
that fell with the shock of the Reformation, and then
go on decorating Christmas trees and giving Christmas gifts, and roasting turkeys. And when the
happy toil and laborious mirth is all over, these same
little ones find us in our own cozy rooms, buried in a
great arm chair, with our feet on the fender, tranquilly digesting our Christmas dinner, and reading—
Dickens' Christmas stories. As we follow the fortunes
of little Dot or Polly, we think what a beautiful
thing Christmas is, and have no idea of being inconsistent. Of course not—*we* are never inconsistent.
But Christmas is the very heart and soul of those

exquisite sermons on the text of humanity—those
sermons which rise so high above worldly philosophy
that they just touch the horizon of Divine Truth;
and for an hour, like all the rest of the world, we
forget that Dickens is—yes, *is*—an apostle of humanity, and not a disciple of Christ—at best but a
sweet alien voice crying in the wilderness of selfishness and sin, to make the path more straight for the
second coming of the Lord.

When we were young, the Christmases were a
long way apart, and very slow in coming, but like
the sun that shines afar off, they cast a golden halo
half around the year; so that there was only a short
twilight of unexpectant, uneventful life between the
Fourth of July and Christmas week, the two great
holidays of the year.   But we have grown older and
wiser since then, and, coming as it does, oftener
now, we have scanned it more carefully, and discovered that there is actually nothing Christian about it.
It is a kind of Melchisedec among days, beginning
with nothing, and referring to nothing, except that
in a vague kind of *retrospective prophecy* (we hope that
phrase may be construed as meaning something) it
refers back to the advent of Christ; and certainly as
far as Time is concerned, it bids fair to be without
"end of days."   Suppose it is not a Christian festival, at least it is a festival of humanity; let us keep
this one day sacred to human sympathy.

Some time we know that the babe was born in Bethlehem of Judæa, and it is good for the world to spend one day looking back to that central axis of all time past, present, and to come, the great miracle-day when heaven and earth were wedded, and God first wore our human flesh.

We look from the mouldering battle-fields of our own Republic, to the blood-stained valleys of Lorraine, and from beleaguered Paris to the six hundred newly-made widows in Berlin, and see no peace on earth. The horrors of the crucifixion are shadowed more than the nativity, and despite the empty Vatican, the Roman sword is still unsheathed in the old world and the new, to wound the living body of Christ.

Ah! if the angels that heralded the birth of our Lord could only come again with the power to sing the fierce passions of the world to sleep, it would be like opening the door of the millennium or the gates of heaven; and whatever is most like it must be good. If for one day we will put away all malice and strife, all anxiety and sorrow, all greed of gain and lust of power, and spend Christmas day like pure and merry children, we shall be sure to hear on Christmas night the angels singing, at least in our hearts, ''Peace on earth and good will to men.''

Let us put ourselves in tune with this merry song that is sung wherever civilization has borne the cross.

From Rome to the Rocky Mountains, from Merry
England, across the globe to Australia, where the
December midsummer brings Christmas and the
roses together, and happy children watch through
the long summer Christmas Eve—Christmas, Merry
Christmas, rings round the world.

WHAT OUR SOULS TELL US.

What do our souls tell us? Oh, many things, possibly; but that depends *entirely* upon education. In other words, thoughts, of which we build our faith and opinions, are the direct products of the material thrown by accident or intention into that great thinking-machine, the human mind.

Some people believe this, and rely upon it to such an extent that they regard their children as if their heads were hollow, and, like unfurnished rooms, were waiting to be fitted out with just such thoughts and feelings as their parents' mental wealth or poverty suggests as appropriate furniture for the dwelling of the young soul.

Some vital question of life is discussed, and you say: "I thought long over this matter once, and at last came to this and that conclusion, and I intend to instill into my children just the opinion I *formed for myself.*" Very likely you do, for you are an egotist; very well meaning and unconscious of it, but still an egotist. The cause is this: you were taught in early youth to believe many things which, had it dared, your reason would have rejected then—but it did not;

for your parents were true, good people, and you
grew up to believe that all their views and opinions
were a part of that goodness from which it would be
sacrilege in you to depart.

So time went on, and your soul lived in the old
house furnished with the faith of your fathers, every
article complete; but year by year it became more
unsatisfactory and inconvenient, until one day in despair you turned out every article of the old faith, and
fitted it up with a new set of opinions for yourself.
You had often before been tempted to do this, but
you were deterred by reflecting how wise and good
those parents were; and some way, when you
thought of this, or, indeed, when you thought of
them at all in connection with the unwieldy furniture
of your soul-house, every article grew symmetrical
again.   Then you gave up for the time the project of
refitting, until at last you 'decided that it was only
the lights and shadows of memory that played tricks
with your eyes to deceive your reason ; and, fortifying
yourself with the old argument (that is so often un-
true in its application) that each generation is wiser
than the last, with one mighty effort you turned
every article of the old faith out of doors, and wondered how you could have put up with it so long,
and how it ever could have seemed for one moment
anything but unreasonable.   The true reason was,
that, without knowing it, you recognized the fitness

and harmony of the old views of things when you thought of them in connection with the grand spirits who had dwelt among them.

The unwieldy furniture that encumbered your soul in its free passage from room to room of your thought-palace, was but a part of the expression of their massive characters.

Upon the broad tables they spread out plans of human life which your delicate hands and feeble muscles could never work out, and in the massive chairs their solid virtues sat in state, and harmony was over all.

But when all this was bequeathed to you—ah! there was the mistake—you found yourself advocating views you did not live up to, and professing opinions not honestly your own, for they were not the outgrowth of your character, and they would have embarrassed your spirit forever. In your own blind way you saw this, and emptied your soul-chambers of it all. And what did you put in its place? Something better and more satisfactory, of course! This is doubtful; for how could you, who had never thought for yourself in all your life, make the first effort a success? But you observed one rule: that was, to get as far as possible from the original style and plan. You were tired of the stern old furniture your soul grew up with. The very shadows lay like great beams across the pathway of your restless fancy, and forthwith you furnished your house with a faith that did not even bear the pressure of your own heart as you tried to settle down upon it, although you had chosen it not only for rest in life, but for repose in death. So it is likely that your first set of opinions did not long outlast the wear and tear of your restless soul pacing up and down the halls of thought.

Then you began a series of repairs, patching up old opinions with new ones ; for a faith we choose for ourselves we are not apt wholly to renounce. This repairing went on for years ; but, being possessed of considerable depth and strength of character, you at last settled down into a state of tolerable composure, and enjoyed the first rest your soul had ever known. Your opinions are all decidedly comfortable articles of furniture, each in its place, bearing its true relation to truth and you. If you have some little weakness in the shape of fancies, you are not now ashamed to range them in a pleasant row on your mantelpiece, like little China dogs and horses. Suppose they are childish and silly, as you half suspect them to be, you do not care, for the rest of the furniture will not frown them down or stare them out of countenance, for everything in the room is on good terms with everything else, because all is on the best of terms with you. Look around. All is satisfactory—yes, very,

from the little China dogs and horses on the mantel,
to the great mirror of truth, before which you com-
pose your soul's dress every day, and take an extra
look now and then, to be sure that your "mantle of
charity" is not awry.

But best of all the furniture in your soul's dwelling, is the great arm-chair of your religious faith. It
is not as straight-backed as your father's, but more
like the one in which your mother used to sit; not
quite like hers, because it is yours.   But it is much
the same; and when you are world-weary and task-
worn, your soul turns to this precious thing, and your
heart leaps forward to the sweet repose as the wide
expanse of arms seems a visible picture of the holy
words: "Come unto me all ye that are weary and
heavy laden, and I will give you rest."   What a
beautiful, blessed rest!   There is nothing like it on
this side of heaven.   To be at peace with your own
soul, while it goes singing up and down the broad
halls of its palace-home, or sits down to rest in the
great arm-chair of your Christian faith, where often
it comes for repose, and where sometime it hopes
to die.

Well, you view this home which your soul has
fitted up for itself, after years of struggle and change
and toil, and you say: "My children's souls shall
not struggle as mine has done for rest.   I will begin
at once, and teach them to believe what I believe,

and think as I think." But here is your mistake. They are not exactly like you, and their souls would be restless where yours is at peace; and do not be shocked if even your old arm-chair would require a little refitting before they would find it a faith in which to rest and die. They will differ from you even in their views of religion. Let them do it. They can not differ much, if both are right. All truth is a unit, and all faith must be the same; it differs only in the opinions with which we deck it out. Still you can not give your child your faith; he must find it for himself. Do not seal him with the infant baptism of prejudice and error.

God is calling every human soul; he calls your child. It may be through a way your feet have never trod. But be silent; keep truth before him, and falsehood and prejudice behind; tear up, as you would a noxious weed, every root of sophistry. Keep the soil of his heart soft and free, and the dews of heaven will water it. This is work enough for you to do. Do not try to form the plant; that is God's work, not yours. Keep every evil thing away; let the sunshine of God's love and yours shine upon the plant, and all will be well. God speaks to him; do not dare to interpret the sacred message. Tell him where the truth is found, and let him talk with God; then retire, and to reassure yourself, repeat: "He has hid these things from

the wise and prudent, and revealed them unto
babes."

As surely as God speaks to your child, he will answer; that is his faith. It is pure and perfect and
simple, and identical in all essential points with the
faith of every human soul who has listened to God
alone, unbiased by the voice of man, who has dared
to be his interpreter.

The formation of our religious faith is the most
thrilling of all the important soul-changes through
which our beings pass; but it would be well indeed
if all our opinions came to us in this unbiased way.
"What!" you say, "am I not to mold my child according to my own ideas and preferences?" No;
certainly not. You must not expect your child to
accept your views for no better reason than *because
they are yours*. If he is educated properly, the time
will come when he must accept them if they stand
the test of truth; if they do not, he never will. He
may try and cheat himself into the belief that he
does, but they will wage an eternal warfare with his
own convictions, or else float lightly upon the sur-
face of his mind, while he never dives deep enough
to find a genuine idea of his own.

"Then," you say, "our children are not to believe and sympathize with us at all." Yes; certainly
they will, for like begets like, and our children
inherit from us peculiarities of mind and character

that will naturally incline them to think and feel as we do in many things besides matters of right and wrong, where, of course, we meet upon the common ground of truth. They will be like us in many respects, and probably they would be more like us still, if we were more *like ourselves*, our *natural* selves ; more as we would have been had not early education, wrongly directed, changed our character in after-life. But they are still enough like us to commune with us in all our thoughts—all pure, good thoughts —and learn wisdom from our experience ; and unless we are arbitrary bigots, the communion will not be the less sweet because they can not yet grasp all we grasp, nor because we can not force the pure water of their reason up the rugged hill of our eccentricities.

You know what it is to fight against something you can not believe, and do n't see why you should, and to struggle against something you must believe, and do n't see why you should not. You have toiled over the road—do not force them to travel it. After all, the surest way to make them differ from you, is to endeavor to make them think exactly like you.

Some souls can not bear too great a pressure, and your pious, patient efforts to lead your child up the steep, rugged way of Calvinism, out of the slough of total depravity in which you assure him that he stands, may offend his reason, and end at last in

making him an infidel. Other efforts, equally well
intended, may result in a hopeless dissatisfaction, as
though his life were set to the wrong music ; an endless longing for the key-note of the true music
which, through the weary march of life, his straining
ear never catches, but in discordant notes that drown
the hymn of the angels, that else would lure him up
to heaven.

What do our souls tell us ? Many, many things
which we would be all the better for hearing, and
which, if listened to, would bear us many soul-
leagues nearer heaven. But in early infancy we begin
with our philosophy and religion to drown the
"still small voice" of the young soul which, if we
allowed it speech, would speak in the language of
God, from whom it so lately came. We take it for
granted that Satan begins at once at one ear, to pour
all manner of wickedness into the heart of a child ;
and we see no other way to turn the balance but by
pouring all manner of righteousness into the other.
This is the theory ; as if life were a race as well as a
battle between the powers of good and evil, and the
child a passive prize to be contended for, If this
were true, we see at once our immense disadvantage ;
for, while Satan and his promptings are wholly bad
and wrong, we ourselves are never sure that our influence is wholly good and right. Our principles
may be in general quite correct, but we who have

been in the world so long, often mar the great truths of God by giving them expression in the dialect of earth ; in other words, discolor and distort them with a little prejudice and sophistry.

We may quote Scripture for every position we take ; but so did Satan eighteen hundred years ago, and it is wonderful with what success his followers have quoted it ever since. But this is our fault, not God's ; for among all its perfections, the crowning glory of the Bible is, that it is a perfect compilation of answers to every question with which the human mind reaches out after Deity. But from early youth we, or those who educate us, mix with the "good seed" so much error and prejudice, it is not singular that the wheat and tares grow up together in the best of hearts ; and when they ripen, they fall together into the hearts of the next generation, to produce in time another harvest ; and so on forever, in endless succession, come the seedtime and harvest of error. This error, too, is not that of which the world takes cognizance, but the more respectable and pretentious sins of prejudice, bigotry and pride. Yet God has commanded us to be perfect, and we must be if we expect to enter heaven. Of course we shall often be overtaken in some sins as long as we remain on earth, but it must not be deliberately and systematically that we sin. The truth is not so far from us as we are from it. God never leaves himself without a witness in the human heart, to say amen to all his words : and in the education of our children, let us be careful how we set aside or do violence to this divine witness, who is our only hope in the unequal contest with Satan. If a child is crippled or deformed, how we grieve over the physical blight ; and yet how often we deform the soul, whose nature it is to grow erect and fair! How many persons who aim to teach their children morality and religion, distort them with selfishness, worldly wisdom and prejudice, until at last, when the backbone of their moral sense will bear no more curvature, it breaks, and they go crawling through life, moral cripples.

In vain will God spread out the illumined pages of his revelation to a blind and distorted reason.

God is a grand builder. In all his works there is no failure. In the dim ages before time began, there was no light because there was no eye to receive it ; but when the eyes of Creation were breaking from their long slumber, light was born ; and when reason came forth, truth was developed.

Call it reason or conscience, it is the same ; and it will surely guide us on to heaven, unless we use it for a sail instead of a rudder ; and then, although the tide is setting heavenward, adverse winds may drift us on to the rocks of Death. But the principle always remains the same ; and in the beautiful adaptation of our senses to the revelations of Nature, and our reason to the revelations of God, lie our hopes of wisdom in this world, and happiness hereafter.

A very common-sense writer in the *Atlantic Monthly* says that whatever has, in some form, been believed by men in all ages of the world, must at the bottom have some great truth. We might take the converse of this, and say that every great fundamental truth must, in some way, assert itself to the human mind, at least in the form of a question. All races and ages of men have had some belief, however shadowy, in a divine Being who embodies all power and wisdom. Going back to the age of Socrates, it is doubtful if he owed his persecution as much to the disbelief of his persecutors, as to their internal conviction of the sublime truth for which he died. Men are rarely persecuted for error as they are for truth.

Without believing in what is called "natural religion," still, account for it as we may, it is impossible not to know that, from the dawn of reason, the young soul is filled with eager questions, unformed and shadowy, but yet bearing on the great subject of divinity and immortality. These are questions we must answer ; these are the roots we must nourish. Not in our own way and our own time, but in God's way, in his very words, and at the time when the young soul asks them—not before, or the answers will be practically useless ; and not after, or else that Satan whom we so much dread may step in and settle the question on a false basis.

To have a soul saturated with theology is not to be good. To have a mind crowded with facts is not to be wise.

To read a child never so good a lesson upon the grand subjects of duty and destiny, before his mental appetite has shown that he is ready for the food, and able to digest it, is about as promotive of his mental and spiritual growth, as a double dinner to-day because he will be hungry to-morrow, would be of his physical growth.

This is no scientific theory of education, but plain, true common sense—too plain to need proof, and too solemn to be unheeded or gainsaid.

Children do not die of mental dyspepsia, but they suffer from it in various ways. We often give them a surfeit of the very mental food for which we are anxious to cultivate their taste ; and curiosity, which is nothing more than mental appetite, becoming cloyed with what is good, seeks other food less wholesome, perhaps wholly bad. Then, in our inscrutable ignorance and far-seeing blindness, we insult our own souls and mock our Creator, by exhibiting our wayward children as living evidences of the truth of the doctrine of "*total hereditary depravity,*" or pay a compliment to Satan by telling him he has succeeded in his teaching better than we who had the aid of God, succeeded in ours.

Day by day, before our eyes, Nature is showing us how she works in harmony with God's laws, and yet we do not walk in her ways. The child is born. God has made a human body and soul, and laid it in the nursing arms of Nature. Forthwith she establishes a just proportion between food and growth, and makes the appetite the regulator. Brain, bone and muscle are crying, " Build us up;" and patient Nature goes on building, with the food God prepared for it. There is no cramming or starving ; the appetite is a nice regulator, and asks food at just the time and in just the proportion that the body needs it for material to work up. So the house of the body goes on building, and all is well. But when the young soul looks out and asks for food, then we begin the cramming or starving, often both, in alternation. What appetite and digestion are to the body, curiosity and reason are to the mind ; and as God has prepared the physical, so he has the mental food, and established the immutable laws by which both must be appropriated, if we expect it to be food indeed— not poison or clogging waste, but material for our growth.

The little soul must sleep for a while. Let it alone, and soon it will wake with the question : " Who made the stars and the flowers, and who made every-

body ?" Then open the text-book of our lives, and
read the grand but simple story beginning thus : "In
the beginning God created the heavens and the
earth." This is God's answer. Then close the book
and lay it away, for this is food enough for once.
Let him think and talk about it for a while, and then
forget it for his play; for the little soul must have
sleep, food, exercise, and then sleep again, in regular
succession. The lesson was food ; thinking and talking about it was exercise ; and then forgetting it was
mental sleep. To-morrow, perhaps, the little soul
will awaken again with the question : "Where is
God ?" or, "Where did baby brother go ?" Then
open the book again, and repeat, in language he can
understand, the description of the "New Jerusalem ;"
then stop again for exercise and rest. But soon the
question will come, "Can't we go there, too ?" This
will be the text for another sermon ; and so on till
youth and manhood, when the mind can take longer
lessons, and understand them better. Every word of
God's revelation to man will be nourishing food to the
full-grown soul. He will not form opinions, and go
to the Bible *afterward* for proof, or elaborate theories,
and go to God's revelation to cull corroboratory
texts ; but the result of his education will be seen in
a stronger power to grasp good and reject evil, and
he will go to his Bible simply to see what it says, and
know what it means and would have him do.

In his theology there will be no hard knots to untie, and in his piety no selfishness and prejudice. A faith formed in this way will last through time, and defy all the efforts of worldliness, bigotry and sectarianism to move one timber of its strong foundation : and Infidelity itself will be ground to impalpable powder between the millstones of man's perfect faith and the immutable truth of Jehovah.

"THE REALM OF CHANGE."

" Let the great world spin forever down the ringing grooves of change."

In the ship of Life, Conservatism may do for ballast, but not for sails.

"Old things shall pass away, and all things become new," is written upon the face of creation.

Nothing in the universe is unchangeable but God, and those grand attributes and laws which are the steps of His throne.

Light, which of all material things most nearly approaches the infinite, is the most evanescent and changeful. A cloud obscures it; or the night cometh, and to-morrow is a new creation.

The trees bud and blossom, and the leaves of to-day draw their life from the decay of half a century ago. The everlasting hills, with their rock-bound sides, are but the sepulchers of the dead things of centuries past, and wise men read the inscriptions and tell us when they died.

All things must be drawn at last into the inexorable orbit of life, death and resurrection. Nature learned this lesson when Time began, and in the beautiful order of seedtime and harvest she brings her annual offering, and swears allegiance to the immutable laws of change.

We would stand still, but we can not. To-day is crumbling beneath our feet, and we must step upon the new to-morrow, though we can not take our treasures with us; and on, and on, over to-morrows without end, we must pass into the far future, leaving a part of ourselves behind at every step.

Our very bodies change. Their essential particles are scattered to the earth and air, and from year to year we put new bodies on, like new garments for the soul. Human will, which is stronger than life or death, is powerless to keep intact these frames of ours; and the very bodies in which we walked a score of years ago, are not the bodies in which we walk to-day. Nor do they change alone; our hopes, loves, rewards and ambitions make mighty revolutions.

It is curious to know how the care-worn skeptic of fifty, who denies the possibility of identity in the resurrection of the body, could prove that, either physically or mentally, he is the veritable little boy who cried over a broken top forty years ago.

But while Nature glides so smoothly through her vast mutations that even our bodies move in unconscious obedience through her marvellous changes; spirit is the only rebellious subject, where all else

bows in willing submission to the inevitable law
which nature and revelation alike proclaim the will of
God. Yet the changes through which visible things
pass, are few and small when compared to the many-
rounded ladder up which our souls may climb to
Heaven.

Change is the very angel of God, sent down to
earth to make his paths straight, and the ascent
easier from human weakness and sin to immortality
and honor. It is this when we learn its laws, and
through their discipline reach its end. We call this
a sad world of change; but in this world God could
give us no more terrible punishment than the power
of standing still. Were this within our grasp, He
would call us in vain. Though we looked up to the
glory of Heaven, and stretched out yearning arms to
its infinite rest, yet we would shrink appalled from
the only path that leads there. We shudder when
we think that, as we toil up the steep and broken
way of labor and self-denial, from step to step, we
must leave something valuable behind, and, at last,
stripped of all, wend our way through the lone desert
of old age, down to the shore, in some hour when
the waves run high, to be borne out upon an ebbing
tide—where? Oh! imagination has borne us on
where Heaven is out of sight. Dying grace is not
promised to the living. We are tempting God, and
upon the cold horizon shines no promise—for Heaven

has sunk down behind the hills of doubt; and we gladly turn back to the idols of *Now*, content to take a perpetual lease upon To-day, satisfying our restlessness by viewing the panorama of a world moving on while we alone stand still. We would be like a little boy in a boat lashed to the shore, afraid to venture out, yet with dizzy eyes watching the tide as it bears its freight to breast the sea; fancying *we* are sailing too, yet ever and anon turning with a sigh of content to realize that our boat, with all our playthings on board, is tied to an everlasting Present. So, not in judgment, but in love, God removes his hand from each successive present, and lets it fall; and not in repining but in love, should we move on.

Sometimes when our faith is small, He takes our idols from us, and removing them to the safe shelter of His rest, bids us follow on. Sometimes, when we dally on the way, He touches us gently and a gray hair or a failing sense remains to tell us where His hand was laid when He moved us farther on. Sometimes His hand is laid more heavily upon us, and a bodily infirmity, like Jacob's shrunken sinew, constrains us to lean upon the staff of His promise, "My grace shall be sufficient for your day." No matter: the staff will bear us through. Though we stumble, we shall not fall; though the way is rough, we shall not be over-weary. And every change leaves us further on, even as every hill we climb leaves us further up and nearer the ineffable glory of the end.

We *must* go on; we *may* go up. Change is a universal sovereign, and the resistance of soul is the conflict of ages. Change is a royal sovereign, too, and has for us many grand possibilities in her gift, and one of which she little recks: by obeying her laws we coöperate with God, who rules all change, and from subjects we become kings. Our realm is the infinite future; thenceforth the race set before us is but an eager march into our kingdom.

When the inertia of the soul is thoroughly overcome, there is something grand in a running race with Time; not resisting the changes as they come, not even standing at the door like patient Nature, to see what to-morrow will bring forth, but strong in the strength of Him who ruleth Time and Change; and safe in the arms of Him who overruleth all things for our good, and wise in the knowledge of Him to whom all things are revealed, we may stand on the outer verge of Time and step grandly into the future, like prophets, in the name of God.

KEEPING TIME.

Not long ago I attended church where I was a stranger. It was a neat little chapel, and the congregation appeared to feel quite a pride and pleasure in the temple they had built for the Lord. All were bright and cheerful, presenting quite a refreshing contrast to some pictures memory furnished, of long rows of men and women with inane faces, seeming to imply that they were not guests in the house of God, but spectators, resenting this omission on the part of our Divine Host, by looking on with an air of well-bred indifference, as if *they* were not hungry for the bread of life. It was a rare satisfaction to see so many whose faces proclaimed that they were indeed invited by divine love, and could not forget that they were the guests of the Lord of Hosts. Their hearts were so full of prayer and praise, that, during the assembling hour, their zeal burst forth in a prelude of song.

It was the Old Hundred, Luther's music to the hundredth psalm—called *old* when it was new; but which will be *new* still when it has been sung by fifty generations. The words are remembered, but when those grand notes rolled out upon the listening air, they seemed to breathe the spirit of that ancient poem to whose words of holy inspiration their music first was set.

But, alas! despite the harmony of soul and sound, even here was something to forgive, something to remind us of that jarring chord which was struck when the gates of Paradise were closed, and will vibrate till Time shall die.

One voice, which might have been full and rich, soared perhaps on the wings of zeal far above the rest—so far that it always descended to the long notes at the end of the line just half a note too late, so that we seemed to have a kind of echo to Old Hundred, as if the singer could not trust the walls to do their ancient duty.

Yet no one heeded the discordant voice. It is singular how, after frequent repetitions, pleasant and unpleasant things are apt to fall alike on inattentive or deaf ears. Not having heard the voice before, it discomforted *me*, and in the interval before service, I began to speculate upon the character of one who, with such serene unconsciousness of results, could continue to

> " Crack the ears of harmony
> And break the legs of time."

I at once decided that the singer must be one of those tranquil spirits who never feel the power of great temptation, but move on through life in the straight path, because it is the nearest way to heaven; often sinning in little things against the order of God's universe, but never hearing the discord or feeling the jar. Such characters rarely become very wicked; for it is one of God's merciful laws of compensation, that those whose avenues of moral sense are dull, can never feel the keenest power of strong temptation. So, at last, the Great Judge may find in them no more to forgive than in those whose quick ears catch the harmony of Heaven, even while singing the psalms of the Earth. Those discerning souls who see all the wrong-doing in the world, often find·their mantle of charity not broad enough to cover it; and with a blindness strangely at variance with their otherwise sharp-sightedness, they fore-seal their own condemnation by piling up mountains of transgression for the wrath of God to kindle: nor do they spare themselves; their praises for redemption are drowned by the ceaseless wail of their confession of sin.

Compared with the harmony of Heaven, our songs of life are all out of tune. We are laggards in the heavenly measure, and the Great Time-keeper notes the discord.

The man of the world feels this when he returns home after a long day; his heart holds a vague consciousness of something wrong; and when he has given six busy days to the world, and the first day of the week comes, bringing the hours which he has always devoted to the accumulation of treasures in Heaven, then he finds what the wrong is—his thoughts make a discord in the holy place. He has not been keeping time. Perhaps he has even lost the key-note of the holy song, and then he wonders how all the discord of the earth could ever make him forget that. But all is right now, and he goes his way re-joicing, keeping time in *his daily life* as a visible sign that he is making melody in *his heart* to God. He speaks gently, tenderly to his wife, and restores the harmony of her spirit, if, in the confusion of earthly things she too had lost the key-note, and was not keeping time to the song of Divine compassion and human charity. He does not reprove her, remember-ing that *his* soul was full of discord; and perhaps it is because she kept time with his mood yesterday, that she is out of tune to-day. So he speaks gently, tenderly now. The children hear it, and petulant words die unspoken, and selfish thoughts are still-born. Without understanding the measure, they have joined in the song which the redeemed of God are singing wherever infinite mercy and human love have gained a victory over sin.

We know that we are not our own; we are God's instruments, and our lives are set to the music of His glory. How can we make such discord when we know the sound goes up to Heaven? How dare we stretch forth careless or impious hands to smite the chords of other hearts, when He who tuned them to his praise is standing by to listen?

We are not all strong, and some weak notes that linger long behind, make no discord on the ear of God. They shall "learn the new song." They were weak, but did not falter in the long strife, whose end is victory over Sin and Death.

Some loud songs are never heard in Heaven, but float out and are lost in the infinite silence.

The psalm of life is not an idle song. It is the grand march over the plains of Armageddon, where we are fighting for the victory over the world, the flesh—yes, and the spirit too—the spirit of selfishness and all evil.

The great pulse of the universe is keeping time to that song; and the great heart of God is grieved when we make a discord even in the heart of a little child.

THE BROKEN EVERGREEN.

In one of the Eastern States there is a beautiful home, where the sunshine always seems brighter, and the flowers fairer, than in any other spot in the world. It was here that my sister and I were born, and lived with our parents, a happy family of four, until three went to heaven, and one went out into the wide world to wait until God should send for her.

I have another home now, and little children that call me "Mother;" but when they ask for stories, I like best to tell them something of my childhood in the old home, just as it was before my parents and sister went from there to heaven.

I had told them all about our flower-garden, our pet lambs, and the curious cave we used to visit; all but one thing, that I never related until to-night. Though often in my thoughts, it always made me sad, and I could not give it words.

Beside our mother's garden, sister and I had one of our own, with trees and shrubs and flowers, quite perfect in itself. This was the best of all our treasures. Our parents managed the more difficult matters of planting and transplanting, but we watched and tended it, and were never weary of arranging it to suit our changing taste.

One fine spring morning, my birthday, father and mother came out with us to work among our flowers. Well I remember how happy we were, planning two little mounds at one end of our garden walk ; how busily we worked cutting the green sod for the borders ; and how delighted we were when the myrtle and Wandering Jew were planted on the top of both, and mother said that in the summer they would grow very fast, and their long sprays trail over the sides of the mounds like a green fringe. Before sunset our work was finished. We spent the evening in mother's room, sitting at the window from which we could see our mounds with their bright green borders ; and, though we were reading, we looked out every few moments until it was quite dark.

After a while sister asked father why that plant was called by so odd a name—"*Wandering Jew.*" He replied that it was probably on account of its strange growth, branching out in every direction, and forming new roots from its branches, yet nowhere a deep root, as though it was always in readiness to move. Then father told me the strange old story of the "Wandering Jew," who, in punishment for a terrible sin, could never die, but must wander the earth through all the centuries, till our Saviour comes again.

The next day was sister's birthday, and we rose
early and hastened out to view our garden treasures,
and see if their dew-washed eyes were opened. But
the sun had been there before us, and every leaf and
blade of grass was the brighter for his coming. The
myrtle looked quite contented and happy in its new
place, and even the Wandering Jew seemed as much
at home as could be expected of such an unhappy
vagrant, although we imagined that it had already
decided in which direction to send out its first wandering roots and leaves.

Although we talked an hour about it, in one moment we saw all this and something else; too, which
surprised and delighted us. On each mound, in the
center, was a beautiful little evergreen tree. We
guessed at once that these were planted in honor of
sister's birthday. While we were admiring them,
our parents came out and told us that the trees were
called "Norway Spruce." Then father showed us a
little pale green bud that pointed directly upward
from the top of the center branch or stem, and bade
us be very careful not to injure that, or the trees
would lose their beautiful proportions, and the
branches grow out in disorder ; and he wished them
to grow perfect, and be always pleasant reminders of
sister's birthday and mine, for she was eight years old
to-day and I was ten yesterday. We promised to be
very careful, and then mother said, with the old

beautiful smile, "My children, keep your hearts like the evergreen : in the spring, summer and winter of life always the same—changeless amid all the changes of earth ; and let your thoughts be like the evergreen branches—ever arranged in beautiful order around *one center*, and that center pointing straight to heaven."

I can never forget how mother looked as she said this, and how very beautiful the garden was. I thought then that Eden must have looked like it, and I wondered how Satan dared to walk through it ; but he did, and it is not strange that he came and walked through ours.

It happened soon after that father and mother took a long ride to the next town. Sister went with them. I was to remain at home. I pleaded to go, but in vain ; and then, after they left, filled with anger and disappointment, I ran out into the garden, heedless of my steps. Stumbling against one of the mounds, the evergreen scratched my face. In my blind rage I struck the tree with all my might, and, looking up, saw I had broken a large piece of the top branch of sister's tree, and in breaking it had peeled a long piece of bark from the stem. I sat down, saying, "I am glad of it ;" but I did not feel glad, for the sweet, bright flowers were looking up at me, and the sun was smiling down, and I could not help feeling that I was the evil spirit working in our Eden. The flowers were blooming, and the leaves were green, and all seemed to be smiling back their thanks to the great Creator who had made them beautiful and called them good; yet I, who had received most of all, was wicked and unthankful. I felt very miserable until my parents returned in the evening; then I told them of my anger and its sad results. They were grieved at my willfulness and sin, but told me of One who was far more grieved than they, and whose pardon I must ask. Then they left me with a goodnight kiss, knowing my heart was punishing me; and it was so: we may escape every other punishment, yet that will always follow us.

In the morning I took sister to our garden and showed her what I had done: her tears fell upon the mound, though she kissed me in token of forgiveness. But her grief was not so deep as mine. She wept for a broken evergreen. I wept because I had been selfish and wicked. I knew my sister had forgiven me, and I prayed that God would—and I think he did; but from that time I never played or worked in sight of the evergreen without a feeling of sadness, for it was sister's birthday tree, and I had broken it; and then I always thought of Eden and the evil spirit that walked through amid the bloom and flowers.

Time passed on, and summer made our garden greener and brighter. Sitting one day on the grass,

I told sister my old fancy about the garden of Eden when I felt like the evil spirit; and pointing to the tree which had grown very crooked and straggling, I said, "See, I left my mark in Eden, not on the people, but the trees." But she only smiled, and said, "Try to forget it, dear;" then kissed me as she laid her flowers in my lap, and walked slowly up the gravel walk to the house.

She looked like an angel to me then, and my heart took a picture of her that it can never, never lose. In a moment I remembered that she looked flushed all day, and, running to the house, I found her laying her head in mother's lap. That night she was ill, and for three days she grew worse. Sometimes I was told to be very quiet, and then I feared she would die.

At last they told me she was dead. With flowers on her breast, and some of our myrtle in her beautiful hair, they laid her away to sleep.

Our home was very lonely after this; it seemed as if our angel had left us, and taken the sunshine away.

One day I stole out into the garden to weep, but, alas! the first object that met my sight was the broken evergreen, sister's birthday gift. My wicked anger against her was all remembered; the mutilated tree seemed still to reproach me with my sin.

I sat down and tried to recall her face as she said,

"Try to forget it, dear;" and I felt as if she was saying it to me then, and my heart grew brighter, and my tears were dried; but the tree never grew straight.

Years after, my parents went to heaven, and left me alone with the sunshine and the flowers; and now strangers live in the old home, and I am far away. But I often think of it, and sometimes visit it, and the rooms look familiar, and the trees like old friends. Even the flowers smile, as if in welcome to an old companion. The myrtle now covers the mounds, for the Wandering Jew disappeared long ago. It must have been killed by some winter's frost; but my little daughter thinks it has only wandered away after the fashion of its old namesake.

Among all the flowers and trees there are none but pleasant memories for me, until I see the two evergreens. Year by year one has grown taller and more beautiful, but the other irregular and straggling still. The broken tree ever reminds me of my sweet sister and my foolish anger, and leaves a regret that can never be wiped out; but then, looking up with the tall, changeless evergreen that no willful hand has marred, I think of my mother's words on sister's birthday morning: for the center branch, with its spiral cone, still is pointing "*straight to heaven,*" and I know that they are all there in that beautiful country, where nought is ever broken or blighted, and the good never die, and no sin or sorrow works through among the bright trees and flowers, to mar their beauty, forever.

RAYS FROM AN OLD MEMORY.

" We know that we have passed from death unto life, because we love the brethren."

It was a cold night, twenty years ago; there was a cold new moon shining, and great heaps of snow lay on each side of the beaten foot-track that led over the plank walk, like a straight and narrow path to the old Methodist chapel.

More snow was falling ; but this was prayer-meeting night, and in every direction were fresh footprints in the snow, all tending to the little church ; for cold, like tempation, is easily resisted, when it only assails us from without; and so in the old chapel were gathered a pleasant number of those whom memory labels the salt of the earth. The lesson, the prayers that were offered, the songs that were sung, have been borne away from memory and sound, except it be in the heart and ear of Him who never forgets. But one figure rises distinct through all the mists of twenty years. It was a strong, calm, reposeful figure, as if it had grown firm by battling with the world and all the evil therein. The face had a lifted expression, as if all the soul's anchors were dropped in Heaven, and his iron-gray hair seemed a perpetual suggestion, that in his calm reliance on some hidden power he had disputed, inch by inch, the aggressions of time.

"Where two or three are gathered together in my name, I am in their midst to bless them." Are these idle words? Are they simply an expression of God's lofty approval, looking down through the vista of untraversable space? or is this promised presence an actual, spiritual halo, like a fragment of Pentecost among us? Wiser heads than mine among God's warring children, have made of this a rallying point of difference; and here, in the name of God, have been dealt some of the heaviest blows of religious politics. But twenty years ago these blows fell far over the head of the child at the Methodist prayer-meeting; and when, just at the conclusion of the services, the iron-grayhaired man arose and repeated, "We know that we have passed from death unto life, because we love the brethren," it seemed as if the words must have come of the inspiration of the hour, if they had not been uttered centuries before.

To the child, whose eyes and ears were uneducated by the world, and open to impressions, there was something in the spiritual atmosphere of that room that suggested the gates of pearl, the streets of gold, and the feet that walk thereon. If indeed the

Spirit of God had descended like a dove upon the open Bible, it would have seemed to the believing heart and intensified imagination of the child a fitting time and place.

The services were over, but the charm was not broken. In the lingering of feet and the clasp of many hands, the child saw the seal of love which the world knows not of, and in her heart of hearts thanked God for the visible sign which might be hers, when in His mercy He should call her into the circle of His love.

Ah! well indeed, if the interpretation of God's message to man were as clear and distinct as his seal upon his children. The child saw the seal and heard the message; but in the windings of a religious theory the message was lost, and, for long years, only the seal remained in her memory, a perpetual witness of what might have been, if the children of God would only be content to have the doors of Heaven as wide open as the Christ did when he entered in.

"Except ye become as little children"—ah! if we all became as little children, should we be able, or care to elaborate or accept long codicils to the "will and testament" of Christ, and call them creeds?

And we of the "Reformation"—we, who have stripped Christianity of its gorgeous trappings; we, who have divested it of the darkened counsel of many words, until it shines undimmed, like the "Star in the East," directly over the place where Christ awaits our coming to fall down and worship Him—are we sealed with His seal, as we bear His charter to a dying world?

"Ye are the salt of the earth." "Ye are the light of the world." Can the salt of the earth and the light of the world blush for the logic of facts, when the world quotes to them: "We know that we have passed from death unto life because we love the brethren"?

"Go into all the world and preach the Gospel to every creature, teaching them to do whatsoever I have commanded you." Dare man repeat the holy commission and leave out its most reiterated injunction—"Love one another"—and dare he preach what he does not practice? He has indeed an altar whereon to make sacrifices for all the shortcomings which, like dropped stitches, mar his daily life. But the brazen altar is outside of the holy place, and he has no altar of indulgence whereon to sacrifice for deliberate sinning, that he may cultivate the roots of an old bitterness whose pungent fruit may please him.

In the olden time it was only consecrated hands that might bear the Ark of God's covenant; this was but a symbol of the purity of his soul who would be a representative of Christ. It is true, that no mortal man is pure enough to honor this profession; and in proportion as a man is lifted by office or capacity above the level of his fellows, he is lifted into the sifting gaze of the world. And yet, the world has a right to expect much of those who have professed to turn their backs on the world, the flesh and the evil one; to have put on Christ, and with his sacred charter in their hands, to work for Him till He calls them home.

The world has a right to expect, at least, perfect love and harmony between those who stand before them as the ministers of the Prince of Peace, and the heralds of the Cross.

Religion has no argument unless we can tell good men it will make them better. The observance of. civil and social law would be a gospel of improvement to bad men: can Christianity promise nothing more in this world? This would be to proclaim it a vast pretension, and us a vast body of pretenders. And if the Christ which is in us is not patient enough to do His will through our members, dare we tell men that we rely upon this power to move our bodies when they are senseless dust, and raise them in the first resurrection for our reward? Who is able for these things? Who dare decide how much of this practical infidelity God will pardon? Any divergence the world more willingly overlooks than an unloving spirit among Christians. A contentious Christian is a recruiting officer for the grand army of infidels, in every true practical sense; in all except the sentiment (for religion has its sentiment), he crucifies the Lord again, and puts Him to an open shame.

When we consider the Church of Christ as a commonwealth, a community of interests, a partnership of capital, an insurance of happiness here and hereafter, with privileges as broad as the powers of man, with promises as high as Heaven and deep as the grave, and added to this the æsthetic beauty, the sentiment of religion, which is the concentrated essence of all poetry, we stand appalled by the magnitude of our pretensions compared with the meagreness of our realization.

Nothing but the densest of all ignorance, or Satan's chains welded never to be broken, could impede the progress of an intelligent and consistent Christianity. Religious controversy would be narrowed to one issue, that between those who are, and are not, stockholders in the commonwealth of Zion, whose dividends are sure for all time and all eternity.

In a country like this, where there are no Goliaths of Church and State to be slain, Christianity should sweep with the double *momentum* of divine and human love; the brotherhood of Christ should spread from the Eastern borders of civilization, to where the Chinese are coming to us through our Western gates, and the world see a second Pentecost.

This is not a vision of Utopia, nor a result incompatible with the imperfections of men. When the eyes of men are pure enough to see the Christ in their fellow-men, the divinity in their own hearts will expand and the small errors of to-day will sink down into utterless depths of nothingness before the great interests of the Christian commonwealth.

We shall not then hear Christians and teachers of men talk over in private the petty gossip of an old bitterness, or rush into print to expose or correct the fancièd errors of their fellow-laborers in the vineyards of God. It is written, "Prove all things and hold fast to that which is good;" but men are not things, and it is not written, "Judge all men, and make of your desks and pens thrones and scepters, judging the tribes of Israel." O heralds of the cross of Christ's humiliation—proclaimers of the gospel of peace, if you could rush to the pulpit, the rostrum and the press, and before the eyes of men tear from your brethren the rays and tinsel of error and pre-tension, it would not draw them heavenward. If the pearly gates were opened as wide as the mouth of hell, men could not be pushed into heaven.

Could we strip a man of all his human errors, till only his poor humanity remained, we should only fill him with resentment, or perhaps humiliation, so that, like Adam and Eve, he would know that he was naked, and hide himself from God.

The time and talent wasted among religious teach-ers in useless controversy, in attack and defense, would reduce the ranks of infidels, and go far toward elevating Christianity from the dead level of a religious theory, to the higher inclined plane of the will and love of God, whose summit is the Mount of Transfiguration, where the full-grown Christ within us puts off its earthly robe to enter into glory.

UNDER THE DOME.

Years ago, a party went for an afternoon's excursion from Albany to Greenbush, to visit the roundhouse. Perhaps there is nothing peculiar about the place, but just as it loomed up in my childish fancy then, it stands in my memory to-night — vague, strange, awful, suggesting the idea of human action petrified, by time and God's inevitable justice, into inexorable decrees of fate.

It was, however, only a large building with several dozen great arched doorways, through which ran railroad tracks, all crossing at the center. The building was very lofty, the roof rising in the center into an' immense dome. And in this dome centered all the wonders of the round house. Just beneath it, where the tracks crossed, was a turntable, and one standing on this could utter quite a long sentence, and hear his own words repeated after him in a voice which seemed to be hundreds of feet above him, but so loud and distinct that it marked every pause and intonation with the accuracy of a deliberate speaker, and the sonorous tones of a church-bell. To the gay party that afternoon it scarce seemed an echo, but more like invoking the ghosts of dead voices that had made their graves in the air; and as one after another stepped upon the magic square to test it, the merry laugh was hushed, and gradually all the life of the party seemed to be absorbed by some weird spirit in the dome above. They stood for some moments in silence, watching through the great arched doorway the last beams of the sunset break into fragments and disappear, then slowly moved away, and I stepped alone on the turn-table and looked upward with some vague, childish idea of catching a glimpse of the echo; but seeing nothing but the great, shadowy dome, growing darker each moment in the waning light, I translated all my courage into words to say: "Good-night, old dome! I shall remember your everlasting echo"—"remember your everlasting echo," pealed out the iron tongue of the ghostly wonder, and I turned and fled as if pursued by the demon of the dome, and somewhere in my latent memory that echo has hidden ever since; and when, as to-night, sitting by my fireside in the waning year, my thoughts go out into all the odd corners of consciousness and recollection to find food for reverie, I conceive all the world to be a great round-house, with a dome above and an echo in the future. Standing on the turn-table of the shifting present, I catch the echo of things to come.

I am startled by no ghostly repetitions now, but listening under the dome where human volition invokes infinite echoes, the words and actions of the world come back to me in the shape of consequences and results. I hear the great bell of human events ringing in the cathedral of time, and thinking of all the human hands that somewhere are pulling the wires, and ropes that swing its iron tongue, I wonder how many would tremble and fall nerveless, if from the dome above a terrible voice should cry—"remember your everlasting echoes."

When the Atlantic cable was laid, Dr. O. W. Holmes said: "The clock of time struck;" and when the last rail of the transcontinental railway was riveted down with a golden nail, some one said it struck again. Useless information; dullest ears could hear that, and all along this overland acoustic tube men stood leaning on their spades and pick-axes to listen when that hour was struck.

But what are the echoes under the dome of the impending future? Here comes down to us a perfect babel of replies. Bending my ear to the loudest, it says: "An immense increase of the facilities of trade—the improvement of our western wilderness—increasing means of paying our national debt, and, after a while, the removal of our republican tabernacle and our congressional tent a day's march nearer the Pacific Ocean." Then, in the din of echoes, I hear something about the annexation of Cuba, and Canada falling at last into our yearning arms ; but to me the connection is no longer clear; and the classical story of the " House that Jack Built " can never be improved by a political paraphrase. So I simply attach the wires of communication, and pass this echo on to Washington. To-night I would rather hear the moral echoes struck out by years of toil from these tons of railroad iron. Slowly they come, and dropping quietly into my ear, they say—" First, you will realize this line to be a great spinal cord of human sympathy, social and political, running through these iron vertebræ of the western world, gathering up impressions from all the nerves of the body politic, for the benefit and preservation of the whole. After a while we shall come to you in the shape of car-loads of Chinese, with their pig-tails and their idolatry, the first to ornament your work-shops and your kitchens, and the latter to be wholly swept away by the irresistible force of your Christian civilization. You need not instruct them. To allow them to stand behind your chair will be sufficient. Did you not in this way succeed in educating and Christianizing the heathen from Africa, receiving in return the small compensation of a few generations of labor? True, you will find the Chinaman very faithful to the god he worships ; but if you are, as usual, a little lax in your

Christianity, it will encourage him to see that your God requires so little service. And as he inclines to a plurality of gods, he will be all the more easily converted should you show him that you worship mammon, too. No matter what a few ultra Christians may say ; you will perhaps ask them how much of trade and politics, how much stock in the Pacific Railway they control; and if they reply, ' My kingdom is not of this world,' then of course you will tell them that they can not reasonably expect a vote or moral influence therein ; the stained windows of their churches should shut out the glare of the world, and confine their hopes and fears. Then you will go on Christianizing these Chinese heathens in your own way, and they will learn to vote for popular measures and men, to spend the leisure hours of the Lord's-day in reading the last political sensation or learning the price of gold or cotton ; and if any one objects, you will tell them that some of the most liberal and influential members of churches are satisfied with this kind of Christianity, and when Christians step outside of their church-doors they should of course adopt the current views and tastes of the age, and that you should consider it great presumption for the poor Chinese to desire anything better."

But the echo grew tiresome, and then the turn-table swung round, and the gold of New York is under the dome. Sweeping by like a ghost, the echo only wails: "Insanity, ruin, disgrace, suicide, wealth, pride, lost opportunity or millstone, and a curse, dishonesty and greed, like a great cancer, eating the muscles of industry and the nerves of trade." And the turn-table swings round again. I see the funeral of George Peabody: first a long train of poor who weep, and of rich who praise and follow this example of loving charity to the grave. And then the train sweeps by, and I see little school-houses dotting the green valleys of the South, and in the sweet hour of children's voices, the echo grows confused, and as it dies away in the distant future, the last words I catch are—"the gold of George Peabody—it is more blessed to give than to receive." And the turn-table swings round again, and under the dome I see other school-rooms full of happy children, and hear a voice read from the sacred Book: "The fear of the Lord is the beginning of wisdom," and then the book is closed and fastened with a Roman chain like the Bible of Martin Luther, and darkness falls over the scene with the mantle of Roman power, until it is lit again by the lurid flames of final disaster—Mexico is brought to our doors—the great republic is rocking to its center; its forum is rent in twain, and into the gulf men are throwing their chained Bibles and their faith, and yet it will not close, and this great government, which has gathered so many alien children under

the shadow of its "living vine" and fig-tree, is
falling apart by its own weight, and there is no bond
to hold it together.

In vain Rome stretches out her palsied hand to
gather it to her bosom. The new generation has forgotten alike the law that went forth from Jerusalem,
and the edicts that came from Rome. In Washington they are worshiping power; in Boston, reason;
and in New York, a golden calf. The dust of the
old world is shaken off upon the new—the republic
is crumbling; the disintegration beginning at her own
heart, she is broken beneath the weight of civilization that was greater than it was good. Above
this chaos a voice cried: "The heathens of old
recognized a grand truth which at your peril you
lost sight of—the children belong to the State;
as you educate, they will legislate. You have put
words of justice into hands unskilled to use them.
Once, in Florence, I gave you a picture of what
this country might be, when you had no longer a
common ground of mutual appeal against the injustice and oppression of ambitious men. Your
religions are diverse, your politics lie on one side
of a great gulf—no tie remains. You have destroyed the old landmarks, and virtue has become policy, and goodness success. The State
failed to teach her children the duty and wisdom
it exacts from their maturity, and in them shall

its punishment be found. You are numbered with the nations that 'forget God.' As France closed the eighteenth century in desolation, the nineteenth shall close with you." Louder and louder swelled the echo, until I stopped my ears and cried in terror, "Where are the echoes of the Church? There are faithful ones in Sodom." For a moment there was silence, while the turn-table swung round again, and then a veritable valley of Shinar was reproduced to my wearied ears; listen as I would, I could only now and then distinguish—"ritualism," "Calvinism," "orthodox,' "evangelical churches". —and then I saw a great church, and the preacher rose and told them of the children's chained Bibles. And while I heard the soft rustle of heavy silks, and saw the sparkle of jewels, they rose and solemnly replied: "Our kingdom is not of this world." Then the preacher told them that gold had reached one hundred and fifty-one, and a murmur ran through the congregation; and as they started to their feet, it rose to a clamor that reached the dome, and its resonant echo pealed out: "Not all that say unto me, Lord, Lord, shall enter into the kingdom of heaven." Louder and louder pealed the echo, until, appalled, I started up to find that I had been dreaming till the fire had burned low, and the resonant echo was the clock striking twelve on this Saturday night. And so, in spite of our weakness and sin, again the angels are letting down the golden bars between six days of dust and toil, and the green pastures where our Shepherd waits. And the Church is safe in the bosom of Him who will also bear our republic safe to the "Saturday evening of time," where the golden gates of the millennium shall unclose the Sabbath of the second coming.

A PAGE OF HISTORY AND A LINE OF REVELATION.

The writer of Ecce Homo, whatever may be said of the book, has certainly impressed upon the reader, with unwonted power, one thought—that the knowledge of God and the spread of Christ's kingdom is in itself, as a vast whole, a far greater marvel than the physical miracles wrought by his personal power or in the apostolic age.

With the combined assistance of reason and revelation, it is difficult even yet to understand that from the highest round of human intelligence we can catch no glimpse of God, yet from the lowest round may touch the hem of the garment of Him who goes before us into heaven.

Craving pardon for the sake of the motive, let us lay all reverence aside, put the miracles out of sight, and make a legend of the resurrection and a fable of the flaming Pentecost. The infidel is now satisfied; and we can view what remains together. We see a harmless wanderer, an ambitious man, always talking of himself, and yet with strange impolicy always offending his most influential friends, and at last dying a violent and shameful death, followed by only a few half-faithful Galilæan fishermen. And yet, eighteen hundred years after, this man, who has been dead for so many centuries, is an acknowledged power in every enlightened nation on the face of the whole earth. And this power unsupported, except by the memory of its dead author, and without the conscious volition of the mass of men, lives in our language, animates our literature, moves in our senates, controls in our laws, and molds our peoples; and, whether we will or not, it is the great engine of progress, bearing the long train of civilization over the track of human destiny.

It is all this, and no man can tell why. We strip Christ of his divinity, and deny every miracle, and yet, denuded of all this, he himself stands a greater miracle than all we have swept away.

Men may reject him. They do. But no enthusiasm haloes them, no power opposes; for Christianity is aggressive, not defensive, and right and left the stream divides and leaves them standing like pillars of salt all along the way between the Sodom of the world's wickedness and the purest civilization contemplated by the closest followers of Christ.

The religion of Christ is simpler than all philosophy, and yet a problem so deep that, in this broad noonday of the world, human reason can not solve it, yet rarely dares reject it, for fear of that sword of vengeance which, but vaguely visible to the conscious eyes of men, always hangs suspended by God's providence, ready to fall on an apostate people or an apostate Church.

To those who read the pages of the world's history side by side with the revelations of God, the whole story of mankind from Eden to Mount Sinai, from Canaan to the Cross, all down the torpid centuries until now, are but a sermon on the text, "The world by wisdom knew not God." Egypt, Greece, and Rome, and China with her thirty centuries of civilization, borne not as a light ahead, but as a burden in the rear of the march of nations, all proclaim it true.

But lest the bewildered eyes of men should fail to read aright so vast a page, it would seem as if Divine Providence had massed the elements of human wisdom and folly to epitomize this truth in the tragic burlesque of a day. The stage was France. Long years of political and religious corruption had prepared an applauding audience, and in 1793 and 1794 was enacted the most grotesque tragedy that the world ever saw.

If we desire to measure the heights and depths of human depravity, we may sink our plummet here, where wickedness became frenzy and infidelity became enthusiasm, and where even the masterminds of the French Revolution, from the heights of reason, education and refinement, alternately ignore, insult and patronize their Maker.

It was just after the execution of Louis XVI. and Marie Antoinette, when, as William Howitt says, "France was one great mad-house of bloody, raving maniacs." The throne was gone. The Church, which had sailed from Jerusalem with its snow-white banner, to be the ark of the world in every deluge of distress, had mutinied long ago, and now, sailing under the flag of Rome, foundered on the rocks of the French Revolution. The gates of hell prevailed against it.

Without uncovering the past to discover just when Christ withdrew himself from a Church profaned, we may simply lift the curtain of the holy place and find that he is gone. We see the purple and fine linen, the gold and frankincense, and the lights upon the high altar; but the key-stone is gone from the arch above, and while we gaze the whole vast edifice of grandeur and sin falls in upon itself and disappears in the vortex of a sinking throne.

Wherever we must now look for the true Church among those followers who so divide the living body of Christ, certainly it is not here; for their light has gone out, St. Bartholomew's eve is avenged, and Christ is vindicated—the gates of hell prevail.

They did not abolish the Church because "it was weighed in the balance and found wanting;" they did not virtually abolish it at all. It simply died, and they swept it out of the way to make room for a better thing. There was no opposition, or, at least, none worthy of the name, except Gregoire, Bishop of Blois. But dead bodies do not resist; they regarded the Church as an old idol fallen prostrate at the feet of Truth.

And now we have before us the strange spectacle of France, an enlightened nation, without a government, a religion, or a church, but with the legislative power vested in the hands of the wisest men of France; men, too, who were pouring out in impassioned sentiment their love of liberty, justice and virtue. The world looked on. What would these wise men do? There was no law to compel, no religion to restrain, no Church to hinder. Above the waste of what had been and was not, they had absolute power to will and to do. They might decree, and no man reverse; they might build, and no man pull down.

They held in their hands the experience of the past, the wisdom of the present, and the revelation of the future; nor were they blind to the hour. Beholding the grand possibilities before them, they believed themselves standing on a modern Sinai to give laws to a waiting people. But they invoked not God, but Reason, and a cloud passed before their eyes hiding the Lord from their sight. Rousseau,

Voltaire, Talleyrand and Mirabeau had prepared France for Anacharsis Clootz, who, at the head of a party, now appeared before the Convention, proclaiming the necessity of "destroying all the pretended sovereigns of earth and heaven." "There is," said he, "no other God but Nature, no other sovereign but the human race; and Nature kneels not to herself." And yet in the next act we see that Nature did kneel to herself, when the busts of Mirabeau, Marat, and other apostles of the republic, were put in the place of the images of saints, to be worshiped in the churches. Clootz claimed that by dethroning God, as they had already dethroned their king, they would abolish together all necessity for taxes, public officers, or executioners, while Reason would unite them in a common brotherhood. The Convention received this impious proposition with transport. Gobel, Archbishop of Paris, after some hesitation, not of conscience but of caution, was decided by the more courageous conduct of Parens, a country curé, and appeared at last in his pontificals, followed by many of his clergy, and exchanged his miter for a red night-cap. Talleyrand, Bishop of Autun, with a host of others, followed, and then the Commune joined the popular tide and renounced Christianity for the worship of Reason. On the 10th of November, amid a wild orgy of sentimental frenzy, the Convention and the assembled multitude formally deposed the Almighty, and set up to be worshiped in his stead a goddess of Liberty and Reason. The scene of this unparalleled mockery was the Church of Notre Dame. An opera-girl served for a goddess to receive the worship. Howitt says "it was a genuine theatrical scene, burlesquing scandalously the rites of religion." To the true worshiper walls are not sacred things, and nothing holy can ever be actually profaned; but the Church of France has taught a different doctrine, and in reading the record of this crazy jubilee one feels a vague kind of disbelief that these men could so soon have outgrown every vestige of respect for a place whose very threshold they had once considered holy. True, they had burned the Pope in effigy, but the Pope had withstood them. It would seem that God himself must have chosen to utterly desecrate those silent incense-saturated walls, so stained by a polluted worship; and the purple and fine linen with which for ages men had veiled the eyes of men, and covered out of sight the ark of His holy covenant, were now thrown out to become the filthy rags of the Revolution. They altered the computation of time, and dated not from the birth of our Saviour, but from the 22nd of September, 1792, the birthday of French liberty. After changing the names of the months, they divided them

into periods of ten days, instead of weeks—less kind
to themselves and each other than God had been,
they robbed man and beast of one day of rest in
every month ; and every decade they met to worship
Liberty and Reason, professing to rise above every
form of ignorance, injustice and fanaticism, to become a loving brotherhood, with their republic for
their religion.   But the guillotine was their altar, and
their religion was blood.

A deputation from St. Denis, with a cart-load of
images and vessels of the sacrament, which were
gathered from all the churches, to be destroyed or
melted into coin, is said to have apostrophized them
thus: ''O you instruments of fanaticism and
blessed saints of all kinds, serve your country by
going to the mint to be melted, and thus give us
in this world the felicity you promised us in the
next !''

Had these reforms been only directed against some
of the perverted forms of religion, the nation at
large must have felt some unfortunate effects of this
loud and reckless iconoclasm; but directed, as they
believed, against the very throne and existence of
God, it assumed a form and shape of such awful
magnitude that it has overshadowed France till now.

While they were drenching their land with blood,
this nation of maniacs seem to have had but one
other desire—to wipe out, if possible, the very idea

of God and a hereafter. For this purpose Fauchè and Chaumette carried the work into the cemeteries, and destroyed or obliterated every emblem or inscription presenting the idea of God or immortality, and placed over the gates the words, "Death is eternal sleep." If it were ever permitted us to pray for the dead, human charity would constrain us to pray that they might have found it so—

> "For e'en the dread power of dissolving in space
> Would be bliss to *such* souls."

It is impossible for these men to take shelter in the heathen's refuge. Mercy spreads no shadowy wings of ignorance over the crimes of their lives which prepared the horrors of their death. They stood amid the "nations that forget God," and defiantly working out for themselves the companion character, they invoked the fate of both. The bloody and impious abominations of the "Reign of Terror" were not committed, or, at least, not directed, by an uneducated mob, but by men who were the lights of France, the friends of Talleyrand, Mirabeau and Paine, the latter of whom was all this time sitting quietly in prison writing his "Age of Reason," perhaps an unconscious rival of the arch-fiend who outside his prison walls was writing down *his age of reason* in bloody columns in the book of time. It is difficult to believe that less than a century ago, with every human reason for a guide, men could have transformed civilized France into this fiendish chaos of confusion, carnage and terror, destroying alike the Republic and its foes, and even forcing each other under the uplifted ax of doom. When we think of Paris weltering in blood, of Nantes breeding pestilence from the stench of its victims, of the Loire bridged with its floating corpses, we sink down in helpless agony and shame, and lay our human reason at the feet of God, imploring him to save us from ourselves. We read of the butcheries of India, and the cold-blooded sacrifices of the Hindoos, and thank God that we live in a civilized land, and have heard the name of Christ; and yet in France, where the sacred symbols of the body and blood have told the story of the cross for centuries, we find the most cultivated minds planning and exe cuting atrocities on a scale that finds no parallel among the South Sea Islanders or the brutal tribes of Central Africa. And all this in the name of human liberty and reason. Human Liberty! a virago with her cap dyed red in the purest blood of France, instead of a white-robed angel on the walls of Zion. Human Reason! a drunken despot enthroned upon a guillotine, instead of a Paul on Mars' hill.

If, in the wise economy of God, this sanguinary chapter serves any purpose, it must be to show to the world, for all time to come, how unutterably low they fall who make a god of Reason.

Nor was the carnage of this frenzied Age of Reason the sum of its crime; that was only the outward and visible sign, written in blood, of that abomination of desolation which swept away a polluted religion and a prostituted Church, and put in their place the flowers of Mirabeau and the logic of Paine, while in and out among them glided that old serpent whose sting is death.

And if the blood of the Revolution rose above the high-water mark of human fury, it was not so much the intention of its leaders; still less the crime of a brutal mob resisting tyranny; it was rather the legitimate result of a corrupt Church on one hand, and, on the other, the teachings of men who had long dethroned God in their hearts, and now sought to lay profane and violent hands upon His earthly scepter.

Liberty and Reason were enthroned, but insanity and terror reigned, and this wild flood of human disaster drowned alike the bodies and souls of men, sweeping away the bulwarks of religion and the landmarks of law.

And now high over this chaos sat the great Robespierre, great even in his littleness. The thunders of Danton were silenced, and Robespierre, enthroned in terror, sat alone—triumphant, calm, satisfied? Triumphant, certainly; but neither calm nor satisfied. It would seem that in the blackest human heart God never leaves himself without a witness; and

so this human fiend, who more than all others had
trampled humanity and outraged Divinity, was made
the vindicator of that God to whom his whole life
was an insult. He had conquered all opposition ;
his delicate white hands were the levers of the Republic; his word was the ax of the guillotine ;
but above and before him frowned the shadow of
death. He could not destroy that. It did not
oppose him; it only waited for him. Why did it
wait? His compatriots had said death was an
eternal sleep—had he not sent them, by hundreds,
to prove it? Yet he had not affirmed it—if it
were that, he was not ready to fall into its arms.
Why did it wait? Was he not master of France?
And so Robespierre, the most pitiful coward of the
Revolution, at last dared the loud wrath of this
insane reign of Reason, rather than the silent curse
of God dethroned. Cautiously, at first, in the Ja-
cobin club, he asserted, in view of the ungoverna-
ble excesses of the people, that " if there were no
God, a wise legislature would invent one " to restrain them. Finding this speech well received by
a majority, he next denounced the extreme atheists,
and finally appeared before the Convention with a
carefully prepared paper, deifying Liberty, Virtue
and Reason, and echoing all the putrid sentiment
of the Republic; and then, having sacrificed unto
the gods of Canaan, he proceeded to argue the ne-

cessity for a belief in a Supreme Being, not as an undeniable truth, but as a theorem tending to the solution of their political problem, which was already beginning to startle even their callous hearts by its vast proportions and the awful momentum of its unmanageable elements. He asserted nothing, but endeavored to prove the advantage to be gained by assuming the existence of Deity. "The belief," concluded Robespierre, "in a Supreme Being, and the immortality of the soul, is a perpetual recall to justice; it is, therefore, social and republican."

Had he exorcised the shadow, or did it still wait? And now the noble senators, who in the cathedral of Notre Dame dethroned the Almighty amid the acclamations of the people, received this speech with the same demonstrations, and the people voted addresses to the Convention, thanking them for the restoration of the Supreme Being.

It would seem that such impiety must appear almost too weak to be wicked in the estimation of Him who is "the same yesterday, to-day, and forever." But this was the wisdom of France; and, as Robespierre said the people needed festivals, they decided that every decade throughout the year should be a festival in honor of something—the human race, patriotism, liberty, virtue, agriculture, and a long list of abstractions; but the first was dedicated to the Supreme Being, as though he, too, were but an

abstraction. "It hardly appeared," says the historian, "a restoration at all, but the erection of a pan-
theon of worshipable things, with the Supreme Being
at the head of them."

The first festival, that of their reinstated Deity,
was appointed for the 8th of June, or the 20th of
Prairial, according to the new computation. Great
preparations were made, and again blood-stained,
woe-begone Paris forgot its aceldama for a few brief
hours, to thrill with a new sensation.

In the garden of the Tuileries a large mound was
raised for the festival, and graced with three statues,
Atheism, Deism, and a veiled statue of Wisdom.
But the mound, erected in haste, proved too small
to afford standing-room for the Convention, and the
rites began amid much elbowing and cursing among
that noble body.

As high-priest of the Supreme Being, stood Robespierre, with torch in hand, awaiting the moment of
the unveiling of the statue of Wisdom to set fire to
the statues of Atheism and Deism. Here, standing
upon the mound above the heads of Paris, just as he
towered over France, we take our last look at Robespierre the Great: the shadow is closing round him;
henceforth, vain, weak, cowardly, and unutterably
wicked, he crawls through another page of history,
and then—drops from the guillotine into the bottom-
less pit of eternal infamy. But at this moment he

stood in his sky-blue waistcoat, carrying an immense bouquet of flowers and wheat, the central object of the eyes of Paris, and half-insane with vanity and the sense of power, perhaps unconscious, or, for one brief moment, unmindful, of the mutterings of hate around him. His arm was raised, that arm potent enough to crush the liberty of France, and, in the words of the terrible St. Just, "send the vessel of the revolution plowing its way through a red sea of blood," and yet, afterward, too weak to let out his own life, when, in the brutal sense of an awful fear, he would have escaped from the horrors before him into the arms of that haunting shadow that followed him to the end.

At the appointed moment Wisdom was unveiled and the statues fired, and once more in Paris reigned a Supreme Being, whose restorer and high-priest was Robespierre. "But, unfortunately," says the historian, "the smoke from the burning of the two images so blackened Wisdom that she looked more like a demon than a divine creature, and the whole appeared more like a burlesque on the Deity than a festival in his honor."

O God of wisdom! in that smoke-grimed statue we see not Thee, but the Spirit of France, blackened by the smoke of Atheism, till all its divinity was hid, lost beyond redemption; and it stood like that statue, a reproach to the hand that raised it.

But now, in that wild ecstasy which marks every event of this insane period, the members of the Convention embrace and kiss each other, and the hoarse multitude roar and shout as they did at Notre Dame. Then in procession the assemblage wend their way to the Convention, where the leader of the section of Marat appeared at the bar and addressed them (in complimentary reference to the Republican party called in the Convention the "Mountain"), beginning: "O Beneficent Mountain! O Protecting Sinai! accept our expressions of gratitude for all the sublime decrees which thou art daily issuing for the happiness of mankind." They do indeed recall Sinai, not the lawgiver or the law from its summit, but the golden calf, the idol at its base, inaugurated in this a more sinful age by the bloody dance of death.

And here we leave them, bloody infidels congratulating their peers on the restoration of a Deity! And the tragedy goes on. It is a record for demons—for demons laugh; and surely never, in the world's history, were the absurd and ridiculous so inextricably mixed with horror and infamy.

We close the page. The lesson is over; the sermon is ended—that sermon preached by human events on the text of Divine inspiration, "The world by wisdom knew not God." The logic of facts is conclusive. The argument is unanswerable, and we turn from the contemplation of this reign of Reason with a most tender reverence for the boundless patience and immeasurable love of Him who, in passive strength and silent majesty, still "stretched out His hand when no man regarded."

If all the writings of French infidels in the eighteenth century were bound together, they must be harmless, if only the simple facts of this bloody, grotesque and inconsistent "*Age of Reason*" were added as a second volume. In this the theory was tested, and there was obviously nothing extrinsic to prevent the most perfect realization of its Utopia. Human wisdom sought and found an utter social, political and religious vacuum, and filled it as it would. But instead of liberty, justice, virtue, equality and peace, there ensued the worst tyranny the world ever saw: men saturated with sentiment preyed upon each other with the appetite of cannibals, and the smoke of the abomination rose to heaven in a dense cloud of human agony and sin, which dropped blood, *blood*, BLOOD, until the air grew thick with horror, and we turn shuddering away, to wonder if indeed there is any earthly limit to Divine love and patience.

But the God of Sinai is terrible as well as great. The world has not known Him, and he who would measure His attributes or limit His power must dare the thunders of Sinai; and he who would have human reason sit in the seat of Moses to legislate in his name, would break the balance-wheel of human society, and open the flood-gates of hell to inundate the world. And the God of Calvary is great, but the world by wisdom has not known Him. Throughout the Old World men have groped their way through centuries to find Him, and only been answered by the hollow echoes of Rome. Though in and out like a golden thread for eighteen hundred years we may trace the true succession, yet the world looked on, and never knew their prophets till the hour was past; and temples have grown hoary over worshipers that returned to dust and never knew Him. And the new world, born of the best inspiration of the old, and carried forward on the tidal wave of the grandest civilization—can it be that it is even now forgetting the Source of its power?

From the Atlantic to the Pacific we have carried the wisdom of the knowledge of God, and yet how powerless it is in our hands. From the negative morality of Chinese idolaters we might learn lessons of consistent practice and patient fidelity to that Power which alone can make us the light-house of the world.

But if from our schools and colleges we remove the Bible and devise other corner-stones, and in our practice forget God, we shall but invoke another *Reign of Reason*, with perhaps its deluge of blood, or else go down like a ship in sight of land when all the waves are still.

The church only can interpose and teach the nations, by a living faith, that "Christ with us the hope of glory" is no poetic abstraction, but a changeless living Power that walks beside us day by day.

What care we for the wordy wisdom of the British House of Lords, or the Ecumenical Council of Rome? For Christ is here; a little child has found him, not in the council of nations or the wisdom of senates, but in the sweet old story of the Babe of Bethlehem, the Wanderer of Galilee, the Jesus of Mount Olivet, the Prisoner of Pilate, and the Christ of Calvary. This is the Healer of many nations, the perfect Giver of a changeless law—"The Christ of Calvary, our Prophet, Priest and King."

Lead us, Father, by Thy counsel. The night of the world is past. The morning has come. The ages have waited, and now the old world turns over from its slumber to face the rising sun. But it is weak and shines afar off, and still the abject children of men sit under the high altars of bigotry and power, and hear Presumption "teaching for doctrine the commandments of men." And still the nations sway to and fro, and make of the whole earth a Calvary, and "crucify the Lord again" between Mitred Tyranny and a defiant "Age of Reason."

www.ingramcontent.com/pod-product-compliance
Lightning Source LLC
Chambersburg PA
CBHW030905270326
41929CB00008B/585